Mobile Apps FOR DUMMIES®

There's a Dummies App for This and That

With more than 200 million books in print and over 1,600 unique titles, Dummies is a global leader in how-to information. Now you can get the same great Dummies information in an App. With topics such as Wine, Spanish, Digital Photography, Certification, and more, you'll have instant access to the topics you need to know in a format you can trust.

To get information on all our Dummies apps, visit the following:

www.Dummies.com/go/mobile from your computer.

www.Dummies.com/go/iphone/apps from your phone.

Ayurveda

FOR

DUMMIES®

A Wiley Brand

by Angela Hope-Murray

Ayurveda For Dummies®

Published by:
John Wiley & Sons, Ltd
The Atrium
Southern Gate
Chichester
West Sussex
PO19 8SQ
England
www.wiley.com

For general information on our other products and services, please contact our Customer Care Department within the U.S. at 877-762-2974, outside the U.S. at (001) 317-572-3993, or fax 317-572-4002.

For technical support, please visit www.wiley.com/techsupport.

A catalogue record for this book is available from the British Library.

ISBN 978-1-118-30670-3 (pbk); ISBN 978-1-118-30667-3 (ebk);

ISBN 978-1-118-30668-0 (ebk); ISBN 978-1-118-30669-7 (ebk)

Contents at a Glance

Table of Contents

Introduction

My search for a medical system that truly encompassed the whole being began when I was 19 years old and studying the biomechanics of the lower limb at podiatry school. A sense of deep unease was growing within me because I realised that a problem in the knee, for example, may be related to the whole of the skeletal structure and not just to the part of the body we were allowed to take care of. Alongside this was the realisation that a disease entity can present a very different picture in people with differing constitutions.

Help arrived for me in 1986 when a doctor came to the hospital to give a talk on Ayurveda, called the mother of all healing systems. Dawn broke for me and shone a light on a system of healing that is so elegant yet so simple in its formation.

Coming from at least 5,000 years of human experience, Ayurveda really is the 'prima materia' (first matter) of all medical modalities. Ayurveda is a system in which the healers have a responsibility to keep themselves well, along with their patients. Encompassing wellness of body, mind and spirit, Ayurveda encourages vitalisation that extends into your every cell.

I hope this book fuels in you the enthusiasm to try Ayurveda for yourself and incorporate it into your daily life, which will benefit and be enhanced by it.

About This Book

Ayurveda For Dummies gives you the tools to comprehend the basic building blocks of Ayurveda. Use it as a basis to progress on the journey to well-being using simple instructions and interventions, which you can implement immediately into your daily routine. I give you tools for recognising problems as early as possible and treating them with both diet and herbs. I provide a lot of general information for maintaining your well-being. Everyone deserves better health.

Conventions Used in This Book

To help you get the most from this book, I follow a few conventions:

- *Italic* is used for emphasis and to highlight new words or terms that I define.

- Web addresses may split over two lines – if so, ignore the hyphen that links them when you're typing the address into a search engine. If you're reading this on an enabled device, the web addresses are hyperlinked and will take you straight to the site in question.

- **Bold** shows the action part of numbered steps.

What You're Not to Read

Of course, I hope that you'll read the entire book, but in some cases I offer information that you may find interesting but that's not essential to your understanding. Sidebars (shaded boxes of text) are an example of this kind of text and may include anecdotes, history or other titbits that I find juicy but you may not! And when I go deeper into the principles or science of Ayurveda, I use the Technical Stuff icon to let you know you're perfectly welcome to skip that paragraph.

Foolish Assumptions

To generate this book, I made a few assumptions about you:

- You're keen to learn more about Ayurveda but don't know exactly what it is and how to practise it.

- You're very busy and you want a simple, clear understanding of the fundamentals of Ayurveda.

- You've already delved into other types of complimentary therapies and would like to expand your knowledge.

- You're interested in optimising your health and are ready to try a few Ayurvedic suggestions.

How This Book Is Organised

I've organised *Ayurveda For Dummies* into six parts. Each part contains a variety of chapters to instruct you further on various aspects of Ayurveda.

Part I: Getting Started with Ayurveda

In this part I explain the belief system and philosophy behind Ayurveda, which can appear quite esoteric at times. Getting to grips with the basics won't take you long and the rewards will be worth it.

You probably want to get cracking straight away with learning your constitution according to Ayurveda from the questionnaire in Chapter 4. This enables you to put the interventions that I list into practise. Armed with this information you can better navigate the rest of the book.

Part II: Living in Harmony with Ayurveda: Promoting Good Health

In this section I take you on a journey to learn how disease develops in your system according to Ayurveda. Completing the questionnaire in this part can determine how healthy your system is. You also look at the health of the senses and how time affects your well-being.

This is the core of the book where ways you can promote good health are clearly laid out. I cover the daily routine, seasonal routines and evening procedures. There is a great chapter on yoga postures for individual constitutions as well as yoga as medicine for problems you may have. I include breathing exercises from which you can gain immediate benefit if you try them for as little as ten minutes a day. You're sure to find advice in this part to suit your lifestyle needs.

Part III: Appetising Approaches to a Healthy Diet

Diet is of utmost importance to your health. In this part I share my enthusiasm for the Ayurvedic approach to diet and I provide you with ways to improve your digestion using food. I give dietary advice for different doshas (constitutions), because we all have different dietary needs. In Chapter 12, I share ways to optimise your diet and make it more nutritious. *Bon appétit*!

Part IV: Fitting Ways to Enhance Healing

In this section I present you with Ayurvedic suggestions to improve common health problems such as digestive disorders, respiratory problems, musculoskeletal ailments and skin and hair issues. If you're experiencing difficulties in any of these areas, I provide helpful prevention advice you can put into practice.

Part V: The Part of Tens

No *For Dummies* book is complete without the legendary Part of Tens. In this part I present bite-size chunks of information about herbs and spices, including their amazing healing properties.

Head to www.dummies.com/extras/ayurvedauk for a bonus Part of Tens chapter: 'Ten Wonderful Ways To Enhance Your Health with Ayurveda'.

Part VI: Appendices

Last but not least are three short appendices: a glossary of Sanskrit terms (Sanskrit being the language of Ayurveda), a botanical index, and a list of suppliers of all things Ayurveda.

Icons Used in This Book

Sprinkled throughout the book you'll see various icons to guide you on your way. Icons are a *For Dummies* way of drawing your attention to important stuff, interesting stuff, and stuff you really need to know how to do.

This icon highlights important concepts in Ayurveda or concerning health in general.

I love science, but maybe you don't. That's okay – you don't need much of it to understand how Ayurveda can help you. When I delve into specialised info, I use this icon to let you know that the material is esoteric and skippable.

When I provide a way for you to do something more quickly or easily, I use this icon.

This dangerous-looking symbol lets you know when trouble may befall you, as when an ingredient I discuss is known to cause allergies. You won't find many of these icons, but please do heed their messages.

Where to Go from Here

I've written this book so that you can dip in and out of it as you please. However, if you're new to Ayurveda, starting at the beginning is most helpful. For the rest of you, take a look at the Table of Contents and see what takes your fancy.

Head online for special bonus content at www.dummies.com/extras/ ayurvedauk, and visit www.dummies.com/cheatsheet/ayurvedauk for the cheat sheet created specifically for this book.

I wish you a happy excursion into the world of Ayurveda, which has enough breadth and depth to satisfy those of you who are hungry for knowledge to help you improve and sustain the well-being of your body, mind and spirit.

Part I

getting started with
with

Ayurveda

In this part . . .

- ✔ Discover the incredible 5,000-year history of Ayurveda.

- ✔ Identify your constitution – your type of skin, hair and body shape – so you can tailor the advice in this book for you.

- ✔ Get familiar with the amazing energy systems in your body.

- ✔ Meet the centres of awareness that are your chakra system.

- ✔ Go to `www.dummies.com/extras/ayurvedauk` for online bonus content, including an extra Part of Tens chapter: 'Ten Wonderful Ways to Enhance Your Health with Ayurveda'.

Chapter 1

Introducing Ayurveda: The Science of Life

*W*elcome to the world of Ayurveda – a vast treasure house of knowledge of natural healthcare given to us by holy men called *rishis*. Literally meaning 'science of life', Ayurveda encompasses all aspects of your well-being, from breathing to digestion.

In this chapter, I introduce you to the ancient art of Ayurveda.

Living Well and Maintaining Health

Ayurveda is a truly holistic health system which supports you from the cradle to the end of your life. The Ayurvedic mode of living aims to maximise your lifespan by optimising your health through interventions that care for your body, mind, spirit and environment. Ayurveda places a great emphasis on the prevention of disease and on health promotion, as well as on a comprehensive approach to treatment.

Looking into Ayurveda's origins

The genealogy of Ayurveda traces back to about 5,000 years ago in the Indus valley, where the *Vedas*, or oldest Ayurvedic scriptures, originated. Legend has it that the knowledge within the Vedas was downloaded, so to speak, to a number of sages in deep meditation. This was experienced as an act of divine love to help us manage and maximise our lives on earth. For centuries, this knowledge was passed down from one generation to the next in the form of memorised chants known as *sutras*.

There are four Vedas, the oldest of which is the Rig Veda, which refers to three great beings governing the universe, in the form of Agni, Soma and Indra, which are personifications of the sun, moon and wind. These in turn become what are known as the *doshas*, which govern all activities in your body and are called *pitta*, *kapha* and *vata* respectively. (You can become acquainted with your own unique balance of these forces by referring to Chapter 4.)

Known as the fourth veda, the Atharvaveda (meaning 'no vibration', or how to make the mind stable), contains the knowledge of Ayurveda. Two systems of medicine are described. The first is a compilation of drugs used on an empirical, rational basis, while the other describes a type of magical spiritual medicine.

Yet another version of the origins of Ayurveda is given by Sushruta, considered the founder of surgical medicine. Sushruta and other sages approached Dhanvantari, the god of Ayurveda. Dhanvantari imparted to them the wisdom of Ayurveda for the betterment of mankind and to help rid it of the suffering of disease.

These legends aren't so far away from the divine origins of the healing arts in contemporary cultures closer to home in the West that Apollo gave us from Greece and Thoth from Egypt.

If you want to delve deeper into the origins of Ayurveda, the three very important texts that all scholars of Ayurveda can't manage without are: the Charaka Samhita, Sushruta Samhita, and Ashtanga Hrdayam by Vagbhata.

Unlike some other systems of medicine, Ayurveda is not just concerned with the absence of disease. As Sushruta, a physician in the sixth century BC informs us, you are only considered healthy when your appetite is strong, your tissues (*dhatus*) are functioning normally, your humours (the *doshas*: vata, pitta and kapha) are in balance, bodily wastes are eliminated well, and your mind and senses experience joy. If these Sanskrit terms pique your interest, head to Chapter 3 for an explanation of the dhatus and Chapter 2 for the basics about the doshas.

An extensive body of knowledge describes the therapeutic use of minerals and plants in Ayurveda. Throughout this book, I recommend different herbal remedies for different ailments or as rejuvenating tonics. If you can't find the particular herbs or spices in your grocers, you can find suppliers in Appendix C.

Ayurveda places great emphasis on the effects of the different seasons and your diet on the equilibrium of the body. Different doshas, or attributes, are prevalent at different times of the day, and during the seasons these cause physiological changes in your body. Ayurveda understands that moving with the times and climate is a mainstay of good health because you are a microcosm of what's going on in your environment. I discuss these cadences of time and what you can do to ensure optimum health throughout the seasons in Chapter 9.

Talking of the environment, Ayurveda recognises the importance of the environment to your health: in Ayurveda, everything is part of the same consciousness. How can we be truly healthy when the environment is being brutalised by development, forests are being cleared on a massive scale and farming practices are employed that disrespect the lives of sentient beings?

The food that we eat has often been packaged, chilled and reheated until it contains very little vital force. Your immune system operates at top capacity when your fuel is so poor. Immunity, known as *vyadhishamatva*, or 'disease forgiveness', is the starting point for good health, and Chapter 12 addresses eating the best food to improve your immune system.

Health is described by the word *swastha* in Sanskrit, which means 'to be established in the self'. Health is really moment-to-moment awareness, and this can be obtained through meditation. Details on how you can put this life-changing practice into action are provided in Chapter 6.

Surveying the Scope of Ayurveda

Within the practice of Ayurveda are specialities – just like in Western systems.

Here are the eight primary Ayurvedic specialities (I don't cover all of these in this book – certainly not surgery, you'll be relieved to know!):

- Toxicology (*agada tantra*)
- Childhood diseases or paediatrics (*bala tantra*)
- General surgery (*shalya tantra*)
- Internal medicine (*kaya chikitsa*)
- Psychiatry and mental disorders (*bhuta vidya*)
- Management of diseases of the head and the neck (*salakya tantra*)
- Fertility treatment (*vajikarana*)
- Rejuvenation and the treatment of geriatrics (*rasayana*)

Speaking of Sanskrit

Ayurveda cannot be separated from the Sanskrit language. Sanskrit is a sister of Greek and Latin and one of the Indo-European group of languages. It's an extraordinary and very precise medium of expression. More epics, sagas and scriptures are written in Sanskrit than in any other language, including English.

The word *Sanskrit* means 'perfected', or 'perfectly formed'. (In fact, Sanskrit is so rigorous and precise, and hence so unambiguous, that it's used in computer-processing projects in the domain of artificial intelligence.)

The complexity of Sanskrit in its level of sophistication and scientific accuracy is only mirrored by mathematics. The process of perfecting the language has taken thousands of years. In the past, Sanskrit was the language used by all the sciences, which were all orientated towards the study of the self in all its aspects.

The use of the language itself is an instrument for healing. Its beautiful resonances, which you can experience without even having to understand the meaning, can reach the very core of your being. All languages vibrate the being, but Sanskrit somehow enables you to keep currents of energy flowing so that you can enter into and maintain an inner harmony. I've used the Sanskrit terms for this reason throughout the book.

The bible tells us in St John's Gospel that 'In the beginning was the word, and the word was God.' The Vedas concur with this view and say that the whole of creation was *sphota*, or spoken into existence.

In some places in India, medicines are still produced using Sanskrit mantras, because it's believed this makes them really potent and much more deep-acting than ordinary preparations.

The forte of the approach of mainstream medicine is in diagnosis and acute medical conditions such as trauma. If a bus knocks you down, you need to be in the accident and emergency room at your local hospital.

However, in the management of deep-seated chronic ailments, mainstream medicine sometimes lacks the sophistication of Ayurveda, which always takes the underlying causes of pathology into consideration. Ayurvedic interventions can deeply purify your body and eliminate toxins from your system.

Iatrogenic diseases – those that are unintentionally caused by medical treatment – are on the increase and were estimated as being the third-largest cause of death in a study by Starfield in 2000 in the United States. Ayurveda's more subtle and individualised approach to treatment shows no such ill effects. However, I'm not suggesting you ditch your doctor for Ayurveda – far from it. But as long as your doctor is happy for you to follow the remedies in this book, Ayurvedic treatment can be very effective.

Primary healthcare is considered as very important in Ayurveda. This book gives you the tools to stay well throughout your life. In Chapter 6, I give you very simple lifestyle recommendations called *dinacharya*, which keep your diet, digestion and sleep – considered the pillars of your health – in good order.

Locating the Practice and the Evidence

Ayurveda has been the only system of medicine in some rural parts of India for thousands of years. Under the rule of the British, Ayurveda was undermined in the belief that the more mechanistic Western medicine was more efficacious. Thankfully for us, the poor continued to use the tried-and-tested native treatments for their ailments, and Ayurveda survived underground until 1947. This is when India became a free nation and Ayurveda received full recognition as a medical system.

In the past 20 years, Ayurveda has undergone a resurgence. It's now practised all over the world and often works in harmony with a more modern approach. Qualified Ayurvedic physicians are medical practitioners, and many hospitals treat patients using solely Ayurvedic tenets, without causing any of the adverse reactions of modern treatment.

To find a qualified Ayurvedic practitioner near you, see Appendix C.

A wellspring of research is available for those of you who are interested in the science and efficacy of Ayurveda. Over and over again, studies have validated the efficacy of this system using the stringency of Western approaches to research and statistical analysis. To get you started, visit:

- ✔ www.hindawi.com/journals/ecam
- ✔ www.oxfordjournals.org (search for 'Ayurveda')

For the countless systemic reviews of Ayurveda, try:

- ✔ www.systematicreviewinayurveda.org

To begin following the tenets of Ayurveda is to enter a realm that can be truly life-enhancing. Here's to your personal journey.

You're a star: Being at one with the universe

The philosophical system of Samkhya was originated by Kapila around the ninth century BC and laid the foundation for Ayurveda.

Samkhya philosophy is the backbone of Ayurveda and gives you a clear schema for how all things come into being. The word *Samkhya* literally means 'number', and is so-called for reckoning up the 25 entities (*tattwas*) that make up the universe. According to this understanding of reality, there's a continual flow into 'becoming' in all life, from the finest essence to the corporeal world.

This idea was mirrored in the West by the Greek philosophers in the phrase *panta re*, which means 'all things flow'. The early sages had the same notion, using the term *samsara* to mean the 'world of becoming'.

Charaka, an Ayurvedic physician and one of the main commentators of Ayurveda, tells us that 'Each individual is the unique expression of a recognisable finely tuned cosmic process occurring in space and time.'

Putting it in modern terms, Newton, in his first law of thermodynamics, states that the sum total of energy in the universe does not diminish or increase, but continuously transforms itself from one state or level of vibration to another as the flow of life manifests itself into many forms.

Because you are formed of the same substance as the creation, you are truly a microcosm of the universe.

Chapter 2

Focusing on the Fundamental Principles

*I*n this chapter, I aim to give you an understanding of the fundamental building blocks of the whole system of Ayurveda, as well as the language you use to understand and investigate the subject in greater depth.

I explain the heart of Ayurveda – the five elements, which you see and experience by using your five senses – and how these five elements make up the world. Forget your school science lessons and embrace the science of Ayurveda.

Fixing on the Three States of Energy and the Five Elements

Samkhya philosophy, one of the oldest philosophical systems and the philosophy that underlies Ayurveda, holds that the creation of the universe enabled three states of energy, or pure consciousness, to come into play. These three states are known as *gunas*, which literally means 'ropes that bind us to the physical world'. Which of these states predominate in your mind contributes to determining your psychological constitution (you can discover your constitution in Chapter 4).

The gunas are as follows:

- **Sattwa guna,** or potential energy, is a state of equilibrium and balance. It gives rise to purity, truth, creativity, happiness and knowledge. Predominantly sattwic people are calm, spiritually minded, quiet, intelligent and health conscious.

- **Rajas guna,** is best described as kinetic energy that results in activity. This has the qualities of restlessness, aggression and effort. A predominantly rajasic person is ambitious, driven, egotistical and perfectionist.

- **Tamas guna,** which is aligned with inertia, is a state where nothing happens and rest ensues. It's a state of dullness, heaviness, materialism, self-interest and depression. Predominantly tamasic people tend to be lazy, attached to things and bad humoured.

The interaction of these three forces creates a unique and harmonious flow of creation, maintenance and destruction.

Together, the gunas form the five elements that compose the building blocks, or proto-elements, from which everything in the material world is constructed. The next sections talk about each element in turn. I talk about the *qualities* the elements contain in the upcoming section 'Examining the Twenty Qualities'.

Each element contains the one before it, so each of the five elements contains ether, and earth holds all the elements – ether, air, fire and water. Each element is connected to a taste. Taste is extremely important in Ayurveda, and I explain it further in Chapter 10.

As gunas descend into matter, they manifest as the finest substance, or ether. Gunas become denser and denser until they form earth. Gunas are known in Sanskrit as *mahabhuta*, which means 'great element'.

Ether

Ether is known in Sanskrit as *akasha*, from the root *kas*, which means 'to radiate'. Ether's predominant quality (I explain qualities in the next section 'Examining the Twenty Qualities') is its ability to convey energy without resistance. Take sound waves as an example: by virtue of ether, sound waves are able to expand and resonate so that we can hear them.

Molecules and atoms need space in which to operate, and ether provides that environment throughout your body. Ether inhabits the alveoli of your lungs so that you continue to breathe. Within your colon, where absorption and assimilation takes place, ether maintains the integrity of the process.

When combined with the air element, ether produces a bitter taste.

As an element, ether has no dimension, because its atomic particles are very loosely put together. Its characteristics are fine, soft and light. Ether is the equivalent of nuclear energy, which is the power released when minute atomic particles are split.

Air

In Sanskrit, air is known as *vayu* and means 'movement, vibration and gaseousness'. You can think of air as atoms of oxygen floating in the ether.

You can easily see the effects of air when you put your washing on the line; air is dry, light, rough, cold and fine.

All the hollow spaces of your body, such as in your throat and bones, contain air. Air serves to activate and stimulate essential processes in your body, such as respiration and the exchange of gases at a cellular level.

When combined with ether, air's associated taste is bitter; mixed with earth, it produces an astringent flavour; and it's pungent when combined with fire.

Air is the equivalent of electrical energy in modern terms.

Fire

The Sanskrit word for fire, *agni*, means 'to radiate', so you can picture fire as radiant energy. Fire's qualities are light, hot, sharp, fine, dry and clear.

All the enzyme functions that take place in your body are related to fire, and fire controls your metabolic rate as well. Fire governs all transformative processes in your body, from your digestive process to your thought process.

Combined with air, fire gives a pungent taste, and allied to earth, it results in a sour flavour.

In Western terms, agni is thermal energy, where two substances come together and create friction, which in turn produces heat.

Water

In Sanskrit, the water element is known as *ap* or *jala*, meaning watery.

The water element governs all the fluids in your body. Its qualities are slow, cold, oily, soft and liquid.

Water is found in all the cellular fluids in your tissues, and in your spinal and brain fluids. *Synovial fluid*, which lubricates your joints and provides the moisture in your lungs that prevents them from drying out and sticking to the inside of your rib cage when you breathe, also contains water.

Because water embraces all that comes in its path, it has a cohesive effect on the tissues of your body. Along with this, water has a moistening and dissolving effect, which you see, for example, when water prevents the surface of your skin from drying up. Tears have a solvent effect if you get something in your eye.

Combined with earth, water produces a sweet taste, and with fire it produces a salty taste.

In terms of modern chemistry, water would be allied to chemical energy. This type of power is generated when a substance undergoes transformation by the breaking of chemical bonds, such as when you chew your food, releasing nutrients into your body.

Earth

This element is known as *prithivi* – 'that offering resistance' in Sanskrit.

In the earth element, all the elements reach their material state and become solid. The attributes of earth are solid, coarse, heavy, stable, slow, rough and hard.

The influence of earth in your body is that it relates to all your structural elements – your bones, teeth and nails. Earth plays a supportive role in your body and provides you with compactness, strength and stability.

Water and earth together produce a sweet taste; when combined with fire, earth gives a sour flavour.

In Western parlance, earth is the equivalent of mechanical energy – the type of force that's liberated when potential energy and moving energy operate together, such as when you lift an object.

Examining the Twenty Qualities

According to Ayurveda, everything you can see, hear, smell, taste and touch is experienced as a mixture of the 20 different qualities, or attributes. They describe everything in our physical and mental world. Each pair listed in Table 2-1 represents two ends of a spectrum.

The best way to remember the 20 qualities is to familiarise yourself with half of them, because the other 10 are their opposites. So if you know *hot*, you know its opposite *cold* as well. Table 2-1 lists the 20 qualities with their opposites, side by side.

Table 2-1	Ayurveda Qualities
Dull	Sharp
Hard	Soft
Heavy	Light
Cold	Hot
Wet	Dry
Dense	Subtle
Rough	Smooth
Slow	Quick
Solid	Liquid
Oily	Brittle

These opposite features point the way to effective diagnosis and treatment of illness in Ayurveda. Ayurveda believes that if the treatment is *like* the ailment it's treating, it will only increase that ailment. Only an opposite quality can combat it.

For example, oil massage is not advised for kapha individuals (Chapter 4 helps you determine your constitution) on a regular basis – it increases their tendencies towards oiliness, heaviness, slowness and cold. A better option is a dry powder massage, which increases light, dry and hot qualities – all of which reduce excess kapha dosha.

Similarly, if you're a pitta dosha and visit a hot country, the hot, dry qualities of the weather increase those tendencies in your body. To find relief, you can counter the situation with opposite qualities – try a cool glass of lime juice or sugar cane juice for its cold, wet qualities, an application of coconut oil on your skin for its cooling qualities, and eating herbs such as green coriander and fennel for their cooling and moistening properties.

Differentiating the Doshas

The doshas are the golden triangle of Ayurveda, formed when the five elements with all of their attributes come together to produce what are known as the three doshas. In a nutshell, a *dosha* is a form of biological energy. The three doshas – vata, pitta and kapha – govern all the physical, mental and psychological systems, and every person has a unique combination.

Chapter 4 offers checklists to help you discover your dominant dosha, so use the information in this section along with Chapter 4 to get a rounded view of your constitution.

In addition to describing types of energy, vata, pitta and kapha also describe types of biological constitution. Every person on the planet has a combination of all three doshas in a unique configuration. Generally, one type of dosha dominates. So, if the pitta dosha dominates in you, you're said to have a pitta dosha or pitta constitution. Most people are governed by two doshas; pure types are fairly rare.

Your doshic balance is determined by a synthesis of four elements (air, fire, water and earth – all the elements minus ether) in combination with consciousness. The diet of your parents and their hereditary tendencies also contributes to your dosha.

Each dosha exists within you, but the amount you have (which is 'allocated' at birth) is unique to you.

When you're healthy, all the doshas are in a state of balance in your body, mind and emotions. But what makes up that balance is unique to you and your constitution.

Vata

Composed of half air and half ether, vata is known as the governor because it moves everything in your body; all nerve impulses, the movement of food in your digestive tract, muscle contractions, heartbeats, and so on, would be impossible without it.

Vata's characteristics are lightness, dryness, mobility, subtleness, coolness, roughness, clarity and inconsistency. Vata is associated with the taste of astringency and saltiness.

When vata is in balance, you think clearly, move easily and are very flexible. If vata becomes disturbed, you experience muscle cramping, all types of pain and paralysis, tics, fear and anxiety.

Because it's so light and subtle, vata is the dosha which most easily goes out of balance.

If your primary dosha is vata, you're quick to grasp things but also quick to forget them as the agility and natural curiosity of your mind darts from one thing to the next. Irregularity is the name of the game for you; sometimes you feel constantly hungry, sometimes you don't. Like the wind, you change from one state to the next. You tend to be slim and gangly, your eyes are quite small and active, and your hair is dry and wiry. Mentally, you're very creative but you get bored easily.

Pitta

Pitta dosha is predominantly made up of the fire element with a little of the water element. It mainly governs your enzymes and hormone reactions, and without pitta dosha metabolic processes would cease.

Pitta's characteristics are sharp, hot, liquid, strong smelling, slightly oily and spreading. Pitta is associated with pungent and sour flavours.

Pitta dosha promotes proper digestion and assimilation of both the ideas and food you take in. It regulates hunger, thirst and body temperature. Your capacity to see is attributable to pitta dosha.

When your pitta dosha is out of balance, you can fall prey to disorders such as jaundice, conjunctivitis, fevers and inflammations.

If pitta is your primary dosha, you have a sharp intellect and a matching appetite. You're of medium build and tend not to put on weight easily, but if you do you can lose it easily too. You're endowed with passion, enthusiasm and vitality. Mentally you're able to focus and you usually enjoy studying. In general you have good leadership skills, but when your doshas are out of balance you can be a bit fanatical.

Your skin is sun-sensitive, and you have freckles and moles. You have light-coloured eyes with a steady gaze. Your hair is light and very silky, and you have to wash it fairly often because it can get greasy. You love sweets and cold drinks, which both pacify your hot attributes.

Kapha

In kapha dosha, you have the elements of water and earth in equal quantities. Kapha keeps your joints lubricated, produces cerebrospinal fluid and protects your cells. It gives lustre to your skin. Kapha's power of cohesion holds your musculature and skeletal systems together.

Kapha's characteristics are hard, gross, sticky, cloudy, soft, static, slow, heavy, dense, liquid, slimy, oily and cold. Its tastes are sweet, sour and salty.

The conditions of this dosha include general swelling, diabetes, obesity and lassitude.

If your primary dosha is kapha, you're probably laid-back and easy going. You have strong bones and good teeth. Your skin is pale and thick, so you don't wrinkle easily. You're prone to weight gain and have a job to shift it. Because of your natural tendency not to move much, your metabolism is slow, along with your ability to digest both ideas and food. It takes quite a time for you to commit facts to memory, but once there you'll never forget them.

Your strength is legendary, and you're capable of hard, heavy work. You are by nature very loving and kind, but in excess this dosha endows you with attachment and greed. You have cravings for sweet and salty tastes.

Navigating Your Body's Networks: The Srotas

Your body has a complex system of passages known as *srotas* that deliver nutrition to your tissues and conduct wastes away. Women have extra srotas associated with childbirth.

Ayurvedic health practitioners pay close attention to how the srotas are functioning to help them effectively diagnosis and treat disease.

Looking at srota states

Srotas can exist in five states:

- **Normal:** Regarded as the optimum healthy state. With normal srotas, all your bodily systems are suffused with oxygen and nutrients, and wastes are removed effectively. This is regarded as the healthy state.

✔ **Hyper-functioning:** This situation occurs when your srotas are overloaded. Things are running too fast. For example, in a hyper state, your body may not have time to extract the vital nutrients from the foods you eat. This hyperactivity can mean that certain organs or tissues get overloaded and can't function efficiently.

✔ **Blocked:** Also known as *srotavarodha*, in this condition a srota suffers an obstruction due to the accumulation of *ama*, or toxins, in your system – like a dam preventing the flow of a river. A blocked srota can lead to atrophy of organs, or tissues deprived of vital nutrients.

✔ **Hypo-functioning:** Known as *srotakshaya*, this condition occurs when your system is operating sluggishly. Waste products begin to circulate in your blood. As a result, your cells and organs shrivel and become dehydrated. One indication of hypo-functioning is that your breath begins to smell.

✔ **Injured:** An injury to a srota can result in a blockage of vital channels. In trying to find a way past the blockage, vital elements invade neighbouring tissues or organs. Unfamiliar substances in the wrong place can cause damage to your system, for example when internal bleeding causes complications to an injury.

Getting to know the srotas

Essentially, the srotas are your body's plumbing, electrical and waste networks. The following list describes the function of each srota in the traditional order:

✔ **Pranavaha srota:** This channel is connected to the respiratory system and some aspects of your circulation. Its role is to maintain your respiratory function, which helps give vitality to your blood. Its opening is in the nose, and it uses the passages of the respiratory tract and the bronchial tree. As well as residing in the heart and gastrointestinal tract, the pranavaha srota's primary location is in your colon, where *prana* (energy) is extracted from the food you consume.

If this srota is out of balance, you feel as if you've exercised when you're hungry, you feel dry, and your appetite and other natural urges are suppressed. (You have several natural urges, which include sneezing, sleeping and coughing.)

✔ **Annavaha srota:** This is the digestive tract located in your stomach, oesophagus and the left side of your body. Its opening is at a junction between your stomach and intestine known as the ileo-caecal valve. Disruption to this channel is caused by eating unwholesome food, eating at the wrong time, and eating too much.

✔ **Udakavaha srota:** This srota is said to be located in the soft palate, third ventricle of your heart and the pancreas. Its openings in your body are the kidney and your tongue. This channel is disrupted by thirst, fear, excessive alcohol and exposure to heat. Excessively dry foods like popcorn and rice cakes disturbs this channels, as does *ama* (toxins produced by your body).

✔ **Rasavaha srota:** The seat of this particular channel is located in the right chamber of your heart and all the vessels connected to it. It carries blood and nutrients to your cells and maintains your immune system. Its opening occurs at the junction of your capillaries. This srota is closely related to the skin as well as to your body's venous and lymphatic systems. Worry and eating too many heavy, dry and cold foods impedes the flow in this channel.

✔ **Raktavaha srota:** This channel corresponds to your circulatory system and what's known as the reticulo-endothelial system, which operates from your spleen and helps your immune system to function. The main headquarters is found in your liver and spleen and, like the rasavaha channel in the preceding bullet point, its opening occurs at the junction of your capillaries.

The raktavaha srota supplies blood to your body via the arteries and veins. These channels are upset when you consume hot, irritating foods such as chillies, or you have excessive exposure to the sun, fire or alcohol.

✔ **Mamsavaha srota:** This channel relates to your muscles and has its seat in your connective tissue, skin and your small tendons and ligaments. The opening for this srota is located on the upper layers of your skin and its passages are the whole of your muscular system. This channel carries muscle fibres – the components of your musculature. The mamsavaha srota becomes impaired if you don't chew your food properly, if you sleep immediately after eating or eat heavy, dense foods frequently.

✔ **Medavaha srota:** This channel is linked to the fat in your body known as adipose tissue, and can be located in your kidneys, adrenals and *omentum* (the fat in between the organs in your stomach). Its openings are in your sweat glands, and its passages are subcutaneous fat tissue. This srota functions to give bulk to your body, provide energy, give lubrication and transport fat throughout your system.

The medavaha srota becomes upset by lack of physical exercise, sleeping in the day and excessive fat and alcohol in your diet.

✔ **Ashtivaha srota:** In Western terms, this is your skeletal system whose seat is found in your pelvis, hips and sacrum. The ashtivaha srota provides you with support and protection as well as transporting nutrients for bone tissue. Its opening is in your nails and hair, and its passages are your skeletal system. It's disturbed by excessive exercise and a high intake of vata provoking foods – those which are dry, raw and cold.

✔ **Majjavaha srota:** This corresponds mainly with your nervous system, and its seat is in your brain, bone marrow, spinal cord and joints. The openings are at the junction of your nerves in the *synaptic spaces*, or the space between your muscles and nerves. Its course is throughout your nervous system.

The majjavaha srota functions in your body to carry the ingredients of marrow, memory, coordination and cerebrospinal fluid. It's damaged by compression injuries, especially to your bone tissue, and eating food that's difficult to digest.

✔ **Shukravaha srota:** This is the equivalent of the male reproductive system, which has its seat in the testicles and the nipples. The opening is in the urethra. Its passages are in the urogenital tract, prostate and epididymis, which are the tubules containing sperm in the testis. The function of shukravaha srota is to produce *ojas*, a substance that supports your immune system. The shukravaha srota is damaged by excessive or repressed sexual activity.

✔ **Artavavaha srotas:** These connect the female reproductive system, and only women have these channels. Their seat is in the ovaries and the areola of the nipples, with the opening located in the labia. Its channels are your uterus, fallopian tubes and vaginal passage. These channels function to produce reproductive tissues and carry menstrual blood. These networks become impaired if they're either underused or overused and if sex is initiated at an inappropriate time, such as during menstruation.

✔ **Stanyavaha srotas:** These channels are basically a subsystem of the artavavaha srotas, mentioned in the preceding point. They initiate the ability to produce milk during pregnancy, and their function is to carry milk to the baby. They're located in the breast tissue with their openings in the nipples, and they operate throughout the lactation system. Malnutrition is the condition that upsets their ability to function.

✔ **Svedavaha srota:** This channel transports your sweat, sebaceous secretions and liquid wastes throughout your body. It keeps your skin smooth and oiled. The seat is found in your sebaceous glands and hair follicles, and the openings are located all over your skin. The svedavaha srota helps you sweat, which is how you regulate your body temperature, and helps you eliminate bodily wastes and water. It gets disturbed by excessive exercise, anger, grief and fear, and when you expose yourself to excessive heat.

✔ **Purishavaha srota:** This comprises the waste-removal system which you can't live without because it removes the solid wastes from your body. This srota is based in your colon, rectum and caecum (large bowel), with the main opening located at your anus. This channel operates in your large intestine, where you absorb vital minerals and form faeces. This system also provides you with strength and support, and has a grounding effect.

This srota malfunctions if you overeat or suppress the urge to go to the loo to pass a stool. If you feel intense fear or are overly anxious, your purishavaha srota gets off-balance.

✓ **Mutravaha srota:** This srota is another waste-removal system, which removes liquid substances in the form of urine and is headquartered in your kidney and bladder. The main opening is located in the urethra – the point of exit for urine. The channels are the ureter (the tubes that propel urine from the kidneys to the bladder), urethra and bladder.

This srota regulates your blood pressure, fluid and electrolyte balance. Its rhythm becomes upset when you suppress the urge to urinate or eat too many foods high in oxalic acid (spinach is one). If you have sex while having the urge to use the toilet, you can cause an imbalance and create upsets like cystitis.

✓ **Manovaha srota:** This srota encompasses all the channels that help you to think and comprehend the world around you. They find their seat in your heart, brain and the energy centres in your body known as *chakras*. The senses perceive and react to stimuli. This also causes the *marma points* (rather like acupuncture points) on your body to react.

Manovaha srotas operate throughout the body and help regulate emotions and their related systems, including the realms of discrimination, feeling, thinking, desire and communication. They become harmed by excessively loud noises, suppressed emotions and intense focus – characteristic of a vata lifestyle, which leads to anxiety, dryness and erratic digestion.

Chapter 3

Uncovering the Subtle Energy Systems

*I*n this part of the book, I journey into the more subtle parts of the make-up of your body. These elements don't function independently but form an integrated matrix throughout your system, connected by *pranic currents* (energy). Like radio waves, these forces operate within your nerves (*nadis*) and channels known as *srotas*.

This chapter gives you a brief outline of how Ayurveda perceives the energy in your body on a subtle level, and how the food that you eat and thoughts that you think translate into your cellular and extra-cellular make-up. This is pretty esoteric stuff, but vital for your understanding of Ayurveda.

Pinpointing Three Essential Forces

The end products of all the food, images, air and fluids that you take in on a daily basis ultimately end up as *ojas*, *tejas* and *prana* – three forces that are akin to the finest elements of your immune system. The more you have of them, the less likely you are to get sick. I explain each in this section.

Outling ojas

Ojas is the refined essence of all your bodily tissues. It endows you with strong immunity and vigour. Without it, you would cease to live.

Ayurveda identifies two types of ojas:

- ✔ **Para ojas,** which resides in your heart and maintains its activity.
- ✔ **Apara ojas,** which moves around the body; it originates from your heart, nourishes your tissues, and supports your life.

You also derive ojas from pure bliss (or *ananda*) – that which makes you feel happy and content wherever you find yourself. In other words, the more you connect to that pure centre of your being where peace resides, the more ojas you put in the bank. Meditation is a great way to get there, and I explore meditation and its many benefits in Chapter 6.

Although ojas is a benefit to your body, too much can lead to trouble. If it increases faster than your body can process it, ojas is converted to *ama* (toxins) and can then incite issues such as high cholesterol and increased blood sugar.

If, on the other hand, you lack ojas, you leave your immune system weakened, which of course leaves you open to all kinds of illness. You might notice that your level of ojas is low when you have dry skin or feel an unusual level of anxiety or fear.

Targeting tejas

Tejas is connected to the fiery principle in your body – *agni* – but operates on a more subtle level. Visualise tejas as the container for agni. It works in many ways like a director, keeping order within your body through processes like regulating body temperature, guiding cell function, and otherwise maintaining balance. Tejas is the substance that enables you to digest food, emotions, ideas and thoughts.

Tejas helps to create and protect your ojas, which in turn supports prana (see the next section) in its work to defend and maintain the respiratory function of your cells. If the force of tejas is low, then your body produces too much ojas. On the other hand, if the flame of your tejas is too high, it burns ojas and therefore leaves you open to disease.

Your body's innate ability to prioritise is part of what tejas controls. For example, if you're under attack, your stomach shuts down and your blood supply is redirected to your limbs so that you can run away.

Tejas also contributes to the cellular intelligence that maintains the sizes and shapes of your bodily components. It dictates how your hair grows and the order of your cells within your organs and other structures. This same cellular intelligence enables wounds to heal.

More ethereally speaking, because tejas gives luminosity to your skin, eyes and hair, it's said to create a glow. When someone is described as enlightened, they have tejas to thank. For those who can see auras, a halo is the manifestation of this light.

Promoting prana

Prana orchestrates and animates your existence. It's the life force that enters you at birth and exits when you die. In Chinese medicine, it's called *chi*. The *prana shakti*, or force in your body, is created by the food you eat and the air you inhale into your lungs.

Prana governs all the motor and sensory nerve transmissions in your body. All cognitive functions of your mind are related to pranic waves, as is the motion of your heart, which pumps vital nutrients around your body. From the moment of a foetus's conception, prana acts to circulate ojas within it.

Cosmic prana abounds in the universe, which is why all of creation works as one harmonious whole. Prana is made up of air and ether elements, which gives it great qualities of expansion. (Refer to Chapter 2 to find out more about the building blocks of existence.) You can experience this expansion in meditation when you reach a stage of stillness and experience a sense of dissolution of all boundaries.

The seat of your emotional experiences is your lungs, which is where prana is garnered from the atmosphere. Kapha emotions like greed and attachment are stored in the lower lobes, while anger and hatred (connected to pitta dosha) sit in the middle region.

Finally, fear and sadness attributed to vata dosha are stored in the upper lobes of your lungs. No wonder that Ayurveda puts so much importance on the smooth operating of the lungs and the practice of *pranayama* (breathing techniques). Chapter 14 tells you more about pranayama.

Navigating the Nadis: Surveying the Subtle Nervous System

Energy flows around your body through the *nadis*, channels (72,000 of them!) that emanate from a central channel along your spine to create a simmering network of very fine forces. These channels are practically untraceable by direct empirical observation, rather like the meridians in Chinese medicine. They connect at several points of your body to create areas of unique intensity, the *chakras*, which I discuss in the upcoming section, 'Working with the Wheels of Power: The Chakras'.

Three nadis form the foundation of this intricate network:

- ✔ **Sushumna nadi** runs through your core, alongside your spine, and is the central channel from which all others emanate. The chakra system (see the following section) is located along this nadi.
- ✔ **Pingala** is identified with energising masculine qualities and opens in your right nostril.
- ✔ **Ida** has pacifying feminine characteristics and finds its opening in your left nostril.

The left channel is more cooling and passive, while the right is warming and generally more active. You can learn to use this knowledge to help you in your daily life, by the practice of *pranayama* (breathing exercises), which I describe in Chapter 14. Meditation and a balanced lifestyle clear and bring harmony to this network of channels and help unblock it if needs be.

The other principal nadis include:

- ✔ **Alambusha nadi** relates to seeing, especially your right eye and its optic nerve.
- ✔ **Chakshusha nadi** connects to your left eye and its optic nerve; it supports your ability to perceive forms.
- ✔ **Hastajihva nadi** relates to your right ear, ends in your left big toe, and aids speech production.
- ✔ **Ghandhari nadi** relates to your left ear and ends in your right big toe. It aids perception of speech.
- ✔ **Kuhu nadi** connects to your channels of excretion, opening at the anus via the rectum.
- ✔ **Saraswati nadi** is named after the goddess of wisdom; it begins in your tongue and ends in the oral cavity, where it perceives the six tastes. It also gives you the wisdom and capacity to speak.

✔ **Shankini nadi** relates to the prostate and cervix and finds its opening in your genitals; it helps in the production of male and female reproductive tissue.

✔ **Vishvodara nadi** is located in the umbilical area; it aids in the distribution of prana and promotes the healthy working of your pancreas and adrenals.

Discovering the Dhatus: Building Blocks of Your Body

The *dhatus* are the original building blocks of all the tissues in your body. They make up your physical body, the one you touch and see. (I explore your other bodies – yes, you have more! – in the later section 'Placing the Pancha Koshas: The Invisible Coverings'.)

Dhatus are the basic types of cells which make up your body: lymph, blood, bone, fat, muscle, nerve and reproductive cells. They're formed from the nutrient *chyle*, which enters your bloodstream at the thoracic duct. Like a roman fountain, the effective production of the first dhatu leads to the creation of the next one, and so on down the line until your reproductive tissue and ojas are produced.

Dhatus also produce secondary tissues known as *upadhatus*, which don't go on to make other cells. An example of this is your teeth, which are a by-product of bone tissue. So the health of your bones can be observed by looking at your teeth.

 Each dhatu has its own *agni*, which is the fuel that helps to generate tissue elements that make up your unique physiology. When dhatus are formed, waste products are also produced. When the *srotas* (channels – see Chapter 2) are operating optimally, they carry these waste products away, otherwise the waste creates *ama* (toxins; explained fully in Chapter 5) and disease in your system.

The seven dhatus, in the order that they form, are as follows:

✔ **Rasa dhatu:** Meaning 'sap', rasa equates to lymph and occurs in tissue fluids such as plasma and chyle. It feeds all the other tissues of the body.

✔ **Rakta dhatu:** Rakta refers to blood. It functions to preserve life and nourish and oxygenate your whole body, and so brings vigour, good colour and warmth.

✔ **Mamsa dhatu:** Mamsa is the muscle tissue, which covers the bone and provides strength and support, especially to the fat tissue.

 ✔ **Meda dhatu:** Otherwise known as fat, meda dhatu plays a vital role in your body. It lubricates all your muscles, joints and ligaments, and acts as an insulator.

 ✔ **Asthi dhatu:** Asthi refers to bone tissue, which provides support for all the organs and musculature to function effectively.

 ✔ **Majja dhatu:** Also known as bone marrow, majja fills your bones and lubricates the body – especially the eyes, stools and skin.

 ✔ **Shukra dhatu:** Shukra means 'semen'; its female counterpart is known as *artava*. It's the substance that creates life, and it also produces ojas, which guards your immune system.

Working with the Wheels of Power: The Chakras

The word *chakra* means 'wheel' in Sanskrit. The chakras are nodal points where your mental, physical and energy body interact (the next section explains these bodies). As many as 140 of these centres of awareness exist, but I focus on the seven main chakras, which are located along your spine.

The system of the chakras is related to the *mano vaha srotas*, the channels which carry your mental faculties (see Chapter 2). They can become perturbed by negative feelings and create mental ama or toxins. This ama can be stored and may block the movement of energy in the chakra system.

The chakra system's points of subtle energy are located on the *sushumna nadi*, which runs vertically through your body from your head to the base of your spine. The workings of your endocrine and glandular system are intimately linked by a nerve plexus to each of your chakras, shown in Figure 3-1.

A *plexus*, also known as a *chiasma*, is where a network of nerves meet up with your lymphatic and blood vessels. The chakra system passes an electric current from one organ to another in order to maintain balance throughout your system.

Table 3-1 shows you a breakdown of the elements of the seven chakras. Each one is numbered in order of density, so the earth element is number 1 and ether is number 5. Each chakra has a vibration which resonates with a sound; these sounds (*mantras*) are also listed. You can chant these sounds and use them to meditate on to purify a centre.

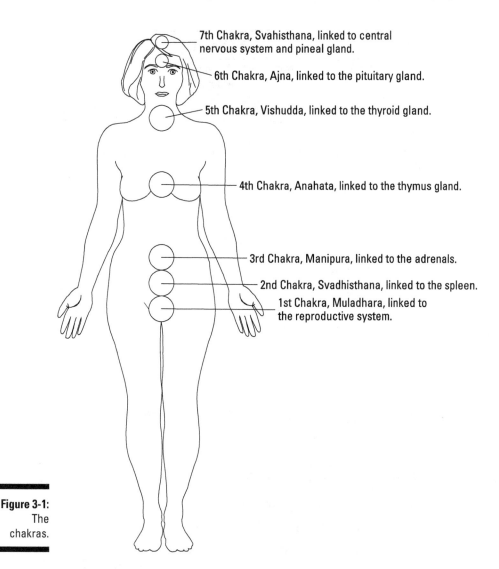

7th Chakra, Svahisthana, linked to central nervous system and pineal gland.

6th Chakra, Ajna, linked to the pituitary gland.

5th Chakra, Vishudda, linked to the thyroid gland.

4th Chakra, Anahata, linked to the thymus gland.

3rd Chakra, Manipura, linked to the adrenals.

2nd Chakra, Svadhisthana, linked to the spleen.

1st Chakra, Muladhara, linked to the reproductive system.

Figure 3-1:
The
chakras.

The chakras also have direction of flow, so by way of example, the 1st and 2nd chakras govern the flow of the downwards energy force known as *apana* (explained further in Chapter 7). In practice, that may mean, if you're constipated, for example, that the muladhara chakra is blocked and may be connected to an unprocessed emotion such as insecurity.

Table 3-1				The Seven Chakras			
Number and Element	Name	Plexus	Activating Mantra	Flow	Disorders	Physiological System
1st, Earth	Muladhara	Sacral	Lam	Apana	Instability	Reproductive
2nd, Water	Svadhisthana	Hypogastric	Vam	Apana	Sexual repression	Urinary, genital, spleen
3rd, Fire	Manipura	Solar	Ram	Samana	Anger, hatred	Digestive, adrenals, pancreas
4th, Air	Anahata	Cardiac	Yam	Vyana	Lack of love	Circulatory, thymus
5th, Ether	Vishudda	Throat	Ham	Udana	Lack of commu-nication, suppressed emotions	Respiratory, metabolism, thyroid
6th, Light	Ajna	Optic chiasma	Sam ksham	Prana	Failure to accept reality	Autonomic nervous system, pituitary
7th, Bliss	Svahisthana	Cerebral hemisphere	Aum	Prana	Psychosis, depression	Pineal

The chakras are connected with emotions as follows:

- 1st chakra: Security, self-confidence and body image

- 2nd chakra: Creativity, vitality, anger and gender identity

- 3rd chakra: Trust, intimacy, status and fear

- 4th chakra: Resolution of feelings, emotional pain and self-awareness

- 5th chakra: Self-expression, joy, maintenance of personal boundaries and integrity

- 6th chakra: Intuition, memory, discrimination and reasoning

- 7th chakra: Transcendental consciousness

Spinning too many plates

If you think of life as a spinning disc, most of us spend much of our time on the periphery of the wheel. This is where the disc is moving the most, and relates to the world of action. However, located in the centre, stillness resides but is largely ignored. Then we become out of balance and get sick and stressed. You can help yourself by building a relationship with this quiet wisdom within you, using the practice of meditation and yoga. (See Chapters 6 and 7 for more on meditation and yoga.) Through meditation, you eventually find *sat chit ananda* (knowledge, consciousness and bliss) within yourself.

There's much to say about the emotions commonly associated with the chakras that is beyond the scope of this book. Perhaps a personal example will suffice. For years I suffered with almost continuous sore throats, because I found it very difficult to really express my needs. Through yoga, meditation and psychotherapy, I found my voice, so to speak, and the throat conditions no longer trouble me.

Placing the Pancha Koshas: The Invisible Coverings

According to Ayurveda, the human form is composed of three bodies: the gross body (physical), which you can touch and feel; the subtle body (mental), which is connected to your nervous system; and the causal body (energy), which links you to the astral world.

As well as this, your body is made up of five envelopes, or sheaths – called *pancha koshas* – creating layers of decreasing density, as shown in Figure 3-2. According to Ayurvedic thinking, you are, in fact, spirit in matter. These sheaths sustain you in the corporeal world until the day you die.

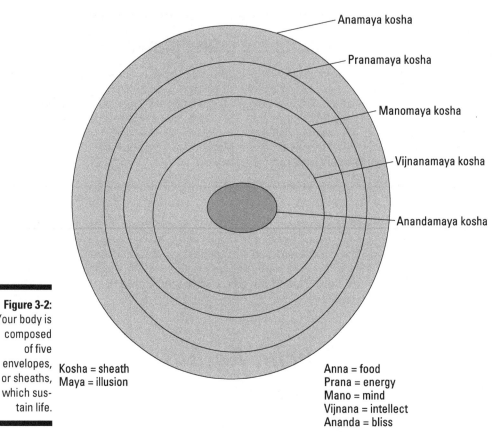

Anamaya kosha

Pranamaya kosha

Manomaya kosha

Vijnanamaya kosha

Anandamaya kosha

Figure 3-2:
Your body is
composed
of five
envelopes,
or sheaths,
which sus-
tain life.

Kosha = sheath
Maya = illusion

Anna = food
Prana = energy
Mano = mind
Vijnana = intellect
Ananda = bliss

The pancha koshas, from the densest to most subtle, are:

- **Anamaya kosha,** or the food-formed sheath, is composed of the five elements. It's intimately connected to the first three chakras (explained in
  the previous section).

- **Pranamaya kosha** expresses itself through the ether and air elements,
  which are invested in the anahata (heart) and vishudda (throat)
  chakras. Here, circulating air in the form of prana finds its home. This is
  also where the vital pranas (see Chapter 2) vitalise the mind and body
  by connecting the senses.

✔ The third and fourth layers share an intimate connection. **Manomaya kosha** refers to your mind, and **vijnanamaya kosha** to your intellect, where discrimination and true intelligence become directed towards the eternal. These two sheaths are closely tied to the ajna chakra in your pineal area. According to Ayurveda, energising this centre gives you innate inner vision – a 'third eye' that perceives things as they really are and recognises divinity in all things.

✔ **Anandamaya kosha** is where you experience supreme bliss that's part of your causal body but transcends all of your the senses and the experience of your physical body.

Ayurveda attempts to direct you towards *sattwa guna*, or the energy of balance, purity and truth, via meditation, yoga and dietary principles. This in turn benefits your anamaya kosha which, once vitalised by appropriate food choices, brings more *sattwa* (harmony) to the next covering, and so on until all the koshas are clear and functioning optimally.

This strategy eventually leads you to live in a state of perfect bliss. And who doesn't want that?

Chapter 4

Determining Your Constitution

In This Chapter
▶ Discovering your constitution type
▶ Understanding vata, pitta and kapha types
▶ Knowing the significance of taking your pulse

*A*yurvedic therapy is based on knowledge of your constitution – of your unique mind–body condition. In Sanskrit, the word for constitution is *prakruti*, or 'first creation', which relates to your constitution at birth. Ayurveda sees illness as a product of your lifestyle more than an invasion by an outside force, and different constitution types depend on different approaches to maintain a healthy balance. Armed with the knowledge of your constitution type, you can select what's best for you from the rest of this book.

This chapter contains information essential to understanding how to put the advice in this book to work for you. If you want to get the most out of this book, read this chapter and determine what type of constitution you have. This chapter arms you with all you need to know to get the best out of the book regardless of your diet and lifestyle choices.

The sensory inputs of your mother had a great effect on you before you were born. Whether your mother was contented or conflicted, listened to Mozart or heavy metal – all these factors can result in an increase of agitation and aggravate vata dosha (see the next section for an explanation of the doshas).

Other influences are hereditary traits – both strengths and weaknesses – along with the age and fitness of your parents. More esoteric influences, such as the position of the planets at the time of birth, also influenced your constitution at the time of your birth, along with the seasonal influences and the condition of the sperm and ova at the moment of conception.

Evaluating Your Constitution Type

The following sections offer ways to determine your constitution type, or *dosha*, from three different aspects: physical type, physiological traits and psychological characteristics. The word dosha actually means 'fault' in Sanskrit, because the elements that make up your dosha are constantly subject to change. Therefore they can very easily go out of balance.

The doshic types are:

- ✔ **Vata:** Classed as an *ectomorph* in Western typology, you're either taller or shorter than average, slim, and not able to put weight on easily. Mentally, you're very agile and curious but quickly bored. You're prone to nervous ailments and anxiety.

- ✔ **Pitta:** You're a *mesomorph* in Western typology, being of medium build. Mentally, you're very focused and can sustain concentration. You're prone to inflammatory disorders of all types, such as mouth ulcers, skin rashes and bouts of anger.

- ✔ **Kapha:** You're closest to an *endomorph* in Western typology – heavy set, and you easily put on weight that you can't shift. Mentally, you can deal with stress well but are susceptible to depression. You have a tendency towards lymphatic problems.

You can determine your constitution type in more detail by going through each table in this chapter and putting a tick next to any description you think applies to you. If you think that none of the descriptions in one row apply to you, ignore that line or ask how a friend perceives you. If you decide that the characteristics in two of the columns pertain to you, then tick them both. You'll almost certainly find that you're a mixture of doshas. I explain what to do when you've discovered your dosha in the later section 'Determining Your Dosha'.

Checking your physical type

You can get started determining your doshic profile by looking at your physical traits. Table 4-1 outlines the physical features of each doshic type.

Table 4-1 **Physical Constitution Traits**

Physical Feature	Vata	Pitta	Kapha
Musculoskeletal Features	Bony; joints crack	Well proportioned, compact	Well-formed, broad shouldered, good muscles
Body Frame/Height	Extra tall/small	Average	Heavy set, stocky
Body Weight	Light; has difficulty putting on weight	Medium	Plump; has difficulty losing weight
Hair	Curly, dry, coarse, dark	Blond or red; fine; oily; goes grey or starts balding at a young age	Lustrous, wavy, thick
Skin	Cool, dry, dark circles under the eyes, tans easily, sparse sweat	Warm; slightly oily; fair or reddish; prone to moles, freckles and rashes; sweats easily; susceptible to wrinkles and sunburn	Thick and pale, few wrinkles
Fingernails	Cracked, lined, brittle	Pink nail beds with a smooth appearance	Well formed with well-defined moons
Eyes	Move a lot (taking everything in), sparse lashes, dry, tics, squints, small/average eyes, brown, black or violet iris	Sharp, steady gaze; green, blue or hazel iris; sclera (white of the eye) tends to be red	Long lashes, large eyes with blue or brown iris, white sclera
Facial Features	Irregular	Prominent	Rounded
Mouth	Thin, dry, dark	Medium, red, soft	Full, velvety, wide
Teeth	Need braces, break easily, loose	Yellowish, medium-sized teeth	Large, strong, straight, well formed
Gums	Thin and emaciated	Bleed easily	Healthy and pink

Looking at physiological traits

The doshas operate in different ways, with vata acting erratically, pitta in an exaggerated fashion and kapha in a slow and sluggish way. Table 4-2 goes more deeply into the physiological traits of each dosha.

Getting your finger on the pulse

An experienced Ayurvedic practitioner can use the pulse to confirm your constitutional profile. This is because the pulse is said to be a true picture of who you are. It represents the rhythm of your life, because all your spiritual, mental and physical experiences are embedded within it.

Taking your pulse holds no mystery – all it demands from you is practice. The best time to take your pulse is first thing in the morning on an empty stomach.

If you're female, begin by placing your right hand, palm facing upwards, under your left wrist just below the thumb, which also is facing upwards. Use the opposite side if you're male. Don't be tempted to take your pulse with your fingers at the top of the upturned wrist, because they'll be in the wrong position. You'll feel a notch at the top end of your upturned forearm just below the base of your thumb. Now place your index finger below it to feel the pulse of the radial artery.

Ayurveda describes the rhythm and course of the pulsation as the movement of animals, so it's easy to conceptualise. Try to get a sense of the temperature, speed and type of movement of your pulse. Your index finger in this position is connected to vata dosha, and the movement that you feel is that of a snake or a leech. It's cool, thready and fast. Now lift your index finger and use your middle finger, which falls just one finger-width beneath it. This is where the pitta dosha resides; the movement here is like a frog or sparrow. You'll experience the pulse here as warm, strong, sharp and fast.

Finally, place your ring finger on the artery so that you're three finger widths from the notch below your thumb. This is often the most difficult to find because it's dull, heavy, cool and distant to the touch, and has the motion of a swan.

If you feel confident with this analysis, then add it to the constitutional tables in this chapter. You'll gain intimacy with pulse taking the more you do it, so keep practising.

Table 4-2   Physiological Constitution Traits

Trait	Vata	Pitta	Kapha
Thirst	Variable	Excessive	Scanty
Appetite	Changeable, easily satisfied	Gets very hungry and has to eat	Can eat less often, grazes when disturbed
Preferred Tastes	Warm food with sweet, sour and salty tastes	Cold food with sweet, bitter and astringent tastes	Dry and warm food with pungent, bitter and astringent tastes
Urination	Scanty, frequent, light colour	Moderate amounts, dark yellow	Large amounts; can be cloudy, infrequent
Elimination	Often constipated, stools are dry, dark and small	Prone to loose bowels; stools are abundant, light or orange in colour, smelly	Stools are large, heavy, slow, soft, sometimes with mucus and brown in colour
Pattern of Illness	Prone to nervous symptoms (such as essential tremor), chronic pain, anxiety	Prone to gastritis, hives, inflammatory conditions, irritability, psoriasis	Prone to excessive swelling (oedema), diabetes, high cholesterol, osteoarthritis, heavy chest colds
Attitude towards Sex	Quickly satisfied, very interested or no interest	Domineering, passionate, quickly satisfied	Likes to take lots of time; romantic and loyal to partner
Speech	Quick, talkative, high pitched, cracked, dry, misses words	Sharp, precise, convincing	Melodic, soft, slow and sweet; monotonous when out of balance

Assessing your mental state

The balance of the *gunas* – the three subtle energies (rajas, tamas and sattwa, explained in Chapter 2) that give you certain characteristics or tendencies in your emotional makeup – determines your psychological traits.

Generally, vata is connected to rajas and movement, hence these individuals' constant desire for change. Sattwa is connected to pitta and associated with the ability to concentrate for long periods. Finally, tamas is connected to kapha and can make an individual slow and deliberate with a tendency to dislike change.

Table 4-3 outlines the various psychological traits associated with the three doshas.

Table 4-3	Psychological Constitution Traits		
Psychological Traits	*Vata*	*Pitta*	*Kapha*
Mental Abilities	Creative, restless and not really sure what he or she wants	Focused, aggressive, goal directed	Steady, slow, calm, dependable
Dreams	Fearful	Colourful, fiery, conflicted	Romantic
Sleep	Light and interrupted	Short (about six hours) and sound	Heavy, difficult to rouse, prolonged
Personality	Indecisive, changeable, lacking constancy, worried, volatile, timid	Sharp mind, intellectual, critical and brave	Steady, even tempered, slow and attached

Psychological Traits	Vata		Pitta		Kapha	
Memory and Concentration	Good short-term memory; finds it hard to focus		Good memory, focused attention		Prolonged memory (once something is committed to memory, it's never forgotten), slow to learn	
Financial Acumen	Spends very quickly		Spends carefully on luxuries		Accumulates wealth and is slow to spend	

Determining Your Dosha

Totting up the ticks in each column in each of the tables in this chapter gives you a rough estimation of your doshic make-up. The column with the most ticks is your primary dosha; the one with the second-most number of ticks is your secondary dosha. There are very few pure types, and most people come under what's known as a *dual prakruti*, where two doshas are fairly prominent.

If one dosha stands out in your analysis, follow the instructions for your diet and lifestyle listed in the rest of the book. If, on the other hand, you have a fairly even score of two doshas, follow the diet and lifestyle changes listed for when one of the two doshas predominates. This is also true for those of you who are fairly evenly balanced between the three, or *tridoshic*. In selecting the right diet, you can always find tastes which are common to both doshas; for example, a naturally sweet taste pacifies both vata and pitta.

Part II
Living in Harmony with Ayurveda: Promoting Good Health

In this part . . .

- ✔ Discover a daily routine to keep you in tip-top health.

- ✔ Stretch and tone your body with yoga – and find poses tailored to your dosha (constitution).

- ✔ Find help with getting a refreshing night's sleep – the Ayurvedic way.

- ✔ Get advice on eating seasonally to keep your digestion and energy levels functioning optimally.

Chapter 5

Ease and Disease:
Health According to Ayurveda

*Y*ou might not have thought a great deal about what health means. Maybe you simply expect or strive for health, but, if you're like most people, it's not something you've carefully defined.

So what is health? In Ayurvedic terms, health is harmony. It's a state of normality and well-being, and means being free from disease and discomfort.

The concept of health gets a little more interesting from here. According to Ayurveda, you're a true reflection of the universe and so can't be totally healthy if the environment around you is damaged and polluted. With Ayurveda, wellness is the ever-changing movement towards actualising your full potential while keeping in mind your abilities and individual needs.

Vagbhata, a physician in the Middle Ages, said that health is a state of equilibrium of the doshas whereby:

✔ Your *agni* or fires are *samavasta* (in equilibrium).

✔ Your *dhatus* (or basic life-supporting tissues in your body) are in a proper state of integrity.

✔ The process of elimination of waste products of your body is regular.

✔ Your *atma* (spirit), sense organs and mind are clean and bright.

Aligning body, mind and spirit

The word used to define health in Ayurveda is *swastha*, which literally means 'to be established in the self' – a true alignment of body, mind and spirit. In this state, the soul uses your body as a temple in which to realise itself and to help you attain four principal objectives:

✔ **Artha:** To be able to have enough resources to live, meaning that you can perform your work and earn money to take care of your needs and those of your family. Meeting this duty without material comfort would be very difficult. The way forward with material wealth is not to become attached to it.

✔ **Dharma:** Rightful duty, or performing the tasks that you're meant to do for the betterment of society, the planet and yourself. Dharma is your true calling, whether you're a driver, farmer, doctor or gardener. You can have different dharmas for different stages of your life.

✔ **Kama:** The pursuit of your desires and satisfaction of your everyday needs. Kama includes your desire to live a long and healthy life. Suppress your desires and you wind up a fully coiled spring that can suddenly release with undesirable consequences. On the other hand, if you become too attached to your desires, you become their slave.

✔ **Moksha:** The attainment of self-realisation or bliss eternal. This is the culmination of your life's journey, or the Holy Grail spoken of for centuries by the mystics. Moksha means 'liberation' and 'the experience of union within yourself', or *ekatvam* (oneness), and it frees you from suffering.

In other words, your body is in a state of functional equilibrium if your hunger, appetite and digestion are not impaired or faulty, and your body can easily and regularly eliminate wastes such as sweat, faeces and urine. Your mind comes into play, too, before you can be said to be fit: true health encompasses a tranquil soul and mind, and sense organs that function efficiently.

In this chapter, I explore the progress of disease and give tips to keep you healthy.

Discovering Ama: Its Journey through the Body

Because a large part of health is the absence of disease, understanding how and why illness happens is important. The nature of disease is known as *nidana* in Sanskrit or *pathology* in the West. And disease has a lot to do with something called *ama* – the juices from food that aren't fully digested. This is why Ayurvedic doctors often focus on digestion. Anything that exists in a state of incomplete transformation is volatile, and ama tends to accumulate as toxins in your system. The result is amaya, or disease caused by ama. Examples of this are joint pain when ama accumulates in the junctions between your bones, and mucous when your nose becomes blocked.

If you're well, the doshas are safely in their homes, as follows:

- Vata is located mainly in your colon.
- Pitta lives mainly in your small intestine.
- Kapha resides primarily in your stomach and lungs.

Flip back to Chapter 2 for the details about doshas.

In Western medical terms, ama equates to:

- **Atheroma:** Plaques of cholesterol in the arteries.
- **Amyloid tissue:** Protein that abnormally lodges in the tissues of the body and causes inflammation.
- **Pannus:** Tissue that settles in the joint spaces of rheumatoid arthritis sufferers, creating inflammation and eroding the articular spaces.
- **Keloid:** Tissue that causes overgrowth of scar tissues.

The effect of vata dosha

Vata dosha (read Chapter 2 for a reminder of the doshas) is known as the king in Ayurveda, because nothing can happen without it. When it's working well, vata dosha gives your nervous system the ability to exchange messages, and enables your body to digest food and eliminate your bodily wastes. That's why so much of Ayurvedic treatment is dedicated to working with vata dosha. On the other hand, when it's disturbed, vata dosha is overwhelmingly important in the active causation of disease. Vata dosha has the attributes of the wind and can, like the wind that you observe in nature, be increased, decreased, deviated or obstructed.

Derangements like these eventually lead to mental imbalance, which promotes sensory deprivation or excess, creating fresh disease in an ever-increasing spiral. An example of this is long-term, unremitting stress, when you become agitated and unsettled. Over time, this can lead you to make poor food choices in an attempt to pacify the feelings. This in turn can give you slow digestion, and then you start to accumulate toxins in your system. Further down the line, you gain weight and, if you continue down that path, it can lead to high cholesterol, hypertension and heart disease.

Almost all disease involves vata. One of its common and most important effects is to diminish the digestive processes and therefore the transformative actions that enable your body to produce new tissue. If your tissues don't get the nutrition they need, ama forms and deposits itself in different parts of your body – especially those places that have already been weakened. Eventually, ama can mix with the doshas and manifests as disease. This is when signs and symptoms arise.

Answer the questions in Table 5-1 about signs and symptoms so that you can determine whether you may have ama in your system.

The symptoms of ama accumulation

So how do you know that you're accumulating ama? Fill in the short questionnaire in Table 5-1 to help you find out. Answer either 'never', 'sometimes' or 'always', with one point for your answer.

Table 5-1	A Checklist of Symptoms		
	Never	*Sometimes*	*Always*
I wake up in the morning feeling tired, dull and heavy. I need a dose of caffeine to get started.			
I feel mentally dull, lack enthusiasm, and am easily fatigued.			
In the morning, my tongue has a coating and/or my breath smells.			
I often experience food as tasteless and have a very small appetite.			
I regularly suffer a feeling of heaviness and indigestion shortly after eating.			
My stools are heavy and sink, and they can smell unpleasant.			
I have a lot of mucus and tend to get many colds over the year.			
I often feel a sense of heaviness in my body, as though it has a blockage somewhere.			
I tend to get constipation.			
I often feel the need to spit.			
I tend to put weight on that I can't shift.			

If you scored between 8 and 11 points in the 'always' section, then you definitely need to address your diet and lifestyle by looking at Part III and Chapter 14. I also encourage you to enlist the help of a qualified practitioner who can really guide you. Between 8 and 11 in the 'sometimes' section sounds like it's time for you to do something about your health before any problems become more serious. If you scored between 8 and 11 in the 'never' section you're definitely on the right track to a long and healthy life.

Tracing the Path of Disease

In general, disease happens slowly. The development of disease is known in Sanskrit as *samprapti*, which means the birth of pain, and in Western medicine as *pathogenesis*. The strength of Ayurveda lies in the fact that it can address an illness at any stage. Each disease follows its own prescribed route because of causative factors such as inappropriate diet and seasonal indiscretions, like eating ice-cream in the winter when you have a cold.

In the upcoming sections, I illustrate the six stages of disease.

Accumulation: The start of discomfort

Accumulation, or *sanchaya*, is when your doshas become imbalanced. One or other dosha begins to increase within its own site, creating disparities.

Temporary disparities are normal, as long as the doshas return to their main homes – vata in the colon, pitta in the small intestine, and kapha in the stomach.

Accumulation causes mild discomfort which, if you're primarily vata (refer to Chapter 4 to establish your predominant dosha), might be expressed as:

- ✔ Anxiety
- ✔ Constipation
- ✔ Distension
- ✔ Dryness in the mouth
- ✔ Fear
- ✔ Flatulence
- ✔ Need for warmth
- ✔ Weakness of the limbs

If you're primarily pitta, accumulation can bring symptoms such as:

- ✔ Aversion to hot food
- ✔ Craving for sugar
- ✔ Burning in the stomach
- ✔ Irritability
- ✔ Rashes
- ✔ Sweating
- ✔ Yellowish tinge to the whites of your eyes

Individuals who are primarily kapha experience the following during accumulation:

- ✔ Craving for astringent and bitter tastes
- ✔ Feeling heavy
- ✔ Lack of appetite
- ✔ Swelling
- ✔ Tiredness

At this stage, you feel an aversion towards the cause of accumulation, so if you're listening to your body, the disease path is easy to change. For example, if you're primarily kapha in constitution, you started to feel slightly nauseous and heavy, especially after eating. As soon as you observe this fact, you realise that kapha dosha is on the increase in your system. The remedy is simple: just lighten your system by drinking ginger tea and abstaining from food until your appetite is restored.

However, your body may be so toxic with ama that it no longer operates correctly. This happens if you lacked awareness in the primary stages so didn't pick up on the subtle signals of the body. In this case, you begin to crave more of the activity or the foods that caused the problem in the first place.

Treating yourself is easier in the accumulation stage than in later stages, and that's why Ayurveda emphasises prevention. Never wait to treat an imbalance, but start straight away to do something about it. Part III gives you all you need to know to stay in balance.

Aggravation: Things not quite right

During the aggravation, or *prakopa*, stage, the dosha begins to move in more pronounced ways:

- ✔ Vata dosha moves upwards into the higher part of the colon.
- ✔ Kapha dosha takes its place in the upper part of the stomach.
- ✔ Pitta moves to the duodenum.

During the aggravation stage, the dosha fills its container or seat – vata in your colon, kapha in your lungs and stomach, and pitta in your digestive tract. For example, if you're a pitta and you eat a hot curry for lunch with a beer in the summer, you're likely to feel hot and realise that you should cut down on spices. However, a friend invites you over in the evening and cooks a Mexican bean dish laced with Tabasco, which you wash down with tequila. After so much spice and alcohol, you probably won't be able to sleep because of terrible heartburn.

If you're a kapha individual, eating cold foods and dairy products during winter will cause aggravation; for vatas, dry, cool and light foods can cause unrest.

If you're kapha, the symptoms of aggravation express themselves as:

- ✔ Congested lungs
- ✔ Desire for sleep
- ✔ Coldness
- ✔ Nausea

Vata individuals are subject to:

- ✔ Coldness of the hands and feet
- ✔ Intense desire for fluids
- ✔ Gurgling in the stomach
- ✔ Pain, especially in the thighs and lower back

Pitta individuals are subject to:

- ✔ Heartburn with accompanying nausea
- ✔ Acidity
- ✔ Constant irritability
- ✔ Thirst

During the aggravation stage, you need to bring the dosha back to its site of origin as soon as possible to prevent more serious problems.

You really need to take action now, because this is the point just before the aggravated dosha leaves your gastrointestinal tract, after which you may need medical assistance. Get the information you need in Part III and especially Chapter 12.

Overflow: Circulation through the system

The overflow (or *prasara*) stage is when the disturbed doshas start to spread around your body via the circulatory system. They settle first in places of previous weakness, like those that have experienced trauma.

During this stage, primarily vata subjects feel symptoms such as:

✔ Aching

✔ Dry skin

✔ Dull eyes

✔ Extreme fatigue

✔ Restlessness

If you have a pitta predominance, you're likely to experience:

✔ Excessive body heat

✔ Burning of urine and faeces

Kapha folks may get:

✔ Increased salivation or water brash (heartburn with reflux)

✔ Loss of taste

✔ Vomiting

In this distribution stage, the doshas lodge in what are termed *khavaigunyas* or defective spaces in your body; these spaces have been likened to potholes in the road. Once the dosha has entered these spaces it invests the tissues with its qualities. For example, when excess kapha dosha enters your lymphatic system, you experience swelling of the legs and ankles.

Relocation: Finding a new home

During the relocation (or *sthana samsraya*) stage, circulating dosha begins to merge with tissues – in an old injury or other site of weakness.

- ✔ When pitta enters a weakened site, it produces an inflammatory change that creates sharp pain and heat.
- ✔ If vata is relocating, it causes atrophy and cracking of the joints known as *crepitous*.
- ✔ Kapha moving from its home results in congestion and heaviness.

Warning bells go off during the relocation stage, and you experience what's known as *prodromal (herald) symptoms* in Western medicine – signs pointing to what's coming. Each disease sends a different signal. For example, in the relocation stage, diabetes makes itself known through increased thirst and urination.

At this stage, you really need to seek medical attention from your GP to stop things getting worse.

Manifestation: Symptoms brought forth

At the manifestation (or *vyakti*) stage, the disease is an entity and has a definite course. It shows signs and symptoms that make its diagnosis beyond doubt. During this phase, the doshas have fully merged with your tissues and made functional changes within your body's systems.

At this stage, your disease acquires a name.

Diversification/specification: How complications set in

The end stage of a disease is called diversification/specification, or *bheda*. During this stage, the site of an illness becomes clear. For example, pneumonia can be viral, intestinal, lobar or broncho-pneumonia, and which type it is won't be clear until the diversification/specification stage.

Complications set in at this stage in the other tissues of your body. These are secondary to the initial problem; osteoporosis, for example, can cause fractures of the bones, because it thins bone tissue.

You're probably taking medicine now and are under the care of your doctor.

Knowing the Importance of Lifestyle for Your Health

You can't control everything – and certainly disease that stems from hereditary factors is out of your grasp – but the good news is that many of the disease-causing elements are firmly under your control.

Diet and lifestyle are the main components of how and whether disease gets a chance to wreak havoc within your body. In Ayurvedic terms, the lifestyle choices you make balance or excite your doshas. Doshic imbalance then leaves you open to disease.

Broadly classified, three major causes of doshic imbalance exist, which I explain in the next sections.

Failure to acknowledge your inner wisdom

It's the rare human who doesn't ignore his or her inner wisdom now and then. Who among us hasn't drunk too much alcohol, or eaten too much chocolate, or failed to get enough sleep? This kind of situation, though, always provides early warnings for you to act upon, but if your mind is clouded by *tamas* (inertia) or over-stimulated with *rajas* (activity – refer to Chapter 2 for more on tamas and rajas), you ignore the red lights. This is when your ego blocks common sense.

Your immune system is eavesdropping on your mind. So the more clarity you have in the relationship with your own inner wisdom, the greater the chance of your mind working in harmony with your bodily functions. The flipside is that if you ignore your inner wisdom, your body can become imbalanced in ways that lead to disease.

When you lead a balanced or *sattwic* life (see Chapter 2), you're more able to make the right choices to maintain your health and do like the oracle at Delphi entreats us to do: nothing in excess. This quality of serenity leads you to the right actions, such as avoiding smoking, drugs and over-indulgence in activities which impair your health.

The senses as master of the body

Indriya, the Sanskrit word for the senses, literally means that faculty that belongs to the 'master of the body'. Modern science seems to support the view that your senses affect your health; in studies such as the work by Yale professor John H Krystal, MD. In 2010, Professor Krystal showed that people with depression have difficulty detecting back and white contrast differences, making their world literally greyer.

Suppressing your natural urges is another way that your inner wisdom comes into play. If, for example, you want to cry or need to urinate, but hold back on these urges, you upset the energy systems in the body.

The effects of time

Bodies just don't last forever. Like anything, the effects of wear and tear over time take their toll and give rise to disorder and disease. Osteoarthritis, for example, is caused by plain old wear and tear on the joints.

Time also has an important effect in terms of seasons and weather. If you eat the same diet in winter that you eat in summer, you leave yourself vulnerable to disease, because you aren't giving your body what it needs. Chapter 9 tells you more about eating according to the seasons.

Sensory indiscretions

Your senses help you navigate the world and can very decidedly affect how you function within it. You reach out to the world using your senses as antennae, and their feedback to your brain determines in large part how you operate in it.

When you misuse your senses, by listening to very loud music for an extended time, for example, you upset their balance. Doing so inhibits your ability to move gracefully through the world. The end result can often be disease.

On a daily basis, you may consume a diet of hoardings, magazines and television. Your nostrils are assailed by a vast array of natural, artificial and sometimes overpowering smells, while your taste buds are bombarded and your ears are incessantly tuned in to the noise of traffic and other sounds. Your senses are coping with far more than they were designed for.

In the following section, I offer tips for taking care of your senses.

Changing your lifestyle to reduce disease

The Lalonde study was a landmark investigation conducted by the Canadian Government into the main cripplers in society, such as cancer, heart disease, suicide and alcoholism. The study identified four independent factors that affect health:

✔ The amount of medical research being done on the disease

✔ The availability of health services for the afflicted

✔ The environment of the disease – such as the workplace

✔ The lifestyle or set of personal choices associated with the disease

The report's most provocative conclusion was that lifestyle changes have the greatest effect on reducing disease for all groups and all age groups studied. Individual responsibility has the greatest impact on health.

Finding Great Tips for Enhancing Your Senses

Your senses are your conduits to the world. Properly respected and taken care of, they can bring great happiness to your life. But you might be thwarting or harming them without even realising it.

Check out the following tips to discover the factors in your sensory life that you can adjust. You can modify most of these elements with very little effort, and may see great benefits from small changes. Look for areas where you have room for improvement, and choose a few to actively work on.

Nurturing your hearing

Making sure your ears are a swift conduit for sound means avoiding loud noise and caring for your ears.

✔ **Keep white noise from fridges, traffic, washing machines, TVs and other electronic devices at a minimum.** Low- and high-frequency sounds can increase vata dosha and your ability to handle stress.

✔ **Adjust your daily schedule to fit in two ten-minute periods of quiet meditation a day.** Meditation brings many life-changing benefits, which you find out about in Chapter 6.

✔ **Embrace periods of quiet as often possible.** Quiet reflection is the most valuable way to really tune in to yourself and attend to your needs.

- ✔ **Use a couple of drops of sesame oil in your ears each day.** Doing so can protect your hearing.

- ✔ **Turn down the car stereo after you leave the motorway.** Extraneous noise often leads to an inadvertent increase in volume while driving, so rest your ears by turning the volume down.

Seeing your world clearly

Because so much of what people absorb comes through sight, taking good care of your eyes is a critical (but easy) practice. Trying to make sure the things you set your eyes on are pleasant is a further way to support your well-being.

- ✔ **Have regular eye exams.** Your optician can tell a lot about your health by looking at your eyes.

- ✔ **Don't wear sunglasses all the time if you don't need them for medical reasons.** Lack of full-spectrum light into your eyes can lead to depression and headaches.

- ✔ **Work in a well-lit room using full-spectrum lighting.** Fluorescent light can lead to fatigue, headaches, lethargy and diminished visual acuity.

- ✔ **If your eyes are strained, rest them or use palming.** Giving your eyes a break enhances visual acuity in the long term. To soothe your eyes, briskly rub your palms together, then cup them over your closed eyes. Feel the heat from your hands, then open your eyes and enjoy the restful darkness of your palms.

- ✔ **Look away from the screen and change your focal length regularly when you do computer work.** Computer vision syndrome is taking its toll on eye health. Try to look away from your screen every 20 minutes.

- ✔ **Create beauty in your surroundings.** You internalise your environment mainly through sight. Textile designer William Morris was right on when he said, 'Have nothing in your house that you do not know to be useful or believe to be beautiful.' A clean, beautiful home increases *sattwa* (balance; refer to Chapter 2 for more on sattwa).

- ✔ **Keep fresh flowers and plants in your home.** Plants and flowers impart sattwa in your environment.

- ✔ **Don't look at the television for protracted periods.** When you do, your ciliary muscles, which control the focusing of your eyes, are held in constant tension.

- ✔ **Get at least 20 minutes of full-spectrum light every day.** Your body seems to run in cyclic harmony with the constantly changing angles of sunlight through the four seasons. Lack of natural light can lead to depression and lowered vitamin D and melatonin levels.

Being good to your skin

It's big, it's all over you, and it's too often neglected – your skin takes in so much from your environment. Take good care of it by giving it attention in the following ways:

- ✔ **Give and receive touch.** Much research has come to light about the skin producing immunological factors. Stimulating the receptors in your skin by massage induces deep relaxation. Human touch can be one of the best stress busters.

- ✔ **Regularly apply oil to your skin.** Ayurveda says that one of the best ways to maintain health and reduce vata dosha in your body is by using oil on your skin daily. Sesame oil is a good all-purpose oil.

- ✔ **In general, wear natural fibres next to your skin.** Natural fabrics like silk, cotton and wool allow your skin to breathe properly and prevent rashes and fungal infections.

- ✔ **Avoid artificial creams and lotions; make an effort to find organic natural ingredients.** Your skin is a large organ of nutrition in your body, so putting unsuitable materials on it transfers them directly to your bloodstream.

- ✔ **Avoid exposure to midday summer sunlight.** To protect your skin from cancer, stay out of the sun between 11 a.m. and 3 p.m., cover up with loose long sleeves and a hat, and apply sunscreen of a minimum of factor 15.

Keeping your nose in order

Where would you be without your ability to tell whether the yogurt had spoiled? Or your ability to breathe, for that matter? Most people don't think too much about their noses until they're stuffed or otherwise out of whack. A few easy practices keep your nose functioning well:

- ✔ **Use a neti pot regularly to cleanse your nose.** Keeping your nasal passages clean helps prevent sinusitis and other kapha-related problems in your head. (Head to Chapter 14 to find out how to use a neti pot.)

- ✔ **Put a couple of drops of oil or ghee in your nose every day.** Nasal/head health is promoted by using pungent oils for kapha, cooling oils for pitta and warming oils for vata.

- ✔ **Avoid using strong-smelling perfumes and body products.** Strong-smelling products not only create allergies and rashes but can incite headaches.

✔ **Use incense and natural aromatherapy oils to create a relaxing atmosphere in your environment.** Fresh scented flowers are another nice way to achieve this effect.

✔ **Avoid using corrosive chemicals and detergents in your home.** Not only are they harmful to your skin and the environment, but the smell can also be noxious.

Bringing general health to your sense of taste and diet

How satisfied your food makes you feel depends in part on the tastes you choose; your ability to taste those flavours is therefore an important determinant of how food functions in your body. Ensuring that your digestive system is in a good state for making use of that food is also important. The following tips address both of these aspects of your diet:

✔ **Use a tongue scraper daily.** In Ayurveda, your tongue is a picture of all your internal organs. Gentle scraping stimulates your internal organs (and improves your oral hygiene).

✔ **Drink enough fluid to keep your urine pale yellow.** Your urine should be a pale straw colour, clear, and without a strong smell (unless you've had asparagus, of course). Make sure that you keep your fluids up when you exercise or when the weather is hot. Vata and pitta people need more fluid than kapha individuals.

✔ **Drink only two cups of regular tea or coffee per day.** Too much caffeine can lead to vata tremors. Most herbal teas are naturally caffeine-free and so are okay to drink throughout the day.

✔ **Don't drink colas and artificial canned drinks.** Colas contain phosphoric acid and other chemicals that compromise your bone density.

✔ **Eat little meat.** Your intake of toxic chemicals drops dramatically when you cut down on meat, because animal fat stores toxins. If you do eat meat, buy organic. Meat raised in a humane way is not only far tastier, it has also had less exposure to manmade chemicals such as antibiotics.

✔ **Include as many flavours and textures in your diet as possible.** Doing so creates satisfaction at all levels and helps you eat healthily.

✔ **Have fewer than five alcoholic beverages per week.** Many studies cite alcohol as the cause of a range of problems, including damage to your liver. Government guidelines state a maximum of 14 units per week for females and 21 units for males. Those units are spread across the week, so no saving it all up for the weekend!

✔ **If you're vegetarian, balance your proteins.** Make sure that you get all the necessary amino acids to make complete proteins, as well as a source of vitamin B12. The chapters in Part III give you heaps of advice about diet.

✔ **In general, consume whole grains and unrefined foods.** They are rich in nutrients and prevent constipation.

✔ **Whenever possible, consume organic and free-range food.** The purer your food, the more nutrient-rich it is and the less likely it is to leave toxic residues. Using organic oils is especially important, because oils are fat-soluble, and therefore their harmful resides are stored deep in your tissues.

✔ **Match your food to the season.** When the weather's cold, vata and kapha doshas are more prevalent. So encourage the opposite qualities by eating warm, cooked food.

✔ **Don't use a microwave to prepare food.** This mode of cooking drives off moisture from food, which increases its rough qualities and vata dosha. It also has a detrimental effect on valuable enzymes.

✔ **Eat only when you're hungry.** Try not to eat just because of the time of day. Check in with yourself and see how hungry you are, and eat accordingly.

✔ **Limit frozen, tinned and processed foods.** As much as possible, cook fresh food, which gives life to your body.

✔ **Take a day to fast or eat lightly on a regular basis.** Many studies highlight the importance of resting your digestive system. Ayurveda suggests fasting as a first line of treatment.

✔ **Thoroughly chew food before swallowing.** Releasing the valuable tastes helps to bring satisfaction with less food. It also helps valuable enzymes in the mouth mix with your food and convert starches into sugars.

✔ **Be aware of how your emotions affect your eating, and adjust what you eat accordingly.** Many people eat to mollify emotions such as frustration and loneliness. Doing so inhibits digestion, and so your body forms ama.

Head to Part III for a wealth of information on getting the most from your diet.

Chapter 6

The Rules of the Day: Dinacharya and Staying in Balance

In This Chapter

▶ Using your daily routine to maintain balance

▶ Discovering the power of meditation

▶ Learning about what's best for your senses

▶ Determining suitable aromatherapy oils for your body type

The daily routine is known in Sanskrit as *dinacharya*, literally 'to be close to the day'. To be close to the day means you are in touch with the cycles of the earth, moon and sun, as well as other planets on a more subtle level. If all that seems a bit airy-fairy to you, just observe how a full moon affects the tides and how sunspot activity affects electrical systems. An undeniable connection exists between us and the elements of our solar system.

Health maintenance forms one of the backbones of Ayurveda, which emphasises harmonising with natural rhythms and the influence that lifestyle has on the *doshas* (your constitution; see Chapter 2). The Ayurvedic *rishis* (the wise ones, who I tell you about in Chapter 1) considered the daily routine to be the most important ingredient of longevity.

Many people are in need of the harmony that the daily routine helps create. For example, the number of new cancer cases now stands at 12 million per year – an increase of 20 per cent in less than a decade. According to the World Cancer Research Fund, a quarter of the cases are preventable, because they're intimately linked with diet and lifestyle. This particular chapter is really important, as following the daily routine can help allay ill-health and may prevent some of the damage caused by poor diet and lifestyle.

Noting the moon's chaotic power

The latest lunar research shows that GPs in the UK are likely to see 30,000 more patients – with ailments as diverse as diarrhoea and gout – when the moon is full. Consultations peak five to six days after a full moon.

Dust mites are also more active, and tiger prawns seem to eat more during a full moon.

One theory suggests that internal body rhythms are affected by increased light on the pineal gland and the slightly warmer temperature. The small change in gravitational effect may also unbalance pathogens, increasing toxins in the body.

It's never too late to cultivate good habits. The organs of your body create a wonderful harmony, but when you lose the connection to daily rhythms and seasonal changes, you begin to get that not-quite-right feeling. You lose awareness of what's good for you – whether that's food, relationships or exercise. In this chapter I offer advice designed to keep you in harmony.

You may want to implement all of the directives listed, or you can simply determine which are the most suitable for your lifestyle and what feels right for you personally.

To make the most of each stage of your daily routine, please refer to Chapter 4 for more information on your individual constitution.

The Right Side of the Bed: Starting the Day with Energy

Beginning your day correctly is paramount, because it sets the tone for the rest of your day. A few tips make maximising this critical time easier and give you a more productive start.

Of foremost importance is the time when you get out of bed. If you get up right away when you wake up, you're more likely to feel good, because you're at your freshest during this time.

If, on the other hand, you go back to sleep, you'll dream, and this can make you tired because you start to return to the part of the sleep cycle known as REM (rapid eye movement). When you have to wake up again, you feel groggy because you're leaving your bed just when you'd be returning to deep sleep.

The time at which you get up depends on your constitution (see Chapter 4 to determine your dosha):

✔ Those with a vata constitution should get up at about 6 a.m. You're easily fatigued and tend to need more sleep to replenish your delicate nervous system.

✔ Pitta people are best suited to 5:30 a.m. You tend to sleep very soundly and wake up refreshed after about 6 hours.

✔ Kapha individuals ought to start stirring at around 4:30 or 5:00 a.m., even though they're the ones who are most likely to want to stay in bed. This is because you need to stimulate an already slow metabolism and you tend to put on weight easily. Rising early and being more active throughout the day will stimulate your system.

Those on a spiritual path, whatever it is, will find 4 or 4:30 a.m. the best time for prayer or meditation, because sattwa (explained in Chapter 2), with its fine balancing energy, is more prevalent at this time and also at dusk.

Try not to rush headlong into the day, and remember to factor in a gentle start with time for reflection, harmonising your inner flow of energy with that of the earth. The following sections show you how to start your day gently.

Reflecting before you start the day

Moving from sleep to activity takes a little doing. A moment of reflection can help to ease the transition.

When you awake, reflect for a few moments before your feet touch the floor. While still lying down, look at your hands, palms up, for a short while and then pass them gently over your face, chest and waist to cleanse your aura and improve awareness. Then briefly say a positive affirmation or prayer for your intention to have a good day. You don't have to get fancy; the important thing is that you use this moment to set the tone for the day ahead.

Before dawn: The time of knowledge

Researchers in Japan discovered that when the first surge of energy happens, 90 minutes before dawn, it's reflected in a change in blood chemistry. This time in Sanskrit is known as *Brahma Muhurta*, or the time of knowledge, and is a period when deep peace prevails and brings a flood of sattwic energy to all of creation. This outpouring of health-giving *prana* (energy) also occurs to a lesser degree half an hour before dawn. So you might as well take advantage of it if you can!

Putting your best foot forward

Every 90 minutes, the flow of breath in the nose switches from the left to right nostril. When it's on the right side, actions such as eating and urinating should be undertaken; conversely, the left nostril activities are more reflective, such as meditating and studying. This is because the right nostril is heating and connected to solar energies, and the left nostril is cooling and connected to lunar energies.

Establish the dominant nostril by breathing on the back of your hand near the junction of the hand and wrist. When you determine from which side the stronger breath is coming, place your corresponding foot on the ground. With this act (known as *swara yoga*), you're literally putting your best foot forward to carry positive energy throughout all your daily activities.

Cleansing your body

When you get up, head right to the bathroom to urinate and evacuate your bowels and remove wastes that have accumulated in your system overnight. Try to educate your bowels to release their contents at the same time every day, because imbalance of the doshas can manifest itself here very quickly.

Finish your body-cleansing routine by drinking a glass of room-temperature water with a little lemon juice. Doing so helps to flush the kidneys and keep your gastrointestinal tract clean.

Drinking from a copper cup removes excess kapha or mucus from the body, because copper ions have a slight warming effect on the body.

Meditation: The Way to Nirvana and the Light in the Heart

Ideally, meditation becomes the foundation of your day. Regular meditation can change your life in a very positive way, leading you to experience the world and other people as being part of the same unified whole.

Meditation is central to the practice of Ayurveda. Note that meditation isn't just about sitting silently with your eyes shut; rather, it's a state of total aware-ness giving focused attention, when both mind and body are in complete har-mony. This state provides deep rest on all levels.

The action of meditation is thought to unlink the cortical and limbic systems, or, to put it another way, it separates the perceiving system and thinking arena from the emotional and autonomic parts of the mind. The result is that you become more wakeful and alert, while in a deeply relaxed state. You also benefit emotionally from a therapeutic effect that helps you cope more easily with the challenges, or slings and arrows, of the day.

Moving into meditation

For your morning meditation, select a place in your home that's quiet, preferably facing north-east, a direction which is considered to be more in tune with spiritual energies. Choose a draught-free and well-ventilated room. Try to use the same space for your regular practice. Doing so promotes sattwic energy (a peaceful quality akin to that in sacred spaces; Chapter 2 tells you more about sattwic energy). Also try to keep away from distractions like your phone or computer, or at least turn them off.

Set aside the same time for meditation every day. Doing so strengthens your practice, because once you have a defined time, you can begin to fit your schedule around it. Sunrise and sunset are ideal times for meditation, because more calm is available in the form of sattwic energy.

Follow these steps to experience meditation:

1. **Sit on a cushion or rug with your legs crossed.** If that's too difficult, choose a comfortable seat or chair that allows your feet to touch the floor.

2. **Now try to still all movement in your body.** Sitting up straight and still enables energy to flow unimpeded through your head and down through your spine, creating a sense of equilibrium in the body.

3. **Focus on your breath, without changing it in any way.** Sense the inhalation and feel the coolness of the air as it passes through your nostrils. Next allow the exhalation of air in its own time and note the warmth of the air as it leaves your nasal cavity.

4. **Try to meditate for 20 to 30 minutes twice a day.** Work up to that duration, and when you master it you can extend it (and perform meditation more often). But consistency of practice is more important than duration; a little every day is more valuable than meditating for huge chunks of time on an irregular basis. The benefits of meditation far outweigh any perceived problems.

A great step to help you towards deep meditation is to focus on a sound. I've included sounds for specific doshas in the next section. The sound 'so hum' is useful if you don't know your constitution or want a general sound to focus on – 'so' on the inhalation and 'hum' on the exhale. This should be sounded internally in a measured and slow way. This enables you to move into a deeper place and enhance your inner awareness.

After finishing your meditation practice, slowly reengage your senses with the outer world and take a little time to reflect and stretch before moving headlong into your busy life. If possible, try to bring to mind how you felt during meditation; doing so will help you to be calm and centred throughout the day.

Using a mantra

A *mantra* is simply a sound, word or group of words that you repeat to help you move into a meditative state and focus your mind. A mantra takes your daily operating awareness to subtler and quieter levels and can affect your physiology in a deep and profound way, leading to an increase in introspection and peace.

You can use one of the tried and true mantras that aligns with your constitution (read Chapter 4 to determine your constitution.) None of the mantras has a specific meaning; each is a natural vibration appropriate for calming and balancing the mind. They are as follows:

- ✔ For vata dosha, use 'shrim' to induce good health, prosperity and creativity.
- ✔ 'Ram', the mantra of truth, righteousness and virtue is suitable for pitta dosha.
- ✔ 'Hrim' helps to purify and cleanse, and it confers joy and energy. It's particularly appropriate for kapha individuals.

Being patient with difficulties

Meditation requires practice. As you become accustomed to meditation, expect some difficulties such as:

- ✔ **An increase in restlessness.** Your mind moves constantly, and you probably don't realise just how true that is until you stop to observe. Don't worry; the jumping around of thought that you're starting to notice is perfectly normal. With practice, you can calm it.
- ✔ **Impatience at the absence of results.** Even though nothing appears to be happening early on, trust that at subtle levels you're ironing out kinks and making progress.
- ✔ **Intruding thoughts invade the mind during the practice.** Don't try to repress these perfectly normal interruptions, but do go back to focusing on your breath or mantra whenever you realise you've lost concentration.

Let patience be your watchword, and treat each meditation period as a special treat.

While the technique of meditation itself is very simple, I strongly recommend the help of a teacher who can help establish the practice and help resolve any problems. Organisations with a proven track record over many years are:

- The Sivananda Yoga Vedanta Centre (www.sivananda.co.uk) is focused in Europe and the United States.

- The Maharishi Foundation has a well-established network of meditation teachers worldwide, who specialise in transcendental meditation. See www.t-m.org.uk (Britain) or www.tm.org (United States).

- The School of Meditation (www.schoolofmeditation.org) is primarily located in Britain and the United States.

Looking After the Senses

Ayurveda places great importance on the care of the sense organs, because their smooth operation ensures clarity and freshness in your experience of the outer world. Part of staying in balance is keeping your senses clear, because they're literally the way in which you take in the world.

Refreshing your eyes

Seventy per cent of sensory experience comes through your eyes, and most of our physical, emotional, mental and spiritual insights are intimately linked to the successful functioning of our visual system. Nowadays, sight is seriously challenged by poor lighting, whether it be too bright or too low, as well as by bad posture, staring at computer screens for too long, and reading small print.

Computer vision syndrome is now an established medical phenomenon, in which concentrating on a computer screen leads to headaches, blurred vision, neck pain, fatigue, dry and irritated eyes, difficulty refocusing and double vision. If this sounds familiar, consider including eye yoga in your daily routine. Chapter 7 gives you the details.

Rotate your eyes in either direction to improve visual acuity and remove habitual strain. You may also want to use a diluted triphala eyewash, which is good for all doshas and cleanses the eyes. Here's how:

1. Mix a ¼ cup of water and a ¼ teaspoon of triphala powder (available from health-food shops; see Appendix C for suppliers).

2. Simmer gently for ten minutes.

3. Cool the mixture.

4. Strain to remove any granules.

5. Rinse eyes with the mixture.

 You may want to apply anjanam, an herbal eye ointment, after your eyewash. This herb is said to be a good coolant, it protects the eyes from bright light and enhances the look of the eyes. Eye drops such as organic rosewater are very soothing, and castor oil once a week really makes your eyes sparkle.

Caring for teeth and gums

Ayurvedic texts explain that the teeth don't exist in isolation, and that they're part of a living matrix, which in fact is linked subtly to end organs in the rest of the body.

To stimulate the connections between the teeth and the organs, try clenching your teeth together. Doing so also aids the circulation of each tooth and maintains the muscles of the jaw. Thirty clenches per day is optimal.

The following tips help you keep your mouth healthy and thereby maximise the connections between your teeth and gums and your mind and body:

✔ Apply sesame oil to your gums after cleaning your teeth, to maintain tooth health. I have a close friend who's a dentist and encourages all her patients to do so – with very good results. Decant raw, untoasted sesame oil over your brush (dipping the brush would contaminate the oil) and judiciously coat your teeth to condition the gums and prevent plaque build-up.

✔ Relieve bleeding gums and gingivitis by massaging the teeth and gums with raw sesame oil four times a day for four to five minutes after you clean them.

✔ A lovely formula for daily use on teeth is one teaspoon each of lodhra, kala namak, triphala and neem, mixed together and kept in a container (all are available from online Ayurvedic shops). This concoction helps to contract the small capillaries and introduce Vitamin C, a powerful antioxidant that stimulates healthy gum tissue. Another useful dental formula is a 50–50 mix of triphala powder with finely ground roasted almond shells.

✔ You can use Irimedali Taila, a special oil which is just for the mouth, to massage your gums to prevent gum disease.

Tongue and mouth maintenance

Two very effective strategies for looking after the mouth are sluicing the mouth with herbal preparations or oily substances, which is called *gandusha* in Sanskrit, and gargling, known as *kavalagraha*. These practices of irrigating the mouth can be performed all year round by all body types. First thing in the morning is the most favourable time of day. They prevent and treat bad breath, all kapha disorders and dryness.

Gandusha

In this procedure, you completely fill your mouth with fluid so that you can't gargle. It's particularly helpful if you've started to lose taste.

Start by preparing one of the following mixtures:

✔ Untoasted sesame oil or ghee with sweet, sour or salty substances such as liquorice powder or a little black salt (available from your Indian grocery) to remove vata disturbances like wasting of the gums and loose teeth.

✔ Ghee with a small amount of a bitter medicament such as guduchi is useful in pitta problems, and particularly helpful in cases of mouth ulcers and pitta-provoked situations such as bleeding gums.

✔ Ghee with a small amount of a bitter, pungent and astringent substance such as eucalyptus oil or neem powder is known as samshodana gandusha and will help to eradicate kapha problems such as infections, dryness and a white coating in the mouth due to candida.

Sit near a sink in a draught-free environment. The ancient texts suggest concentrating while seated in a darkened room with someone massaging your neck and shoulders. If you can arrange this, you're very lucky – enjoy it!

Completely fill your mouth with one of the solutions. Doing so may cause your eyes and or nose to run. That's part of the process of disturbed doshas from your ears, nose, mouth and eyes which are accumulating in your mouth, so that you can expel them.

Kavalagraha

In *kavalagraha*, you half fill your mouth with a decoction of herbs in either water or oil, so that you have room to gargle.

The mixture you gargle depends on your constitution. Check out Chapter 4 to determine your constitution, and then choose the appropriate recipe:

✔ For vata, combine:

- 1 cup water
- ½ teaspoon cumin seeds
- 2 teaspoons sesame oil
- 1 drop lavender oil

✔ For a pitta constitution, mix:

- 1 cup water
- ½ teaspoon turmeric
- 1 teaspoon fennel seeds

✔ If you have a kapha constitution, prepare:

- 1 cup water
- ½ teaspoon honey
- ¼ teaspoon ginger

For whichever recipe you choose, bring the water and herbs to the boil and then simmer for three to five minutes. If you're using the vata recipe, wait to add the oil until after the mixture has simmered. Cool the vata or kapha mixture until it is warm before using; use the pitta mixture cold.

Then gargle, as follows:

1. **Hold the substance in your mouth for one minute and then swoosh around your teeth and eject.**

2. **Fill your mouth again for two minutes and gargle with the head back.**

   Spit out the substance. Your mouth should feel really refreshed.

More tips for mouth care

Other tips for the health of the mouth include:

✔ Chew a mixture of equal quantities of fennel and cumin seeds, or a cardamom pod, after eating, to freshen your breath and aid your digestion.

✔ Avoid crunching on ice in drinks, which weakens tooth enamel.

✔ Refrain from drinking very hot drinks, eating acidic foods and smoking – all of which upset the natural flora of the mouth.

Care of the tongue

The tongue is considered a very important organ in Ayurveda and is known as *jivha*, a word which has the same root as the word 'life'. Treat this organ of perception with great care.

Use a tongue scraper, which you can find at any chemist, to keep your tongue in its best shape. To use it, gently pass the scraper over the surface of the tongue from back to front.

Don't be too aggressive with your tongue scraper. The papillae (the bits that stick up) on your tongue are very delicate and easily damaged. Keep your tongue scraper clean and dry between uses or you may spread infection.

Scraping your tongue:

✔ Aids the expulsion of ama (that's the bad stuff, which I tell you about in detail in Chapter 5).

✔ Stimulates stomach activity, because the stomach is innervated with the same nerves as the tongue is.

✔ Keeps the mouth and breath fresh.

✔ Removes excess kapha.

✔ Improves the taste of food.

Stainless steel tongue scrapers are a good choice. Plastic can be too sharp. Use a silver tongue scraper and you get the extra benefit of silver ions deposited on your tongue; that's a tonic for pitta types. A copper scraper is good for kapha and vata doshas.

Snehana: Loving the Body with Oil Massage

Massage is central to the therapeutics of Ayurveda, which recommends that you should never be far from a bottle of oil. The early texts compared the human body to a leather bag which gets worn out but lasts much longer if it's lubricated. Similarly, the axle of a wheel will also fail to operate unless properly greased.

Charaka, one of the most venerated Ayurvedic physicians, described the utility of oil massage by noting that when a pot is coated with an oily substance, the contents come out easily. This is also the case with the body: when appropriately oiled, the aggravated doshas can be expressed without too much trouble; when the aggravated doshas are left in place, they can create disease. In short, if you massage yourself with oil, you help to promote health.

The most gentle of all the therapies in the book, oil massage brings Ayurvedic herbs deep into the skin tissue. That action enhances your sense of touch by opening the channels through which sensation and *prana* (energy) flow to create a balance between what you experience and how you perceive it.

Ayurveda identifies nine effects of oil massage:

- Strength
- Invigoration
- Fluidity
- Peacefulness
- Gentleness
- Repairing scar tissue and muscular adhesions which create blockages to the flow of prana
- Moisturising skin
- Sensory stimulation
- Accommodation, or your skin's ability to stretch and prevent the formation of fissures and splits

Oil massage is referred to as *snehana*, which also means 'to love'. The ancient texts mention 24 methods of application, covering a wide spectrum of therapies, such as: vaginal/urethral (yes we need moisture inside and out!) douches; gargles; nasal, ear and eye applications; and ingesting oily or sticky substances such as rice and decoctions.

Selecting the best oils for your body type

Both Sushruta and Charaka, the founding fathers of Ayurveda, mention that sesame is a good all-round oil to use because it's subtle, endows satiety, is bulk promoting, aphrodisiac, enhances retention of memory, and acts as a skin and hair tonic.

Sesame oil is one of the best rejuvenators in Ayurveda, because it works on all tissues, or *dhatus*, is widely used as a base for herbs, nourishes the skin and bones and calms the mind. It's said to penetrate all seven layers of the skin. In recent studies, sesame has been shown to have anti-viral properties, especially in the case of the Epstein–Barr virus. Sesame oil keeps for a long time without going rancid and contains a number of essential minerals, including iron, phosphorous, magnesium, copper, silica, trace elements and calcium.

You can buy sesame oil in any supermarket. Just don't get the toasted variety, or you'll go around all day smelling like a Chinese restaurant!

Precious oils in history

Some of the first words uttered in the Bible at the start of creation are 'let there be light,' and in the Chandogya Upanishad, one of the earliest Vedic texts, we're informed that 'light, when we eat it in the form of fat or oil, is changed into three qualities; the grossest becomes bone, the finest speech and the midway turns to marrow.' So oil is pure light and the finest substance or quintessence of the plant, and has all of the plant's properties contained within it.

Depending on your dosha, choose your oil as follows:

- ✔ Vata individuals should choose sesame, almond or nirgundi oils. These are light and warming in quality, which balances vata dosha.

- ✔ Sunflower, coconut and neem oils are recommended for pacifying pitta because they're cooling in quality without being too heavy.

- ✔ If you have a kapha constitution, look for mustard or corn oil. However, if you're overweight, using oil will add more kapha qualities to your already heavy and slow attributes. Therefore use dry powders with silk gloves if you're very overweight, and apply more stimulation to increase the blood flow to areas like your thighs to stimulate the breakdown of fat tissue.

You can find further instructions for oil application and body massage in Chapter 16.

Oil application to the ears: Karna purna

Applying a drop or two of sesame oil in each ear every day protects and vitalises these sense organs, which become aggravated by vata because you use them constantly. So this simple practice should become a life-long habit for everyone.

Headphones, in particular, are hard on your ears. Using headphones increases air imbalance in the body, because sound is carried in this medium. In turn, this leads to dryness and accumulation of ear wax, which can give rise to tinnitus.

The inability to withstand loud noises is one of the first signs that vata is going out of balance.

Don't apply oil to your ears if there's any sign of infection, but see your doctor immediately.

Oil application for the nostrils: Nasya

Applying oil to the nostrils is beneficial to all doshas, but kapha and vata imbalances are particularly helped by it. Applying oil into your nose improves the flow of prana, prevents dryness of your nasal cavity, and is said to increase mental clarity.

Simply apply ghee or sesame oil to your clean little finger and rub gently into each nostril.

Patent nasal oils are readily available; the most common is known as Anu Tailam. Simply tip your head back and introduce three to five drops into each nostril on a daily basis. Doing so gives a sense of calm to the body and relieves dryness of the nostrils, pain in the face, weakness of vision, as well as pain in the neck region.

If you suffer from a blocked nose or sinusitis, then you need a deeper cleansing using a neti pot. See Chapter 14 for details.

Adorning Your Body with Clothes and Perfumes

How you present yourself to the world has a profound effect on how you feel about yourself, so time spent on your appearance is well worth the effort. Here are some simple tips for pampering yourself, using the knowledge of the doshas.

Choosing clothes for comfort

I'm sure you know the lovely feeling that freshly washed and ironed clothes give you. Ayurveda says that such clothing confers *ojas*, or good energy, on the wearer.

Remember the old saying that you never know how someone feels until you've stood in their moccasins? There is literal truth to that. You don't want to wear anyone else's clothes or shoes, because they contain the wearer's energy patterns, and those may be quite negative. This guideline is a hard one for any of us who frequent charity shops, so as a minimum get items dry-cleaned before you put them on.

When you choose clothes, keep the following tips in mind:

- ✔ Choose natural fibres where possible, because they allow the skin to breathe freely and are less irritating.
- ✔ Silk is said to best protect you against negative influences.
- ✔ Underwear made from silk or cotton is breathable and helps prevent fungal infections.
- ✔ Wearing nylon socks and plastic shoes is like putting your feet in polythene bags. A large number of sweat glands are located in your feet, and the result, especially in the summer, can be athlete's foot (and smelly feet!).

Co-ordinating colours with the doshas

Colours are associated with different qualities and can be an important means of warding off bad influences. Dark colours, for example, tend to be heavy and cooling in effect, whereas reds and oranges are warm and stimulating.

Depending on your dosha, follow these tips for choosing colours:

- ✔ Vatas and kaphas are both cool doshas, and therefore favour warm colours such as coral, mauves and pinks.
- ✔ Kapha types should avoid white in general and stick to enlivening colours, because kapha secretions in the body tend to be white and cool.
- ✔ If you're pitta, which means you tend to get hot under the collar and in the body, go for more sombre selections such as greens, browns and blues.
- ✔ The ubiquitous black that's favoured today is a shade that attracts denser, more *tamasic* (undesirable), energies and literally drags you down.
- ✔ Gold jewellery imparts the warmth of the sun to vata and kapha doshas.
- ✔ Silver and platinum suggest the characteristics of the moon and are associated with its cooling properties. These are most suitable for pitta dosha.

Putting your best foot forward with comfortable shoes

How you understand the world is determined in part by how you make contact with the ground. According to Polarity Therapy, developed by Randolph Stone in the 1950s and an offshoot of Ayurveda, the body is electric, with the head being the positive pole and the navel being neutral. The feet are the strongest negative pole in your system and contain 84,000 nerve endings that connect to all the reflex zones of the body. According to the Ayurvedic system, 72,000 subtle channels called *nadis* find their junctions in the feet. So choosing appropriate footwear is paramount to your health.

Indian yogis wear wooden sandals, because the leather of a cow isn't permitted. For those of us who are not concerned by these issues, shoes that breathe are by far the best choice, so that means canvas, cork or leather.

Feet expand by as much as one size during the day, so buy shoes in the afternoon or early evening to get the right fit. Take your shoes off the minute you enter your home and allow your feet to feel the ground.

Change your shoes regularly, so that you're not exposed to pressures in the same part of your foot on a daily basis.

A word also about heel height: irreversible damage can be done to the delicate structures of your feet, legs and lower back if you wear high heels all day. Wear them very, very rarely!

Perfumes and oils

Perfumes and oils are said to confer longevity and charm to the wearer. Wearing a scent isn't only pleasing to the mind, but stimulating to the libido. (So be careful with it, all you would-be Romeos and Juliets!)

Your aromatherapy oils help with stress management, and each dosha has specific characteristics that may be pacified by using a particular oil.

Essential oils work at a primordial level to enhance mood, focus the mind and stimulate the body in a positive way. Introduce your picks from the following list of oils. You can apply them directly to your skin if they're mixed with a carrier oil such as almond oil. You can also use them in your home or office, using diffusers or room sprays.

Vata dosha

Those of you with a predominant vata dosha can benefit from the use of:

- Cedarwood, clary sage, ylang ylang, frankincense and lavender to help dispel the anxiety and fear often associated with this dosha

- Chamomile, eucalyptus and angelica to improve groundedness

- Rosemary, cypress and basil to fight fatigue and weakness

- Neroli, rose, thyme, basil and lavender to remedy sleeplessness

Pitta dosha

The hot tendencies of pitta dosha can benefit from using:

- Coriander, musk, borage, sandalwood, frankincense, benzoin, cardamom and rose to address the propensity towards irritability and anger
- Brahmi and gold chamomile to reduce frustration
- Lavender and peppermint to address stubbornness
- Amber and geranium, which come to the rescue when a domineering attitude is at play

Kapha dosha

Allay the heavy and cool qualities of kapha by using:

- Bergamot, clary sage, geranium, orange and petitgrain oils, especially if feeling depressed
- Cardamom, rosemary and basil oils to address greed and attachment, both common kapha feelings
- Jasmine and ylang ylang to address low self-esteem

Time to Step Outside

Eat a light breakfast (Part III gives dietary advice appropriate to your type), and you're ready to face the world.

The steps in this chapter may seem extensive, but they leave you ready for a full and active day. I allow two hours before I leave the house in the morning for my daily routine: this allows for half an hour of meditation and 90 minutes for completing my ablutions without rushing.

Taking your time with preparations enables you to face the world and all its challenges full of confidence.

Chapter 7

Seeking Union with Yoga

● ●

In This Chapter

▷ Introducing the central role that yoga plays in Ayurveda

▷ Determining whether yoga is right for you

▷ Selecting the appropriate posture for your body type

▷ Breathing the doshic way

▷ Looking at specific postures for healing

▷ Chilling out the yogic way

● ●

*A*ccording to Ayurveda, yoga is an important part of ensuring good health. Concerned with the most fundamental relationships between nature and consciousness, Ayurveda and yoga are involved with purifying the mental and bodily faculties, controlling the mind, and seeking union with the Absolute (God, the divine, a higher power – call it what you will). Put simply, physical yoga can be considered the exercise arm of Ayurveda. For my patients I always prescribe both postures and breathing exercises, without which a treatment seems incomplete.

In the first part of this chapter I point out why yoga is beneficial and how to get started. I introduce you to some very basic postures to help keep your body healthy and in balance. I acquaint you with some simple breathing practices that can help you get the most out of your session.

The great popularity of yoga is related to the fact that when used therapeutically, it has great potential to calm the mind and manage the reaction to stress.

I also look at yoga as therapy. Although yoga isn't an alternative to conventional medicine, it can definitely support the healing process, especially in diseases that can be aggravated by stress, such as asthma, diabetes and hypertension.

Understanding Yoga

By performing yoga postures known as *asanas*, you free up your movement, support your digestion, balance your hormones and soothe your nervous system. Gentle stretches can not only enliven the cells but also encourage the removal of bodily wastes. This ultimately leads you to greater self-awareness and peace of mind. After my yoga class, I always feel that my nerves (known as *nadis* in Ayurveda) have been ironed out.

Remember that the optimum amount of exercise varies from one person to the next. In accordance with this, the Vedic texts say that the best amount of exercise is when sweat comes to your forehead, armpits and spine in small quantities. Don't forget that too strenuous activity depletes *ojas*, which is the good substance that guards your immunity. (See Chapter 3 for more about ojas.)

Don't practice yoga if you feel ill, and consult your doctor first if you have any of the following: glaucoma (inverted postures can increase pressure on your eyes); bleeding of any kind, including heavy periods; neck injuries; previously broken bones; severe osteoporosis; or rheumatoid arthritis. Don't practice on a full stomach; a gap of an hour is adequate after a light meal, or wait three hours after a heavy one. When doing the postures, ease into them gently, and if you start to feel discomfort or pain, stop immediately.

The emphasis is on the regularity of practice and not on how long each session is. A short daily practice is of far more value than a regular burst of activity every few weeks. You'll be amazed how a small amount of effort can yield great results.

Going with the Flow – Understanding Body Energy or Prana

In this section, I introduce the different energies of the body, known as *prana* in Sanskrit. *Prana* means, variously, 'breath of life', 'vital energy' and/or 'the capacity to love and desire'. Prana is where Ayurveda meets yoga, because the yoga postures activate prana to work harmoniously throughout your body (see Figure 7-1).

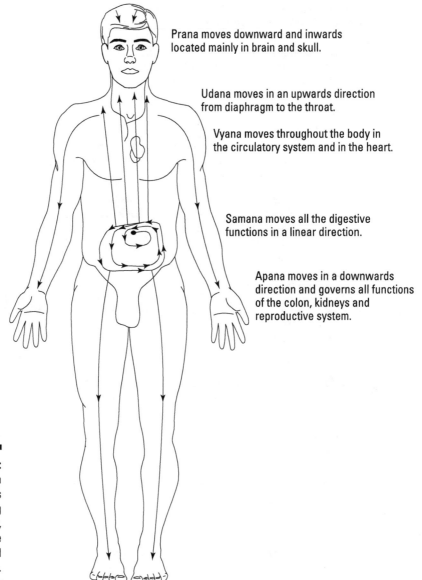

Prana moves downward and inwards located mainly in brain and skull.

Udana moves in an upwards direction from diaphragm to the throat.

Vyana moves throughout the body in the circulatory system and in the heart.

Samana moves all the digestive functions in a linear direction.

Apana moves in a downwards direction and governs all functions of the colon, kidneys and reproductive system.

Figure 7-1:
Prana
animates
everything
in the body,
both visible
and
invisible.

The following list explains the five major *winds* or energies and how they act on the body. These forces which activate your system are divided into five types:

- **Apana,** which literally means 'air that moves away', is focused at your navel. It's the downward- and outward-moving force that moves air and fluids out of your body, including as flatulence, faeces, newborn babies, menstrual fluid and urine. At a more subtle level it aids in the elimination of negative sensory and emotional experience, and most importantly it maintains your immune system on all levels.

  Along with vyana (later in this list), apana creates stability in your legs. All standing and crouching postures help strengthen and maintain this supporting energy.

- **Samana,** meaning 'balancing air', is located one step above apana, at your stomach level, and moves in a clockwise circle. Samana energy governs all movements in your abdomen and colon. It promotes digestive activity and it aids the lungs in absorbing oxygen. On a mental, sensory and emotional plane, samana works to synthesise and digest experience, so it's very busy! All forward bends and spinal twists help to support this vital force in your body.

- **Udana,** which literally means 'upward-moving air'. Its centre is located in your throat and moves in an upwards direction. Its most important function is speech.

  Along with vyana, udana moves your arms and holds your head high.

  Udana plays a part in your growth, both physical and spiritual. It's said to aid in your individual evolution of consciousness, or your journey to self-realisation.

  Postures that help develop this force are the ones where your hands actively reach upwards.

- **Vyana,** meaning 'outward-moving air', is located all over your body, but specifically in your lungs and heart. Vyana ensures that blood circulates to the periphery of your body.

  Vyana maintains the flow of your thoughts and emotions and confers strength and movement to them. So if you're feeling stuck, try poses where you extend your arms out from your sides, as well as the sun-salute sequence later in this chapter.

- **Prana,** located in the heart, means 'forward-moving air'. All sensory perceptions and mental impressions are possible because of this life force. Prana is the vital force which nourishes the brain, and it's the life force or animator of all things.

  Meditative postures and back bends are helpful to support this energy. All chest-opening postures, including the half fish listed later in this chapter, are also beneficial.

Introducing a Simple Yoga Posture for Each Constitution

In Chapter 4, I help you discover which type of constitution you have. Knowing your constitution type points you towards the postures most beneficial to you. If you haven't already discovered your constitution type, I recommend turning to Chapter 4 now. So here goes: stretch your mind and flex your body!

You need to focus on your yoga poses without distractions, so before you start a yoga session, turn off your mobile phone and unplug the landline.

Regulate your breathing while performing the poses, and move slowly and with concentration and focus.

You may like to refer to the excellent *Yoga For Dummies* by Georg Feuerstein and Larry Payne (Wiley) for more postures.

Trikonasana: A vata-pacifying posture

A brief reminder of the special qualities of vata dosha: it's cold and its main seat is in the pelvis; vata dosha is the humour which governs all movement in the body. So the postures most beneficial for vata management are related to the pelvic area:

- Meditative postures that put pressure on the lower abdomen and help the body to be firm and grounded
- Asanas which put pressure on the colon and pelvic area, such as forward bends
- Balancing postures, which increase concentration and help prana to flow in a smooth and directed way

The symbol of the triangle appears in many cultures as an image of the divine. You can observe it in many *yantras*, or symbols used as a focus for meditation. The downwards-directed triangle represents Shakti (the divine feminine) – the force known to be dynamic. Its passive counterpart, the upwards-pointing triangle, signifies Siva (the divine masculine).

In the trikonasana posture, you literally form a triangle. This asana stimulates your digestive system and stretches the spine on either side:

1. **Stand with your feet parallel, approximately 3 to 4 feet apart.**

2. **Turn your left foot slightly in towards the right, and rotate the right foot 90 degrees so that it's in a direct line with your left inner arch.**

   Feel yourself rooted to the ground.

3. **Extend your arms to the level of your shoulders, and then fold your body over your front leg during an exhalation, while maintaining strong contact with the ground through your back leg.**

   Take care that your hips are squarely forwards and that your knees aren't bent.

4. **Point your left palm upwards, keeping your arm and wrist straight, and place your right hand at the side of the ankle on a block or on the floor, on the outside of your right ankle.**

   Check out Figure 7-2.

Figure 7-2:
Becoming a
triangle.

Your spine elongates, and you can focus on opening your chest with the hand extending to the ceiling. Allow your breath to flow smoothly.

5. **Hold the posture for about 90 seconds if you can, then return to standing on an inhalation, pressing even more on your left foot and lifting through the upturned left arm.**

6. **Repeat on the other side.**

Gaining control in this basic posture builds focus for more complex variations.

Ardha matsyendra: Posture for pitta management

The pitta dosha is heat-producing and governs all transformative processes in the body. It centres mainly in the small intestine, so the yoga postures of most benefit are those that affect the navel area to increase digestive efficiency and stimulate gastric juices.

Pitta postures to pursue include:

✔ All postures that involve spinal twists

✔ Inverted asanas (such as shoulder stand), which reverse pressure on the organs, strengthen the liver and small intestines, where excess pitta congregates in your body, and improve digestion

✔ Inner-directed postures that induce a meditative state of mind

People with a pitta constitution are very goal-directed and may try to speed things up, even while doing yoga. If you're a high-energy pitta person who finds it hard to chill out, being very deliberate in your movements, resting between poses and doing poses with your eyes closed can help you achieve balance.

Sometimes called the lords and fishes pose, the half spinal twist is named after one of the Vedic saints. This very useful posture is one of the few in which each of your vertebrae gets to turn to the side. This helps greatly with maintaining spinal flexibility, improving the circulation of your spinal nerves and ligaments. The added benefit is that the main seat of pitta, near the navel, gets a workout too.

To do a half spinal twist (see Figure 7-3), follow these steps:

1. **Keeping your spine erect and shoulders level, sit on your heels and breathe calmly.**

2. **Shift your weight to the right buttock and lift your left leg over your right leg, so that your left heel comes to rest at your right hip.**

3. **Stretch out your arms at shoulder level either side of you, and turn your torso to your left while exhaling.**

4. **Put your right arm on the inside of your left leg and grasp your foot to aid leverage, allowing the spine to naturally twist from the base upwards.**

5. **When you've twisted your torso as far as you can, turn your head to the left, while keeping your neck relaxed.** Remember not to lead with your chin, but to turn your whole head at once and place your right hand to the floor behind you.

6. **Release as you exhale, and slowly untwist.**

7. **Repeat on the other side.**

If your hips are very tight, you can modify this posture by putting several blankets or a block on your right side under your buttock, so that you don't collapse on one side. In addition, resting your left hand on a block helps.

Figure 7-3:
The half
spinal twist.

Ardha matsyasana for the kapha constitution

The kapha dosha tends to be cold, heavy and sluggish. Kapha energy centres mainly in the upper part of the stomach and the lungs. Types of postures helpful to those with a Kapha dosha include:

✔ All postures that open the chest

✔ Postures that are stimulating to the system and increase the metabolic rate, such as the salute to the sun sequence, later in this chapter

✔ Inverted postures, which increase heat in the body and are helpful to stimulate the release of excess kapha dosha in the form of mucus in the body

 To offset the natural sluggishness of the kapha constitution, perform the asanas briskly. (I know that you kapha types think that relaxation is the best part of a yoga session!)

Carrying your heart high

You may notice a tendency to sit or stand in such a way that you're collapsed in around your heart. This is a common response to the many hardships of life, not to mention a natural reflection of being hunched over a computer all day.

If this is the case for you, it really helps to develop what I call the Duke of Edinburgh walk. Walk with your hands behind your back. Breathing from an open chest is good for all your functions – physical, mental and emotional.

Known as the half fish pose (see Figure 7-4), this posture is beneficial in treating asthma, because it really opens your chest and allows for the smooth flow of prana. Secondarily, it tones the thyroid and all the associated organs in the neck, while stimulating the nerves too. Your thoracic area gets a much-needed stretch, which relieves tension and opens the heart.

Follow these steps:

1. **Lie on your back with your feet extended together and your arms and palms facing down, comfortably under your thighs.**

2. **Press your legs and elbows into the floor, arch your back and lift your chest as high as you can.**

   Keep your elbows as close as possible to your sides, to stabilise your body.

3. **Inhale gently, lifting your chest and positioning the crown of your head on the floor.**

   Try to open your chest as much as you can.

   Don't hold the pose too long, because it's quite wearing on the neck.

4. **To release the posture, gently lift the head, extend the back of the neck and rest into the ground.** Release your hands and arms from under your buttocks, and relax.

Figure 7-4:
The half fish pose.

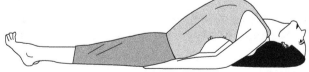

Easing Disease with Yoga

For centuries in India, doctors have prescribed yoga as a therapeutic intervention to help both alleviate and treat medical conditions.

Alleviating arthritis pain with natraj asana

I always enjoy doing this lovely posture, perhaps because it's the pose of Shiva as a cosmic dancer (see Figure 7-5); I always feel light and playful when I do it. The pose activates all the major and minor joints of the body in one single move, and has a beneficial effect on joint mobility. This makes it very useful in the treatment and prevention of arthritis. Your shoulders, hips, ankles, knees and hands are engaged, and the corresponding nerves, muscles and tissues in these areas are mobilised. This is because the synovial fluid in the joints gets a chance to circulate.

This pose has a stimulating effect along the whole spine and can help remove rigidity and pain. It also aids digestion and helps improve your eyesight as well. On the psychological level, this posture symbolises action and can help you overcome feelings of 'stuckness' or stagnation, which in turn improves your determination and willingness to move forwards both mentally and physically.

To achieve the natraj asana, follow these steps:

1. **Stand up straight with your hands hanging loosely by your sides.** Look directly ahead and breathe normally.

2. **Put your weight on your left leg, while bending your right leg at the knee.** Grab the top of your right foot with the palm of your right hand and push your foot backwards into your palm at the same time as you slowly raise your left hand to the front, keeping the fingers together and pointing upwards with your palm down.

   Keep your left arm at about 60 degrees, pointing towards the horizon, so that the whole hand is visible. Look at your outstretched hand.

3. **Bend slightly forwards at the waist, keeping your eyes on the fingers of your left hand, while your right leg is firmly rooted into the floor.**

   Breathe slowly and normally stay in the posture for eight seconds.

4. **Return to standing by slowly bringing your left hand down and lowering your right leg first to the folded position and then down to the floor.**

5. **Repeat Steps 1 to 4 on the left side.**

   The other side may feel completely different, but just work gently as far as you feel comfortable.

If you're a little stiff or unsteady, do this pose near a wall or chair for support. It gets better the more you practise.

Figure 7-5:
The cosmic
dancer.

Dealing with digestive problems with vatayanasana

The posture is easy to perform and is known as a wind-relieving posture. It gently massages your abdomen and stomach as it expels gas from the colon, which can create some merriment in a yoga class, but you get used to it after a while. It's also useful for stretching and toning your lower back.

1. **Lie on the floor, keeping your back close to the ground, arms gently relaxed either side of your body.**

2. **Inhale while slowly stretching your left leg down along the floor and clasping your hands around your right knee as you bring it towards your chest. (See Figure 7-6.)**

Figure 7-6:
Relieving wind and stretching your spine.

3. **Exhale as you use your arms to press your knee to your chest.**

   To work the posture a little more, raise your head to meet your knee.

   You can massage your spine and relieve stiffness by bending both knees to the chest on an inhale, raising your head to meet your knees and rocking gently side to side.

4. **Release the pose, lowering your leg to the floor, then repeat Steps 1 to 3 with your other leg.**

Psychologically, this posture is said to help with self-acceptance; after all, you're literally embracing yourself.

Beating obesity with bhujangasana

According to the ancient yoga text *Gheranda Samhita*, when you practise the cobra pose regularly, the serpent goddess known as Kundalini awakens the spine and brings it suppleness.

This stance tones all the abdominal organs and strengthens your pancreas and liver in particular, which has a positive effect on your gut and helps combat obesity. Regarded as one of the best postures for curing constipation, it also helps ease menstrual discomfort. The cobra pose expands your chest and psychologically opens up the heart, allowing feelings to flow.

Here's how to practise the cobra pose (see Figure 7-7):

1. **Lie face down on the floor, turning your face to the side so that you rest on your cheek, and bring the palms of your hands beneath your shoulders on each side of your body.**

2. **Press down on your palms and raise your chest off the floor, moving your head and eyes forwards.**

   Point your fingers forwards in line with your shoulders, and keep your elbows close to your body. Your shoulders should be down, away from your ears, and your face relaxed. Keep your heels about hip width apart, with your toenails on the floor.

3. **Breathe normally, straighten your head and tilt it slightly backwards.** Inhale, and hold the breath and the pose for 6 to 8 seconds.

   Tighten the buttocks to protect your lower back. Make sure that everything below the navel stays in contact with the floor.

4. **Exhale and lower your head towards the floor, turning it to rest your cheek on the floor.** Relax your body for a moment then repeat the pose three more times.

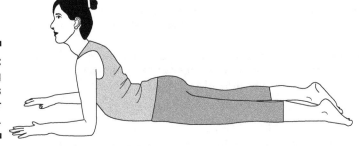

Figure 7-7: Bringing suppleness to your spine.

It's easy to forget that your facial muscles affect all the musculature of your body. This was brought home to me when my yoga teacher said you can really tell a lot about people when you stand in front of a class. So I asked what she could tell about me. Her response: 'Too much strain in the face.' Now, as soon as I remember to relax my face, I can feel my whole body begin to relax.

Looking at yoga for your eyes

Ayurveda states that disease can be caused by under-use, over-use and abuse of the senses. Because most sensory input is through the eyes, I've included some very simple exercises you can do at any time to help take care of these windows to your soul.

The psychological and physiological aspects of seeing are intimately entwined and ultimately affect how you feel. You may put your eyes through a lot of stress, forcing them to work at an accelerated pace instead of allowing them to work in a relaxed fashion.

Studies of rural populations show us that *myopia* or short sightedness is relatively rare, with only about five per cent of country dwellers needing corrective lenses. However, fifty per cent of the student population need help seeing well. Genetics cannot explain the rapid increase in the situation over the last 75 years, but the fact that people used to spend much of their day outside looking into the distance, and now really tax their eyes with close-up tasks and computer use, may offer an explanation.

If you spend much of your day looking at a computer screen, use these tips to ease the strain on your eyes:

- ✔ Look away from the computer – preferably into the distance – every 20 minutes for at least 2 minutes.

- ✔ Start healthy blinking habits. The average blink rate is five to ten blinks per minute. When you're on a computer or reading, your blink rate decreases dramatically, which makes your eyes dry and irritated. (People who are scared or afraid of letting go tend to blink less.)

You can improve your visual performance by shifting your eyes consciously from one object to the next, as in this visual tracking exercise:

1. **Hold one finger of your left hand about six inches in front of your eyes while you hold one finger of the other hand at a distance. Keep your eye on something also in the far distance.**

2. **Shift your gaze between the objects in the near, middle and far distance while breathing slowly.**

Try to pair your breathing with the shifting of your gaze. This coupling really helps to change the focal length and relieves tension in the eye muscles. Try it and see.

Focus on the lines in Figure 7-8 and monitor your breathing as you trace the lines with your relaxed eyeballs.

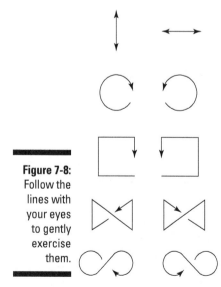

Figure 7-8:
Follow the lines with your eyes to gently exercise them.

Palming your eyes to soothe them

A very good way to relax your eyes after doing yoga poses or whenever they need some TLC is a simple palming technique that gives your eyes a complete rest:

1. Find a quiet space, with a table on which to rest your elbows. Prop your elbows on the table and place the palms of your hands side by side facing you.

2. Lower your head so that your eyes are cupped by your palms.

   The objective is to block light from your eyes without putting pressure on your eyes. You can achieve this by putting the heel of your palm on your cheekbone. Your little fingers rest on either side of your nose, with your thumbs on your temples.

Rubbing your hands together before lowering your head enhances the experience.

3. Relax the muscles in your face and neck while breathing deeply.

   Intoning the word 'Relax' and deepening your breathing benefits your eyes even more. This technique is known as breathing through the eyes.

   As you exhale, visualise any tension leaving your eyes.

Roaring through the lion pose to destroy disease

In the lion pose, known as *simha asana*, which literally means 'the powerful one', you resemble a roaring lion. Mentioned in the *Hatha Pradipika* (a famed book on the practice of yoga), the lion pose is said to be the destroyer of all diseases.

The lion pose helps to release tension in the whole head area, so all the muscles of your face and jaw benefit as well as your eyes. Blood floods into the tissues of your throat, which often carry a lot of tension. Clenched jaws often go with clenched fists, and the fingers and hands benefit from a good stretch.

To accomplish the lion pose, follow these steps:

1. **Sit on your heels with your feet pushed up against your buttocks and your shins flat against the floor. Put your palms on your knees, keeping your arms straight.**

   Keep your spine straight and your head erect.

2. **Lean forwards just a bit and open your mouth as wide as possible. Push your tongue out as far as feels comfortable. Simultaneously stretch out your fingers. Focus your eyes either on a point between your eyebrows or on the tip of your nose.**

   You will look pretty scary – see Figure 7-9 – so make sure that you're alone or with people who know you haven't lost the plot!

Figure 7-9: Imitating a lion relaxes your whole head.

3. **Exhale and hold the posture for 30 to 60 seconds.**

4. **Inhale, allowing your hands to relax, and close your eyes and mouth.**

5. **Repeat Steps 2 to 4 three times.**

This pose is brilliant for getting rid of pent-up anger, and it's said to make you fearless – which can't be bad. If you're really game (so to speak), let out a roar like a lion, as loud as you can.

Practising Simple Routines for Every Constitution

You may not always have time for an extended yoga practice. But that doesn't mean you can't give your system a nice wake-up with a simple routine or two. The postures in this section are appropriate for any constitution.

Saluting the sun

Surya namaskar, performed as a salutation to the sun, is the equivalent of the Gayatri mantra, which is a prayer to this most life-giving force in the universe. When you perform this sequence correctly, it confers all the benefits of solar energy to your body, mind and spirit.

Work up from one to three rounds daily. Remember, to really get the best out of it, to tie the movements in with your breath. Figure 7-10 shows the poses and when to inhale and exhale.

Spoken of as the crest jewel of yoga, this series of postures benefits every Ayurvedic constitution. (Refer to Chapter 4 to discover your constitution, or dosha.) However, you perform the salutation according to your constitution:

✔ Pittas should perform it slowly and deliberately, and focus on overcoming the tendency to rush through everything.

✔ Kaphas should perform the sequence in a brisk fashion, resisting the temptation to take it slow and easy.

✔ Vata types need to practise this at a medium pace while maintaining complete focus and not allowing distractions.

To salute the sun, follow these steps:

1. **Begin by standing up straight with your feet together and hands in the prayer position.**

2. **Bringing your palms apart and arms straight up over your head, arch gently backwards while inhaling.**

   Relax your neck and push your hips out.

3. **Exhale as you bend forwards from the waist, letting your hands touch the floor or as close as they can get to it.**

   Try to keep your legs straight, but bend your knees if necessary.

4. **Inhale, stepping your right leg back so that your bent knee is as close to the floor as is comfortable and your toes are bent. At the same time, bend your left knee, placing your hands palm down on either side of your left foot. Look forwards, lifting your chin.**

5. **Holding your breath, bring your left leg to join the right one, so that you're supporting yourself on your hands and your bent toes.**

   Keep your body in a flat line while looking at the floor.

6. **Exhale as you slowly drop your knees, chest and finally your forehead to the ground.**

   Your spine will be slightly arched at this point and your elbows bent.

7. **Inhale and lower your hips to the ground, gently arching your back. Bend your elbows as you extend your legs, untucking your toes so that the tops of your toes are on the ground.**

8. **Exhale as you push up from your hands, feet and hips to form a triangle.**

   You can have a lovely stretch as you exhale. (This triangle is called the downward-facing dog pose.)

   Try to keep your heels on the ground, but it's okay to stand on the balls of your feet if you can't.

9. **Keeping your left leg back this time, inhale as bring your right foot forward and stretch your left leg behind you and put your hands either side of your right foot. Arch your back slightly and look up.**

10. **Exhaling slowly and deeply, bring both feet together, keeping your knees straight and bending forwards from the hips.**

    Let your head, neck and arms relax.

11. **Inhale as you return to a standing position. Arching your back, stretch your arms upwards, bringing your palms together over your head.**

12. **Exhaling slowly, bring your arms to your sides and close your eyes.**

    Feel the relaxation.

13. **Begin another round, bringing your left leg back first in Step 4.**

I've seen this posture performed on the knees, which obviously isn't as beneficial, but if you want a more relaxed approach and aren't quite flexible enough yet to start the posture standing up, you can try it.

Figure 7-10:
Breathing
through
a sun
salutation.

Moving with the moon: Chandra namaskar

While the sun salutation is expansive and out there, the salute to the moon is a beautiful sequence to follow when you want to direct your energies more internally to become calm and receptive. In the Vedic teaching, the moon rules the *manas*, or mind.

This moon salutation can draw in scattered energies and help you to become more focused; just follow these steps and Figure 7-11:

1. **Stand upright with your feet together. Place your hands, palms together, at the front of your chest. Inhale as you stretch your arms back over your head and lean backwards, remembering to keep your buttocks tight as you arch your back (shown in Step 11).**

2. **Exhaling, bend your knees and come to a full squat, trying to keep your feet flat to the ground and placing your hands on either side of your feet.**

   If you can't keep your feet flat, stay on the balls of your feet – it's important not to strain.

3. **Inhale slowly as you extend your left leg behind you, dropping the knee to the floor.**

   Leave the right foot where it is and keep your hands palm down directly below your shoulders.

4. **Continue to inhale while sinking downwards and arching your back, dropping your head backwards, raising your arms above your head as you look up to your hands.** Exhale, placing your hands palm down under your shoulders again.

5. **Gently bring your right leg forwards while extending your left leg back and dropping your left knee to the floor.** Now come back to the squatting position you struck in Step 2.

6. **Exhale, lowering your buttocks to your heels and resting your forehead on the floor as you stretch your arms palm down in front of you.**

7. **Still on your knees, stretch your arms above your head and place your palms together as you inhale with your buttocks off your heels.** Let your head tilt back a little and watch your extended arms.

8. **On an exhale, fold back down again so that your buttocks are on your heels.**

9. Breathing in, curl your toes under, come into a full squat again, then exhale.

10. Inhaling, stand upright, raising your arms above your head and leaning backwards.

11. Bring your palms together in front of your chest in the prayer position.

12. Repeat the steps, extending your right leg behind you first this time.

Figure 7-11:
The moon salutation.

Easing into Relaxation with Corpse and Waterfall Postures

Many people never feel really relaxed, even after a night's sleep. However, people who practise yoga regularly often testify that one of the best parts of any session is the deep relaxation at the end of the class.

The relaxation postures themselves literally iron out your energy paths (known as *nadis*) – the equivalent of giving your nervous system a soothing massage.

Relaxation poses are a form of conscious relaxation – not a sleep or rest period. If done mindfully, these poses actually make you feel energised and help you overcome fatigue.

Coping with stress starves your body of vital energy. Your muscles become tight as stress becomes embedded in your body. Your contracted muscles cut off the flow of oxygen vital to your tissues and create conditions that promote disease. So, relaxing your mind helps keep your body healthy.

Lying down for the corpse pose

Savasana, or the corpse pose, works on your super consciousness to release stress and tension where it all starts in the first place.

Generally, a yoga class ends with 10 to 15 minutes of relaxation, but I've attended classes where relaxation is implemented in between all the asanas – to let them soak in, so to speak.

Some of the benefits of savasana that may encourage you to take up this practice include:

- Lying in a horizontal position facilitates easy circulation so that your heart doesn't have to pump so hard. All your muscle groups are relieved of strain and your breathing becomes more relaxed and rhythmic.

- When all your joints and muscles are relaxed, your mind follows suit and switches off.

- In deep relaxation, you can observe the rise and fall of your abdomen and practise conscious breathing, which facilitates a greater inflow of prana to your tissues. This has a very soothing effect on the higher centres of your brain. Then you can engage in what's known as *pranadharana*, where you become a passive witness of the breath moving up through your body and out through your nostrils.

✔ In savasana, you progress from broad to subtle levels of awareness and become aware of the difference between relaxation and tension in the body.

Many of us are completely unaware of how much tension we carry around in our bodies. Take a moment now to press your middle fingers at the point where your jaw closes. If it's painful, it's a symptom of the tension you hold in your body just to get yourself through the day.

While you observe your breath getting deeper and slower during the pose, you get less input from your stressed-out brain. Eventually you reach a state known as chitta vishranthi in which you experience super-consciousness and total relaxation.

With continued practice, you become more and more aware of the fact that you're the witness of your own thoughts, and your awareness of your body fades into the background.

The type of relaxation achieved in this practice increases over time, and the benefits are far-reaching. In savasana, you allow mental stress and strain to come to the surface and dissipate. As a result, you feel more centred.

Savasana can help you to reduce the effects of hypertension, insomnia, diabetes, joint disease, anxiety and all stress disorders. Studies have shown that after running on a treadmill for a period of 5 minutes, normal resting pulse can be attained in just 8 minutes using the savasana technique, whereas between 14 and 24 minutes were required for either lying on the floor or sitting in a chair.

To do the corpse pose, start with the idea that you'll give full attention to this posture; don't see it as nap time at the end of a yoga session.

Find a warm place and wear warm clothing. You may want to cover yourself, because you can get quite cool as your metabolic rate decreases.

This posture's deceptively simple, but in fact it's one of the hardest to achieve. Do it for at least ten minutes at the end of a yoga session. Here's how:

1. **Lie on your back, with your legs slightly apart and your arms away from your body, allowing the ground to support them.**

   Figure 7-12 shows the pose.

Figure 7-12: The corpse pose.

2. **Roll your head from side to side then centre it.**

3. **Stretch yourself from head to toe and allow your body to sink deep into the ground.**

   Observe the rise and fall of your abdomen as the breath flows along your body and out through the nostrils. Let this process deepen until your pulse and respiratory rate become very relaxed.

Becoming a waterfall

The waterfall posture is a little more dynamic than the corpse pose. You elevate your legs against a wall in a modified shoulder stand.

This is a great posture if you have swollen ankles and varicose veins. It relieves the effects of stress and refreshes your heart and lungs and is quite useful in alleviating the effects of jet lag.

Locate a wall in a warm spot, and follow these steps:

1. **Sit on a small cushion on the floor, with the side of one shoulder 6 to 12 inches from the wall.**

2. **Lower your back gently to the floor and swing your legs up the wall.**

   Keep the cushion beneath your buttocks, stretch your back out on the floor and place your hands palms up at the sides of your head.

   You can enhance the effects of the posture by tying a scarf around your eyes or placing an eye pillow over them. Blocking your sight quiets the mind as well as relieving fatigue.

The overall sensation has been described as feeling like a waterfall, which I can verify from my own experience.

Chapter 8

Night-time Rituals for Sound Sleep and Fertility

*T*he importance of a good night's rest is one of the three pillars of health in Ayurveda, along with food and sex. According to the Vedas, the sacred texts that underpin Ayurveda, you connect with your innermost being – the divinity within us all known as the *Paramatman* – during sleep.

Sleep is profoundly refreshing because it offers a chance to disengage from the sensory bombardment that pervades your daily life. You let your mind, body and emotions restore themselves and prepare for the day ahead.

To lead a healthy life, you need to get the proper amount of quality sleep. Studies show a strong correlation between the amount of sleep people get and their overall health. People who get less than four hours or more than ten hours of sleep each night tend to be ill more than people who slumber between these extremes. Vagbhata, a famous Ayurvedic physician, points out that poor sleep weakens your digestion, and poor digestion can open the door to disease.

While on the subject of sleep, in this chapter I also take a look at that activity you may do before sleep: baby-making. I explore the part of Ayurveda known as Vajikarana, which focuses on improving fertility, and I offer some practical guidance on what you can do to increase fertility.

For this chapter, you can get away without knowing your constitution type, but it's always helpful, so I recommend going to Chapter 4 to discover your type if you haven't already.

Explaining the Different Types of Sleep

Even though we all spend a third of lives doing it, sleep is something that we know comparatively little about. Until the 1950s, scientists thought sleep was a passive affair, but they now know that your brain is very active during sleep. Certain nerves in the brain produce transmitters which keep the brain alert when you're awake, but then another neurotransmitter, *adenosine*, builds up in your bloodstream to cause drowsiness. Your level of adenosine slowly reduces overnight while you sleep, so that you can wake up again in the morning.

When taking a nap is okay

Sleeping during the day is a no-no in the Ayurveda system. Catching a quick 40 winks is fine, but sleeping for more than 30 minutes during daylight hours creates an increase in tamas guna, which breeds inertia and dullness, making you sluggish and slow. (See Chapter 2 for more on the gunas.)

Like every rule, exceptions exist:

- A nap during the summer when it's hot is okay. In other seasons, daytime sleeping can be bad for people with both pitta (hot) and kapha (cold) constitutions.

- If you're older, napping is okay, and, of course, young children need extra sleep.

- If you're studying hard, a little nap can help recharge you mentally and physically.

- After having sex, you need to replenish yourself with extra sleep.

- If you carry heavy weights as part of your job, you merit a little daytime kip.

- Travelling by any form of transport increases vata dosha (air) and causes fatigue, which is helped by a daytime nap.

- Illnesses all call for extra sleep time.

- During the grieving process or if you're undergoing any intense emotion, including keeping a vigil of any kind, you can benefit from resting during the day.

You'll be glad to know that if you're used to a daytime snooze, Ayurveda has a get-out clause called *satmya*, the concept of the body's acclimatisation or adjustment to something that would normally be unhealthy. So, if you're from the Middle East or Spain, where people have historically slept during the afternoon, you can nap and still be in harmony according to Ayurveda.

According to Ayurveda, there are seven types of sleep, caused by:

- **Tamas.** This – one of the three different forces governing creation – is predominant at night. (Refer to Chapter 2 for more on tamas.) It tends to be dull, dense and heavy, and subsequently causes drowsiness.

- **Kapha.** On the physical level, kapha has damp and gross qualities that induce sleepiness.

- **Certain diseases or a fever.** This type of sleep is caused when illness throws all the doshas out of balance.

- **Fatigue from overexertion of your mind.**

- **Physical exertion.** Sleep induced by exertion is a healthy response.

- **The very nature of the night, when tamas and the darkness comes down.** Sleep attributable to this is cool and has a heavy energy.

- **Agantuka.** This is a particular disease, to which Ayurveda attributes a type of incidental sleep. This type of sleep points to a poor prognosis because it leads to eventual death. Hopefully you won't experience this one!

Considering Causes of – and Cures for – Insomnia

If you suffer from insomnia, you're not alone. Approximately 25 per cent of the global population experience sleep-related issues at some time in their lives. More medication is prescribed to treat sleep disorders than for any other therapeutic use.

Insomnia causes untold misery both at night and during the day, no matter what form it takes:

- **Transient insomnia** is a temporary affair you may experience when you're jet lagged, sleeping in a strange bed or you've had a row with your partner.

- **Temporary insomnia** is when the sleep cycle is upset for a couple of weeks. It's typically caused by an ongoing situation that gnaws away at you in the night, such as work-related stress or a looming divorce.

- **Chronic insomnia** is a persistent medical condition that can relate to an illness or the development of poor sleep habits over a long period.

Getting acquainted with the Ayurvedic types of insomnia

Insomnia can manifest itself in a variety of ways. The Ayurvedic classifications go into the detail of the universally experienced symptoms of this sleep disorder (refer to Chapter 4 for a description of the constitutions):

- **Vata:** You're a very light sleeper and the slightest sound wakes you up; then you have a difficult time getting back to sleep. You typically wake up between 2 and 4 a.m. – the time when vata dosha is dominant. You tend to lie in bed worrying about things, and your mind flits like a butterfly from one worry to the next.

  Your dreams involve flying, falling and being chased.

- **Pitta:** You fall asleep rapidly but wake up between 12 and 2 a.m. You often feel frustrated and angry when this happens, and it can put you in a grisly mood the next day. You tend to feel hot and often sweat at night. Sometimes you're thirsty as well.

  Your dreams involve wars, conflict, weapons and anger.

- **Kapha:** You fall asleep easily but wake up because your sinuses are blocked, which commonly occurs in the early-morning hours. You may suffer with indigestion, because your digestion tends to be slow, especially if you've eaten late in the evening. If you haven't metabolised both emotions and food, you feel heavy and depressed the next day.

  Kapha dreams are romantic, sad, watery and calm.

- **Sannipata:** In this serious condition, all the doshas are out of balance and you find it very difficult to sleep at any time. Thus, you can be very tired and have trouble being fully awake. Thankfully, this is the rarest form.

The next section offers ways to overcome the first three types of insomnia. If you have sannipata, you need to see your doctor to ascertain whether you have an underlying medical condition.

Finding ways to get a good night's sleep

As a general rule, Benjamin Franklin's old adage about sleep works well: 'Early to bed and early to rise makes a man healthy, wealthy and wise.' That said, each doshic type has an optimal bedtime:

- **Vata:** 10 p.m.
- **Pitta:** Between 10 p.m. and 11 p.m.
- **Kapha:** Between 11 p.m. and midnight

How the sun affects your sleep

The sun's energy is expansive and creates activity, while the night is dominated by *tamasic* energy, or inertia, which tends to draw everything inward and slow you down.

Sunlight stimulates the pineal gland (an endocrine gland embedded in the brain) to produce both melatonin and serotonin, hormones intimately connected to the sleep cycle. So if you want to be well and have undisturbed sleep, be sure to get at least 20 minutes of natural sunlight every day – especially in the winter. The sun's effects reach your brain through your eyes, so spend a minimum of 20 minutes exposing your face to the sun without glasses of any kind – even your prescription specs block the sun's benefits. Studies in Sweden clearly showed that exposure to sunlight for at least 20 minutes a day helped to regularise menstrual periods and regulate sleep patterns.

Lack of exposure to sunlight can interfere with many physical and emotional functions. I went to a conference in Las Vegas a few years back and heard casino staff complaining of menstrual irregularity. It wasn't hard to find the reason, considering that the staff worked in buildings with no windows or even clocks for that matter, which is a very disorientating experience for the body.

Getting to a good place – physically, mentally and emotionally – before you go to bed can do a lot to stave off bouts of insomnia. Use the tips in the following sections to make your night-time ritual a soothing one that encourages healthful sleep.

Some people are more vulnerable to insomnia than others. If you're one of the sleepless ones, being aware when you're exposed to physical and psychological stress can help you manage your insomnia.

Spending time winding down

Take some time at the end of the day to reflect on the day's events and contemplate how you can improve things in the future if necessary. Reading something spiritually meaningful can help you wind down to a night's sleep with pleasant and calming thoughts. Save the thrillers for daylight.

Turn off your computer at least an hour or two before retiring. Your electronic lifeline is also a stimulant, and recent studies from Harvard University say it definitely jangles your nerves, preventing calm sleep if you're using it every night before you go to bed.

If you like to play music at night, stick to slow, soothing, melodic sounds, preferably playing on a machine you can turn off from your bed.

Making your bedroom sleep-inducing

Turn your bedroom into a sanctuary. Use restful colours on the walls – pale yellow is ideal because it's a positive colour that reflects the energy of the sun. Remove all clutter from the room to make it a light and airy place.

I use an air ioniser, which I think helps my breathing. Avoid any strong smells in the room – commercial cleaners, for example. Sprinkle a little lavender oil on your pillow to create a restful aroma.

Make sure that your mattress is the best you can afford. Don't scrimp on this piece of furniture; remember that you spend a third of your life on it!

A cheaper and very good option for the financially challenged is a memory-foam topper. These toppers are brilliant for moulding around all the kinks of your body. A small caveat, though: I had a patient with a foam mattress topper who suffered terribly with menopausal night sweats. Because the foam doesn't allow air flow, the mattress can make you very hot indeed.

Reduce visual distractions:

- ✔ Remove your television if you have one in your bedroom. Many people watch intensely violent images before going to sleep, and Ayurveda says that the delicate film of *tarpak kapha* (grey matter in the brain) becomes impregnated with these images, so that your sleep is disturbed by them without you being conscious of it.
- ✔ Turn the bedroom clock to face the wall, or remove it altogether. If you wake in the middle of the night, just seeing the time can cause anxiety.

Avoiding certain indigestibles

Eating a heavy meal before bedtime not only makes getting to sleep difficult, the food also sits there in your stomach all night, leading to indigestion, which blocks the channels (and, ultimately, it can be a factor in obesity). So leave about two hours before retiring after having three courses.

A couple things to avoid before bedtime are:

- ✔ **Alcohol:** A glass of wine with dinner is okay, but leave it at that. Although the initial effect of liquor is to make you sleepy, it can also cause you to wake up in the middle of the night feeling dehydrated and thirsty.
- ✔ **Stimulants:** It's well known that caffeine can keep you awake at night, so avoid stimulants after 5 p.m. The good news is that Ayurveda doesn't consider coffee, tea, nicotine and other stimulants intrinsically bad.

    However, Ayurveda is also about moderation and timing. In countries and cultures where the power of caffeine is recognised and respected, espresso and coffee comes in very small cups and isn't drunk just before bed.

Keep in mind that some over-the-counter drugs for slimming, cold relief and asthma treatment contain caffeine.

Take a look at your medications. Tricyclic antidepressants can cause insomnia, and beta-blockers can plague your night with bad dreams and make you toss and turn. If you're having ill effects, consult your doctor.

If you're on prescription medications for insomnia, be aware that they cease to have any benefit after a few weeks, because the body gets habituated to them. Don't stop taking them abruptly though, because this leads to further bouts of insomnia. Talk to your doctor about how to gradually reduce your dosage.

Harnessing herbal help

Herbal remedies can be of great benefit in subduing insomnia. Table 8-1 lists helpful herbs for the three main types of insomnia. Refer to 'Getting acquainted with the Ayurvedic types of insomnia' earlier in this chapter for information on the insomnia types.

Some remedies work for all doshas: take two Maharishi Peaceful Sleep tablets at night with milk or water. You can get these from the website www.maharishiayurveda.co.uk.

Table 8-1	Herbal Insomnia Treatments	
Vata Insomnia	*Pitta Insomnia*	*Kapha Insomnia*
Add 1 teaspoon ashwahghanda (Indian ginseng; see Chapter 17), 1 teaspoon ghee and a strand of saffron in a teacup of warm milk. Drink it half an hour before bed.	Combine ¼ teaspoon nutmeg, ½ teaspoon jaggery (Indian brown sugar) and a little ghee in a teacup of warm milk. Drink it half an hour before bed.	Chop 1 clove of garlic, and simmer it lightly in half a cup of water. Drink it half an hour after eating your evening meal.
Apply a little warm sesame oil to the top of the head and lightly massage the feet with sesame oil before bed.	Apply coconut oil to the top of the head and gently massage the feet with coconut oil before bed.	Apply Brahmi oil to the top of the head and massage the feet with it before bed.
Take a warm bath before bed, with essential oil of camphor, lavender, musk or clary sage.	Take a warm bath before bed, with a few drops of essential oil of rose, jasmine or sandalwood.	Take a warm bath before bed, with a few drops of essential oil of eucalyptus, sage, cinnamon or cedar.

Connecting Eating and Sleeping

How you sleep at night depends a great deal on how you've eaten during the day and whether your food is well digested. The Ayurvedic idea of ama comes into play with improper digestion. *Ama* refers to the state of a process not yet completed; ama in relation to digestion means improperly or incompletely processed foods, which can produce toxins in the body. (Chapter 5 has more about ama.)

To avoid ama for the various constitutions, follow these rules:

- **Vata dosha:** Meals should be light and consist of warm foods cooked with warming spices such as cumin, cloves, cinnamon and ginger. Those with Vata constitutions should eat at around 6 p.m.

- **Pitta dosha:** Food should be cool and not spicy. Use herbs such as coriander and fennel. It's best to eat your supper between 6 and 7 p.m. if you have a pitta constitution.

- **Kapha dosha:** Warm food in moderate quantities seasoned with warming spices such as ginger, mustard seed and garlic is best for Kapha types. Eat between 7 and 8 p.m. and avoid snacking before bed.

In general, yogurt is prohibited at night, because it's said to obstruct the *srotas* or channels of circulation. (Chapter 2 explains the srotas.) This is particularly true for those of you with asthma, bronchitis or rheumatism.

Here are some more helpful foods for promoting sleep:

- **Shali rice** (rice that matures in the winter) is said to be strengthening, cooling and slightly diuretic, and is recommended to help with sleeping when served with milk.

- **Cherry juice** of the sour variety has been found to encourage the production of *melatonin*, which is the stuff secreted by your pineal gland to regulate sleep. Drinking a glass of cherry juice half an hour before bed may be helpful to you, although if you have a pitta constitution, you may find it a little warming; if so, dilute the juice with water.

- **Warm milk** contains an amino acid called tryptophan, which is a natural sedative. Add a strand of saffron to a cup of warm milk to help reduce mucus production if you're sensitive to milk.

Creating Beautiful Babies instead of Sleeping

Ayurveda deals with two aspects of sexual intimacy:

- Infertility and problems in conceiving.
- The opportunity to avail yourself of sexual energy to explore a part of your nature.

I placed this section here on the assumption that most people make babies in bed at night. But no matter what of time day you choose to procreate or indulge in intimacy, the information in this section can help you.

In the *Ashtangha Hrdyam*, a famous Ayurvedic treatise by a physician called Vagbhata, Vajikarana translates to the strength of a stallion's (vajee's) tool (karana). This wakes up the Ayurveda classes I teach, I can tell you! More seriously, Vajikarana is the science of increasing fertility in men and producing healthy babies. The following list applies to men only:

- **Vajikarana:** The science of aphrodisiacs and substances that maximise sexual satisfaction by acting as aphrodisiacs or heightening satisfaction.

  One example is *Mucuna pruriens* or kapikacchu. Take one capsule twice a day with water or milk after meals.

- **Shukra-Shodhana:** The concept of purifying semen, so that your progeny will be strong and in good health.

  An example is *Saussurea lappa* or kushta. This herb is usually part of a formulation.

- **Shukra-Stambhaka:** This group of medicines help with premature ejaculation by increasing a man's ability to retain sperm during intercourse.

  An example is *Myristica fragrans*, or jatiphala as it's known in Sanskrit.

- **Shukra Pravartaka-Janaka:** These substances increase semen flow in the testes.

  Examples are *Embelica officinalis*, or amalaki, and masha, which is black gram or urad dahl.

- **Shukra Shoshaka:** These drugs dry up semen – useful if a man has copious amounts of semen but a low sperm count.

  Examples are kalinga, a type of watermelon, and haritaki (*Terminalia chebula*), which is commonly taken with long pepper (*Piper longum*) at the end of the winter.

✔ **Shukra Rechana:** This group of compounds aid in the release of semen for men who have trouble ejaculating.

Examples are *Solanum xanthocarpum*, or kantakari, and in the same family *Solanum indicum*, or brihati.

✔ **Shukrajanana:** This collection of herbs promote *spermatogenesis*, production of healthy sperm.

Under this heading fall popular Ayurvedic herbs such as *Withania somnifera*, or Ashwagandha, and *Asparagus racemosus*, or shatavari.

If you're having trouble conceiving, you can choose from a large number of helpful medicines. I strongly advise that you consult an Ayurvedic practitioner/physician.

The great Ayurvedic physician Charaka has the last word on Aphrodisiacs when he states:

All the objects of beauty are assembled in a woman in a compact form, and nowhere else. All the objects of the senses found in the person of a woman evoke the maximum delight in a man. The woman is, therefore, the most lovable object of a man. It's the woman who procreates children. Dharma (righteousness), artha (wealth), laksmi (auspiciousness) and loka (the entire world) are established in women. The woman who is beautiful and youthful, who is endowed with auspicious signs, and who is amiable and skilled is the aphrodisiac par excellence.

Selecting foods for good reproductive tissue

Here's a list of foods that help you build healthy sperm and ova:

✔ Artichokes

✔ Asparagus

✔ Black lentils (masa)

✔ Buffalo meat soup (mahisa rasa; not that there's much of it around, but I have seen it!)

✔ Ghee

✔ Honey

✔ Nuts: Cashews, pistachios and almonds

✔ Meat soup (mamsa rasa; particularly favoured is chicken soup)

✔ Milk

- ✔ Mushrooms
- ✔ Rice (shali variety)
- ✔ Seafoods: Lobster, crabs, oysters, prawns and shrimp
- ✔ Spices: Cumin, ginger, cloves, cardamom, garlic
- ✔ Sugar and sugar cane
- ✔ Wheat

The common feature of all these food substances is that they're *anabolic*, which means they build strong and healthy tissues in the body and ultimately good reproductive cells, or *shukra dhatu* in Ayurveda. Eating these foods gives you strength – which imparts vigour, dynamism, virility, health and potency.

Some substances retard sperm production, so if you're trying to conceive, avoid coriander seeds, tobacco and more than your two permitted glasses of alcohol.

I can't leave the subject of baby-making without mentioning the fact that eggs of all kinds get a frequent mention in Ayurvedic discussion of foods that are good for fertility, and goat's testicles fried in ghee with a little long pepper and salt are said to be legendary in their aphrodisiac effects!

Drinking the milk of kindness

Milk is given pride of place in ancient Ayurvedic teachings about sex, mainly because it's a product of mother-love. In Vajikarana, milk is recommended before intercourse to promote semen. It's also recommended for after intercourse – drinking warm milk with ground cashews helps build up sexual energy again.

Ghee (clarified butter) is given an accolade as a reproductive-health-promoting substance. You can easily understand why when you realise that ghee is distilled from butter, which is made from milk.

Charaka, sometimes called the father of Ayurvedic medicine, recommended placing a gold ring in a saucepan with a little milk and adding a teaspoon of ghee. Stir in a teaspoon of honey and sip the rich, warm beverage. Gold ions from the ring impart warmth and glow into the brew without hurting the ring.

For a tasty treat, sample the milk products from the herd at the Bhakti Vedanta Centre in Hertfordshire, UK, if you're in the area. These cows are raised with so much love that you can taste the sweetness of their lives in every drop of milk. Details are available at www. bhaktivedantamanor.co.uk. The centre treats cows with a great deal of respect. Each cow bears its first calf and starts giving milk at around the age of three. The cows are hand milked, and the calves are allowed to suckle naturally. The herd is fed on natural vegetation, vegetables, grains and grasses.

Evaluating the uses of alcohol

Along with several foodstuffs that have aphrodisiac qualities is the ever-popular alcohol. Wine, specifically, if consumed with pleasant people, can get the 'juices going' for a night of lovemaking. Wine, used wisely – in moderate quantities and with food – exhilarates the system, increasing sexual potency and strength. Therefore, as Charaka states, wine is the nectar of the wise and poison of the unwholesome.

Wine has the reverse effect if drunk with those who get argumentative and rude – who have what's known as *rajasic* behaviour – so bear this is mind. Anger is even more excessive with the tamasic type, leading to stupor and sleep, so definitely no boozing with tamasic types!

Chapter 9

Changing Your Diet with the Seasons

*I*n this chapter, I look at the profound effect that the shifting seasons have on the body. I discuss some of the more intrinsic rhythms of the body and how they follow the seasons, as well as ways to keep your system running smoothly in every season.

It isn't essential for you to know your Ayurveda constitution to make use of the information in this chapter, but it helps, so refer to Chapter 4 to determine your dosha (vata, pitta or kapha).

The Smooth Rhythms of the Body

'The butterfly counts not months but moments, and has time enough.'

– Tagore

Adapting your living patterns to harmonise with the rhythms of the natural world has become ever more difficult in this 24-hour culture. Urban life takes an especially heavy toll in terms of exposing you to the stress of crowds, pollution and noise.

The effects of living in this advanced society include a variety of mental illnesses and a deep-seated anxiety at the heart of everything. All medical authorities acknowledge that illnesses are affected by stress. It's also becoming clear that in addition to physical ailments, some mental disorders and psychosomatic problems have their origins in imbalances in the endocrine (hormonal) systems and in interruptions in the natural cycles of the body known as *circadian rhythms*.

The human body is a miracle in its organisation. Timing cycles in your body range from microseconds in your brain cells, minutes in your muscles, hours in your hormones to days in your blood cells. Your body is transformed from hour to hour, and your vital organs and metabolism fluctuate accordingly.

The *diurnal tempo* is the most important rhythm to us, determining when we sleep and orchestrating the flux in our blood pressure, body temperature, pulse rate and amino acid levels throughout the day. Every woman understands the effects in her body of the changing hormone levels as each month progresses. Seasonally, too, the body secretes more of the hormone thyroxine in the autumn to support us through the winter cold.

Even the most traditional medical practitioner recognises that drugs are more or less effective depending on when they're taken. By way of example, recent findings suggest that flu jabs can be made more effective by administering them at different times of day. Mornings appear to be better for men and afternoons for women. By synchronising the jabs with natural cyclical rhythms, the vaccinations appear to offer improved immunity.

If your systems are functioning well and your circadian cycles are able to flow freely, you remain healthy. However, if your rhythms are thrown out of whack due to stress or trauma, you become more vulnerable to illness and infection.

The ancient wisdom of the knowledge of time is deeply embedded in Ayurveda. According to this worldview, information from the environment and the planets is being constantly transmitted via the *srotas*, which are both virtual and material channels (Chapter 2 explains the srotas). These channels prime your system with information to align your body with the external world. Of course, the external world changes with the seasons, so you need to keep your internal systems in alignment with the external world. The following sections offer advice on how to do that and on how to reclaim your connection between external and internal when you lose it.

Staying in Tune with the Seasons

The seasons evolve because of the yearly journey the earth makes around the sun. The farther away from the equator you are, the more marked are seasonal changes.

Research suggests that the nutrients contained in pasteurised cow's milk vary significantly in different seasons. In 1997, the Ministry of Agriculture, Fisheries and Food in England observed that during the winter, iodine is more prevalent in milk, while beta carotene content increases in the summer. On a similar note, researchers in Japan found that spinach had three times as much vitamin C content when it was gathered in the summer than in other seasons. In tandem with such findings, Ayurveda suggests that seasonal and local foods are best for you.

Introducing the two parts of the year: Adana and Visarga

The earth's cycle around the sun divides into two major phases:

- ✔ **Adana:** The northerly phase, which comprises late winter, spring and summer. Adana, which means 'seizing', lasts from mid-January and culminates in mid-June.

- ✔ **Visarga:** The southerly phase is made up of early autumn, autumn and early winter – essentially mid-June to mid-January. The word means 'the sound that dies away'.

Adana is acknowledged to be linked to disease because of the absorbing effects of the sun and wind on the environment. This absorption and consequent drying during Adana leads to a corresponding increase in bitter, pungent and astringent tastes in vegetation. If that seems a bit far-fetched, just compare the sweet flavour of spring greens with that of their winter counterparts. Spring lettuces are sweet and aromatic; winter greens tend to be more earthy and bitter.

In mid-June, the sun takes a southerly course through the sky. This period lasts until November and is known as the more generous time of year. Moisture returns to the earth, endowing it with strength and mitigating the harshness of the sun. The well-irrigated environment responds with the dominance of sweet, sour and salty tastes, which creates bulk and vigour in animal and plant life. The southerly phase consists of early autumn, autumn and early winter.

The most important junction of the year is at the time when Visarga gives way to Adana, which is known as *Yama Damstra*. This crucial junction takes place between 22 November and 9 December. It is recognised as the king of all crossroads, because it is when Yama, the lord of death, collects the souls of the deceased. It is a period of great vulnerability, when all faults are magnified and all the elements are in flux.

The transitions between Visagara and Adana are important:

✔ During the transition between Visagara and Adana – the end of November and beginning of December – you need to make very careful choices in terms of your lifestyle and food (see the later section 'Warming Winter Foods') to be sure you maintain the proper balances and rhythms. On a more positive note, it can be a time when deep transformation can take place. If your intention is pure, you can grow the seeds of change to encourage a psychological renovation.

✔ Adana gives way to Visarga between 8 and 24 June. According to Ayurveda, you need to supplement your body chemistry with the opposite tastes according to the predominance of Visarga or Adana (see the later sections on seasonal foods). This leads to an optimisation of your health.

The following sections help you to put theory into practice.

Matching your physical condition to the seasons

Table 9-1 shows the cycle of the six seasons according to the ancient teachings. The phase of strength refers to how well your digestion is performing.

Table 9-1	The Cycle of the Seasons		
Season	**Sanskrit Name**	**Time Period**	**Phase of Strength**
Early winter	Hemanta	15 November to 15 January	Maximum strength peak
Late winter	Sisira	15 January to 15 March	Maximum strength waning
Spring	Vasanta	15 March to 15 May	Moderate strength waning
Summer	Grisma	15 May to 15 July	Minimum strength waning
Early autumn	Varsa	15 July to 15 September	Minimum strength peak
Autumn	Sarada	15 September to 15 November	Moderate strength peak

For practical purposes, all you need to be aware of is that at the six seasonal junctions, the body is at its most vulnerable. These gaps are known as *rtu sandhi* (joints of the seasons), when disease can more easily enter the body. These sandhi points occur seven days either side of the intersection, so take extra care at these times by eating well, getting plenty of rest and attending to your daily routine. (See Chapter 6 for details of how to stay in balance.)

During these transition periods, both Sushruta and Charaka, the most famous Ayurvedic physicians, recommend shodhana practices (cleansing processes) to remove the excess doshas (in the form of bile, mucus and dryness) from the body by a process known as *panchakarma*. An Ayurvedic practitioner/physician can guide you in the correct manner.

Adjusting Your Digestion in Autumn

In early autumn, the evenings are still long, your appetite is strong, and the weather is generally cold and damp. While the sun's power is diminished by wind, rain and clouds, the energies of the moon gain ascendancy.

This is the time to get some oil massages, preferably Ayurvedic ones, as well as herbal body scrubs. Warm baths with essential oils are always helpful to soothe away tension and increase vata dosha (refer to Chapter 2 for an explanation of vata dosha).

Looking at the conditions

At the beginning of autumn, vata starts to aggravate the accumulated pitta from the summer by acting like a bellows. As summer pitta leaves your body, you may develop symptoms such as conjunctivitis, gastritis, rashes, headaches and irritability.

Vata-related problems, such as cracking joints, anxiety, irregular digestion and an increased sensitivity to cold, can start to manifest themselves. To combat these conditions, adopt a leisurely and quiet lifestyle during this period so that your system can adjust to the change in seasonal energies. This translates as follows:

- ✔ Don't drink cold water or use ice.
- ✔ Don't sleep during the day.
- ✔ Reduce sexual and physical activity.

These simple strategies also help you to adjust to the prevailing forces of nature. Vata characteristics are cold, light, dry and dispersing, and one of the main ways of pacifying these increased tendencies in the body is by increasing foods that are naturally sweet, sour and salty in taste, served warm and in moderate quantities.

Eating the right foods

This is a delightful time of the year when the autumn tints shimmer in an array of colours. All around you is evidence of the earth's fecundity, with hedgerows filled with blackberries, rosehips and haws, rich in vitamin C.

An often-overlooked autumn bounty is elderberries, which are packed with anti-viral properties to allay winter colds. Add elderberries to an apple pie, put them in oatmeal, brew them in tea. One of the best treats I ever had was at an ashram in Orléans, France, where I was offered elderberry jam (*sureau*). It's glorious on toast or in porridge. Failing that, you can buy it as a syrup called Sambucol in health-food shops.

Colon health should take high priority now, so that accumulated heat can find its way out of the body. Keep your diet rich in fibre. Cooking with both figs and dates helps your colon, and you can also eat them as snacks.

The modern tendency of eating a large quantity of food at a sitting can easily put out your delicate digestive fire, which you need to stoke at this time of the year.

To maintain normal digestion, incorporate into your diet old barley (it's lighter and therefore easier to digest than normal barley), and shali rice, a very nutritious form of rice grown over 60 days, also called red rice. Barley couscous is always a treat to stave off the chill, with the added bonus that it only takes five minutes to prepare. Just add boiling water to a bowl of barley couscous, let it soak for four minutes and then mix in argan oil if you have it, or virgin olive oil for essential fatty acids.

If you're not vegetarian, eat the meat in the form of game such as pheasant, venison, quail and partridge. These meats aren't oily or heavy, so they're easy to digest.

When it comes to beverages, boil pure water, let it cool and add a teaspoon of honey. You want honey in the autumn because of its heating properties. In contrast, unrefined white sugar is cooling to the system, so you can use it in the summer to help you cool down. Take arista (wine with decocted herbal extracts), to ward off dampness and help the digestion.

A note about vegetarianism

Throughout this chapter you notice that my diet advice includes eating meat. Ayurveda is, perhaps surprisingly, not vegetarian; pages of text exist about the qualities of different meats, from peacock to elephant. Food should always be consumed as a sacrament, and if you follow the daily routine in Chapter 6 you notice your desire to consume large amounts of meat products naturally slips away.

Embedded in the practice of Ayurveda are the sage Patanjali's sutras, where the notion of *ahimsa* (non-violence) lies. The industrial slaughter of creatures today produces meat that's filled with adrenalin caused by the fear the animal felt on the way to the abattoir; this adrenalin is held in the musculature, making the meat tough and chewy.

If you need any more persuasion, have a look at a widely available film called *Food, Inc.* by Robert Kenner and you get a real insight into how animal husbandry in the modern world is a rare thing, as well as the mindless cruelty enacted on animals on an epic scale.

As the season progresses, the days get colder and shorter, so add more warming spices to your diet. Ginger holds pride of place in Ayurveda because it has so many wonderful properties and you can use it in both sweet and savoury dishes. Taken at this time of the year, ginger helps prevent the build-up of mucus in your system. Cinnamon, cardamom and clove encourage your digestive juices to flow and enhance the flavour of any dish.

Take advantage of the health-giving properties of beetroot during this season. Its ruby sap is filled with blood-building nutrients that supply iron to your blood, bringing more prana (energy) into the bloodstream. An added bonus is that beetroot has been proven to reduce blood pressure.

Warming Winter Foods

Now the weather is beginning to get really cold, but the good news is that if you paid attention to changing your diet in the autumn, your digestion is as strong as it gets during the whole year. In winter, eat lots of steaming casseroles with delicious root vegetables such as carrots, salsify, celeriac, turnips and swede. Packed with energy from the ground, these tubers are filled with goodness that satisfies your increasing hunger at this time when your body craves calories in order to keep you warm.

Peas and all the types of winter squash also provide heat and energy to the system and taste so sweet.

Winter is the period to reintroduce porridge into your life. Follow this recipe for an Ayurvedic slant on porridge:

1. **Place a pint of water, a little salt, four cloves, one cardamom pod and a piece of cinnamon bark in a small pan.**

   I bite the cardamom pod first to liberate the heavenly aromas.

2. **Boil for five minutes, then add 2 to 4 cups of oats or spelt porridge, depending on how thick you like your porridge, and cook for four more minutes.**

An added delight to my porridge is the addition of my neighbour's walnuts, collected from her tree in October, and then a dash of organic maple syrup. This power breakfast keeps me going all morning.

As winter progresses, kapha dosha is on the rise, and with it come heavy, moist, sticky and cold properties. To stay in balance, you need to counter these tendencies by including warm, light and tangy foods in your culinary choices.

Nuts abound at this time and can comprise part of your daily intake of protein. They're generally hard to digest, but roasting makes them lighter on the stomach. Almonds are best soaked overnight and peeled. They're a very good source of calcium.

Try some sea vegetables at this time of year. Samphire, also known as sea asparagus, has a delicate flavour. On the same lines, add kelp and dulse to cooking rice, mix arami with carrots and put nori in casseroles. Sea vegetables are filled with mineral salts and iodine, which are becoming rare commodities in the modern diet.

The energetics of the Sisira period, or late winter, are much the same as winter proper. Your diet needs to be free from cold drinks and raw foods. Heat any of the abundance of leafy green vegetables available at this time of the year, such as cabbage, Brussels sprouts and kale. These vegetables are all loaded with antioxidants and vitamin U (yes, U!), which is said to heal ulcers in the stomach – something that bitter/astringent substances are said to be able to do in Ayurveda. Try adding warming spices such as caraway or cumin to encourage digestion. And instead of tossing steamed vegetables in butter, use clarified butter in the form of ghee to help make the veggies more digestible.

A slice of good-quality wholegrain bread gives you plenty of the amino acids you require to sustain a healthy body.

Beans are notoriously difficult to digest, but you have the capacity to handle them in winter, and they provide a great boost of body-building protein. They're slightly astringent, and that makes them useful for breaking down the kapha, which is starting to increase in your system now. The varieties of beans are endless, but a few favourites are chickpeas, pinto beans and lima beans. Mung beans and aduki beans are filled with nutrients and are *tridoshic*, which means they're suitable for all constitutions.

To eliminate the gas-producing effect of beans, cook them with a very small pinch of *asafoetida*, a pungent tree resin with a sulphurous odour, which comes in a small pot. Also known as *hing*, the spice is widely available in Indian grocery shops.

Cleansing Spring Foods

During spring, your body follows the cycle of the natural world and is subject to a sort of thawing. Kapha, the energy that invests itself in mucus-like secretions in your body, starts to liquefy and move to the surface. This situation can cause many problems, such as sinusitis (inflammation of the sinuses) and a feeling of heaviness.

Implement a diet that eliminates heavy, sour, sweet and oily products. You can bring in more bitter and tangy foods and take herbal wines like draksharishta before meals to help with poor digestion.

During spring, you're more susceptible to colds, so give your system all the help it can get. One way to protect yourself is to take Swedish bitters before food (as directed by the manufacturer) in a little water. The original recipe for this blend of herbs such as aloe, myrrh, angelica and rhubarb is said to come from the great European physician Paracelsus.

You can also avail yourself of what you can pick from the hedgerows: tender young shoots of dandelion leaves, and roots, birch leaves, blackberry leaves and small plantain shoots. Make a tea of equal proportions of these herbs and drink it daily. Also try making a daily tonic by brewing elderflowers collected and dried in the summer. The great Ayurvedic physician Charaka points out that spring is a time to savour youth, beauty and the woods.

Replace citrus and dairy in the springtime with lots of cleansing hot drinks such as herbal teas and honey water with black pepper. Many commercially available herb teas contain ginger. Keep a supply and use it often to flush your system of accumulated toxins. You can make your own brew using freshly chopped ginger, fenugreek seeds, black peppercorns and black tea.

For the love of asparagus

My personal spring favourite, which I eat whenever it's in season (which is for about six weeks starting at the beginning of May), is English asparagus. Boil a whole bunch in a pan of water for three to five minutes and serve it with butter or ghee. Asparagus holds pride of place in the vegetable world because it contains natural steroids and a wellspring of chlorophyll. Get it as fresh as you can, because after you cut the asparagus the precious natural sugars rapidly convert to starch.

Use herbs that warm the body and increase your metabolism. Garlic is good, although don't use too much if you're on a celibate spiritual path, because it can stimulate passion! Add cayenne pepper, mustard seed, paprika, onion and horseradish to your diet. Try smoked paprika for a real treat.

Sleeping during the day is strongly discouraged during spring.

Cooling Summer Foods

The summer sun now reaches its zenith and with it your appetite reduces and your digestive capacity is at its lowest point, simply because your body needs to metabolise fewer calories to keep you warm. Many of us eat the same amount of food all the year around, but you need less in the warmer months – so give your stomach a bit of a rest at this time. Pitta dosha, with its qualities of heat, oiliness, sharpness and pungency, is on the increase in the body. So emphasise sweet, moist and cool foods as a counterbalance.

Take advantage of the fruit stalls packed with juice-filled treats. Local fruits are your first choice, because they have more flavour and more nutrients than fruits trucked in from far-flung places. Your best choice is local, organic fruits. I often hear people commenting on the fact that fruit and vegetables look great but their flavour is entirely lacking. Gas-ripened fruit may look great, but depriving fruit of the sun during the ripening process creates morsels that are tasteless to the tongue.

Green coriander should never be far away from you in summer. Sprinkle it liberally on all foods. It's not only very tasty but also very cooling to the system.

Ayurveda places great importance on the flavour of food and clearly suggests that good sweet, aromatic flavours feed you in body, mind and spirit. Have you ever noticed that when a food is really flavoursome, you need the smallest amount to satisfy yourself? *Rasa* (flavour) comes from the word for 'sap' or 'juice' and refers not only to what you experience in the mouth, but also conveys a myriad of meanings such as the effect of a piece of music and the very essence of life.

Replenishing your body with fluids is of primary importance in the summer, because your blood thickens due to the drying effects of the sun. If you imbibe alcohol, cut down on the amount you drink. Keep your body well irrigated with lots of water and fresh juices. Try lemon barley water, mint tea and lemon balm. Grow lemon balm in the garden and then you can pluck a few leaves, steep them in hot water, let them cool and add some jaggery (solidified sugar cane juice) to taste.

Eat melon of all kinds in the summer months. Sprinkle a little ground ginger on top to make it more digestible. However, eating melon mixed with other foods creates ama (toxins). So try it as a late afternoon snack – a taste treat that also provides fluid to your system.

Green leafy vegetables are also in abundance in summer, and lettuce of all kinds is a refreshing choice. Try to move away from the boring old iceberg; it only became popular because it keeps well in salad bars, and there are so many much more nutrient-rich choices in the green leafy camp including kos, endive, dandelion greens, romaine and rocket. Chicory really has a lovely bitterness, which you need to increase the precious digestive juices that are so scarce now in your stomach. Lettuce also makes terrific soup.

Bon appétit as another year passes.

Going nuts for coconut

Coconut water is an absolute treat in summer. It's a great tonic for your kidneys and is an excellent rehydration fluid with lots of electrolytes and potassium, which are lost in sweat. It's also an invaluable source of antioxidants and contains cytokines, which are phytohormones that promote cell division and growth. You can get organic varieties from Asian grocery shops, but beware of some of the tinned stuff, because it's so full of preservatives. Buy a fresh coconut, extract the water and then enjoy the sweetness of the flesh as well.

Part III

Appetising Approaches to a Healthy Diet

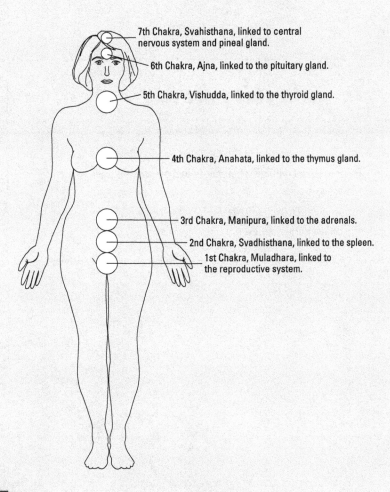

7th Chakra, Svahisthana, linked to central nervous system and pineal gland.

6th Chakra, Ajna, linked to the pituitary gland.

5th Chakra, Vishudda, linked to the thyroid gland.

4th Chakra, Anahata, linked to the thymus gland.

3rd Chakra, Manipura, linked to the adrenals.

2nd Chakra, Svadhisthana, linked to the spleen.

1st Chakra, Muladhara, linked to the reproductive system.

Go to www.dummies.com/extras/ayurvdauk for super online bonus content.

In this part . . .

- ✔ Learn about the importance of taste in Ayurveda.
- ✔ Enjoy the benefits of the right diet for your type.
- ✔ Get au fait with different herbs and spices and their benefits.
- ✔ Eat energy-giving foods, and foods to help digestion.
- ✔ Bake wheat-free bread!

Chapter 10

Stimulating the Palate: A Taste of Things to Come

In This Chapter

▶ Discovering the six essential tastes

▶ Learning about the effects on flavour in your body

▶ Introducing agni and how you can enhance it

▶ Looking at the six stages of digestion

▶ Learning how to determine your digestive capacity

Ayurveda purports that all your senses react to food. Flavours therefore are part of a sophisticated system that yields chemical and emotional effects throughout your mind and body.

You've probably had the experience of smelling a favourite food from childhood and being flooded with memories. That experience supports the idea that your food nourishes more than bodily tissues and fluids.

In this chapter you discover that taste includes a lot more than what happens on your tongue. The whole picture of taste includes your sense of smell, texture and even more – such as how you feel emotionally.

Rasa: Discovering the Six Essential Flavours

The Sanskrit term *rasa* (flavour) shows how the Ayurvedic concept of flavour is fuller than our Western understanding of it. The word divides into two parts:

 ✔ **Ra** means 'to feel, perceive, taste, relish, love and desire'
 ✔ **Sa** means 'to encompass' and also refers to the best part of anything or the juice in the stomach known as *chyle*.

The two parts of the word together – rasa – refer to the prevailing sentiment in human character, mind and heart, giving the meaning of flavour a much wider reach.

Ayurveda not only takes a fuller approach to explaining flavour but identifies six distinct flavours, which I explore in the following sections. An optimal diet is seen as being made up of each of the flavours every day. This is acknowledged as your best approach to building a satisfying diet and helping ensure good health.

Selecting sweet (madhura)

For most people, sweetness becomes embedded in the mind early, because a mother's milk tastes sweet.

The sweet flavour tends to be heavy, cold, sticky and oily. Sweet foods are often slightly greasy and mild, and they bring about a change in your saliva, making it more viscous.

I remember my mother giving me a spoonful of jam after I ate a chilli in a curry. Just as the jam cooled down the heat of the chilli, so a sweet flavour can reduce the power of pitta – the fiery dosha. (Chapter 2 defines the doshas.)

Sweet flavours also reduce vata, the airy dosha. When you feel anxious and all at sea, something sweet immediately calms your jangled nerves.

Finally – and sadly, as far as my waist is concerned – sweetness increases kapha, which is the earthier dosha and confers the ability to build tissues. This makes it heavy, so that extra piece of pie will just add to your figure!

Within your body, sweet food has many uses:

 ✔ Improving memory
 ✔ Removing burning (such as gastritis or inflammation in your throat) from your system
 ✔ Reducing thirst
 ✔ Promoting milk production in pregnancy

If you're fit and have good digestion, sweet flavours act as a tonic to your system. You should increase naturally sweet tastes if you're debilitated. Eat raisins, for example, which are very nutritious and sweet. A tonic wine known as draksharishta is a stimulant for your digestion, particularly if you're run down after a bout of the flu.

Sweet foods are easy to come by. Wheat and other staples in your diet are predominantly sweet, as are:

- Grains, which leave you feeling full and satisfied, including:
    - Barley
    - Oats
    - Rice
- Tubers:
    - Manioc
    - Potatoes
    - Taro
    - Yams
- Oil and oil-containing products:
    - Almond
    - Coconut
    - Peanut
    - Sesame
    - Sunflower
- Fruits such as:
    - Apricots
    - Grapes
    - Nectarines
    - Peaches
    - Pineapples
- Milk and milk products; goat's milk is also astringent and therefore a little lighter to digest
- Sugars:
    - Agave
    - Date sugar

- Jaggery

- Maple

- Sugar beet

- Sugar cane

This list isn't exhaustive, and even certain herbs and plants have a sweet taste. For example, liquorice is sweet with a secondary aftertaste that is slightly bitter. Liquorice can help reduce inflammation, is a great expectorant, and is helpful if you have gastritis. Shatavari is a sweet and well-used root of asparagus that helps improve the memory, vitalise the nerves, promote breast milk production and clear out phlegm from the lungs.

 If you want to include sweet flavours in your diet by using fruit, make sure you wait until the fruits are ripe. Many fruits are picked before they are ripe, and therefore their prominent taste is masked. For example, bananas are often sold green, and if you eat them at this stage they act as an astringent in the body.

Of course, sweet food in excess leads to trouble such as obesity and diabetes, so eat sweet foods in moderation. Interestingly for those of you who are worried about your weight but enjoy a sweet taste, honey is considered astringent and therefore okay.

Savouring sour (amla)

The sour flavour makes its presence known as soon as it hits your tongue. Right away, you start to salivate. This effect does good things for you, cleaning the mouth and causing sweating, which clears the channels of your body.

Sourness is made up primarily of earth and fire elements, which makes it hot, oily and heavy in nature. This is what you taste in acidic fruits and foods that are rich in oxalic acid, like spinach.

In your body, sour food reduces vata and increases pitta and kapha. In moderate quantities, it can improve your digestion and stimulate your appetite. Too much though can promote skin rashes, muscle weakness, jaundice, gastritis, and any inflammatory disorder related to pitta dosha.

Most fruit can be considered sour before it has ripened. Mango is both sweet and sour (and delicious). Other sources of the sour flavour include:

- Ascorbic-acid-rich fruits like gooseberries.

- Lemons, which are particularly easy to work into your diet by squeezing them over your food; besides keeping all the connective tissues in your body in good shape, lemon can help alleviate diarrhoea, cramps, nausea and fever.

✔ Hawthorn berries, which boost your circulatory system.

✔ Rosehips, which are packed with vitamin C.

✔ Sorrel, which is often eaten with fish, and is a good blood cleanser.

✔ Tamarind, which is acidic and sour, and helps if you feel nauseated or have diarrhoea.

Amalaki, which is a type of gooseberry extremely popular in India for its benefits, is more sour than anything but contains all of the other flavours except salty. Amalaki has excellent healing qualities, especially for the digestive system.

Securing salt (lavana)

Salt heightens the taste of anything that you add it to, which is why you find it on so many tabletops. It's always been highly prized; the Latin word *salary* derives from the same root as salt.

Salt is mildly sedative and can act as a laxative and purgative. It can clear any obstructions in the channels of your body. It's used in massage therapy, toothpastes, eye drops and ointments.

The qualities of salt are derived from its elemental make-up of fire and water, which give it hot, heavy, sharp, slightly oily properties. Ayurveda highly prizes rock salt, or *saindhava lavana*, which is rich in minerals such as iron and magnesium and is less likely than other salt to cause fluid retention in your tissues. This salt is mined in the province of Sindh in India and is regarded as a heart tonic and an aphrodisiac; this is possibly due to the fact that it's considered cooling in nature, unlike other salts. Like all salts, rock salt encourages salivation. This means that your enzyme-rich saliva can get started straight away and digest your dinner!

In addition to table salt, you can find salt in:

✔ Celery

✔ Irish moss

✔ Fish from the sea

✔ Oysters

✔ Seaweeds

✔ Samphire

If you're iodine-deficient, try adding a little seaweed to your rice while it cooks, to easily gain a nutritive boost.

Salt-free diets get a lot of attention these days, but Ayurveda states that a little salt not only improves the flavour of other food, but brings the digestive elements to the fore to help digest your meal.

Not everyone who has hypertension is affected by salt. Check your blood pressure over time to find out whether this is the case for you, and speak to your doctor if you aren't sure.

Salt can increase the symptoms of gout and of all pitta issues within your body. In large amounts, salt:

✔ Dries the skin

✔ Induces vomiting

✔ Causes the tissues to hold on to water; sea salt especially increases this tendency

✔ Decreases virility

✔ Creates thirst

✔ Causes wasting of the muscles

So eat salt in moderation.

Broaching bitter (tikta)

The bitter flavour can eclipse the others, but it has great therapeutic value. Many animals know this instinctively and search out bitter herbs to eat when they're ill. (That's why your pet cat or dog eats grass when it's sick.)

Bitter is a combination of the elements of ether and air, which makes it dry, cooling, light and reducing in nature. It reduces the flow of saliva when you put it in your mouth, but it's great for promoting your *agni* (biological fire) and therefore your digestion. It purges all the channels in your body, and because of its drying action will dry up any secretions in your system, like excess mucus.

The bitter flavour works to break down fat, or *meda dhatu* in Ayurveda – great news if you're worried about excess pounds. Bitter also has a blood-purifying action that makes it very useful if you have *septicaemia* (blood poisoning), pus-producing skin problems or wounds.

The active ingredients in bitter-flavoured foods are called *alkaloids* and *glycosides*. They offer therapeutic benefits for adult-onset diabetes (people in India routinely use bitter gourd juice to balance their blood sugar and help with diabetes), digestive disorders, skin complaints, fevers and jaundice.

Don't overuse the bitter taste in your diet if you have a low sperm count and want children, because it can dry up the precious seminal fluid that your sperm swim around in. If vata dosha is aggravated, you should also avoid too much bitter, because this taste has very similar properties because of its drying, lightening, cooling and dispersing nature.

In your diet, bitter comes from:

- ✔ Coffee
- ✔ Dark green leafy vegetables
- ✔ Fenugreek
- ✔ Karela, or bitter melon
- ✔ Rhubarb

Bitter is the flavour most lacking in the Western diet, which might explain our penchant for coffee!

Turmeric is one of the most commonly used bitter herbs in Ayurvedic medicine. Turmeric has wonderful antioxidant properties. You can use it to:

- ✔ Help manage your blood sugar levels
- ✔ Reduce aggravated pitta dosha
- ✔ Clear a sore throat and fever
- ✔ Treat urticaria (if you use it in cream form)
- ✔ Reduce the effects of rheumatism

With so many practical benefits, turmeric is a great seasoning to keep in your kitchen. Coriander's another solid choice for the spice rack; it's ubiquitous in Asian cooking, because it's a very useful bitter taste that you can use to treat fevers and nausea.

Promoting pungent (katu)

The pungent flavour combines fire and air, and it packs a punch by increasing the flow of saliva in your mouth, causing a tingling sensation on the tongue and bringing tears to your eyes. This flavour makes even the blandest food exciting. Some people eat such hot food that it burns the lining of their gut and therefore creates ama in their digestive systems. (Chapter 5 explains ama, or toxins.) As in everything, moderation is the key.

In your body, pungent food works to reduce kapha and dosha while strengthening vata and pitta. It can help all the tissues in your body by improving their individual *agnis*, or enzyme activity. Pungent food has a drying action and can help you eliminate mucus. It can be used to break through any obstruction in your body and improves flow in the subtle channels (*nadis*; see Chapter 3).

You can use this taste to help relieve colds, asthma, obesity and diabetes. However, be very wary of it if your pitta is aggravated or you're in a debilitated state. This is because excessive use of pungent tastes is said to cause giddiness, nerve pain due to inflammation, and debility.

Examples of sources of the pungent flavour in your diet include:

- Black pepper
- Garlic
- Ginger
- Horseradish
- Lemongrass
- Mustard
- Onions

Black pepper is the most popular pungent flavour and appears on tabletops all over the world.

Therapeutically, the pungent taste can be utilised as a decongestant. A very simple remedy for a cold or cough is one teaspoon of honey with ¼ teaspoon of black pepper, taken three times a day, especially after food.

The widely used mixture for low, sluggish digestion is called Trikatu, which is made up of three pungent substances, namely black pepper, long pepper and ginger.

Another pungent favourite in Indian cuisine because of its gas-expelling properties is hing, or asafoetida, formed from a tree resin. Asafoetida helps to promote a healthy nervous system, improves your digestive system and boosts your circulation, among other things.

Appreciating astringent (kashaya)

Within the astringent flavour, air and earth are in combination to give the effect of drying, cooling and lightness in your body. Perhaps the most elusive of the tastes, the astringent taste generates contraction in your system. For example, fresh pomegranate has a mouth-puckering dry quality – especially if you eat a bit of inner flesh. That's astringent. You wouldn't want to eat it, but applying witch hazel closes your pores because it's astringent.

Used therapeutically, astringency draws two sides of a wound or an ulcer together to unite them. It also stops diarrhoea and staunches bleeding. Astringency alleviates pitta and kapha and promotes vata dosha.

You get the astringent taste in your diet by eating:

- Alfalfa sprouts
- Barley
- Chickpeas
- Green beans
- Tea (which contains astringent tannins)

Therapeutically, the following astringent herbs offer benefits:

- Hypericum helps with wound healing if applied externally.
- Arjuna is the bark of a tree and is used for treating heart disease and as a heart tonic.
- Triphala balances all three doshas and contains two substances, haritaki and bibitaki, that are primarily astringent in quality.
- Honey is astringent in quality. It cleans and heals wounds, and also helps with fractured bones. (Remember that it should never be cooked or mixed with salt.)

Too much astringent flavour causes stiffness in your body and constipation.

Looking at the Six Stages of Digestion

The six stages in the process of digestion correlate to the six tastes I explain in the previous section.

The food that you eat enters your mouth and is gently warmed by one of the *agnis*, or 'biological fires', under your tongue. Saliva then mixes with a type of kapha called *bhodak* and between one and six of the tastes are presented to your body. Taste perception lies within you, which is why if you're feeling off colour or your agni is low, your food appears rather tasteless.

Food enters your stomach with a predominately sweet taste. Then after about 90 minutes, hydrochloric acid in the form of pachacka pitta mixes with it and creates a sour substance.

Next, the contents of your stomach go into your duodenum in your small intestine, where pitta in the form of bile salts mixes with them and they are alkalised.

Now the nutrient chyle enters the jejunum, which is further along your small intestine, and the food becomes bitter. Some absorption into your system takes place here.

After your food passes through your small intestine it enters your large intestine and now has a predominately pungent taste. By this stage, most of the nutrients and water have been removed and circulated around your body. What will be eliminated is also differentiated at this stage.

Your body is a great conserver of energy, so by the time the food substances get to the end of your large intestine to the area known as the caecum, any remaining water has been removed from the waste by virtue of its astringent environment, and the rest is ready to be expelled from your system.

The Second Course: When Food Leaves the Mouth

The rasas, or flavours, that I describe in the previous sections have an immediate effect in your mouth that gives a feeling of satisfaction with your food. After you chew and swallow, the next stages of digestion begin.

The stage of digestion after rasa is _virya_ (effect during digestion); then follows _vipaka_ (effect after digestion).

Effect during digestion: Releasing energy with virya

The literal meaning of _virya_ is 'vigour' or 'potency'. The fresher the foodstuffs or herbs, the stronger their potency.

Virya occurs after you've chewed your food and after the enzymes in your mouth have had their way with it. The food heads to your stomach, and your system utilises the active power of what it's taken in.

Virya determines whether the effect of the food is heating (a substance _provides_ energy from the body during digestion) or cooling (a substance _requires_ energy to the body during digestion). Salty, sour and pungent substances are heating; sweet, bitter and astringent substances are cooling.

As cooling substances work to remove excess heat from your body, they also:

- Remove excess heat from the blood
- Enliven the system and act as a tonic
- Reduce inflammation
- Promote firmness of your tissues
- Increase kapha and vata dosha

Heating herbs and foods have a stimulating effect on your body and work to:

- Remove dampness and heaviness
- Make you sweat
- Promote digestion
- Increase pitta dosha in your tissues

Effect after digestion: Vipaka

During vipaka, the nutrient chyle reaches your tissues to be assimilated and absorbed. Vipaka also determines the effect of what you've eaten on your body and mind.

Post-digestively, the two main effects on your tissues are to build them (which is known as an anabolic effect) or the opposite, which is to break them down (a catabolic effect).

Table 10-1 shows how what you eat eventually affects the tissues of your body. For example, if you have an inflammatory condition and you take in a lot of sour tastes, the fiery element known as pitta will increase in your system. This in turn increases your experience of pain.

Table 10-1	Effects of Flavours on Tissues
Taste in the Mouth, or Rasa	*Post-digestive Effect, or Vipaka*
Sweet	Sweet, which increases kapha
Sour	Sour, which increases pitta
Salty	Sweet, which increases kapha
Pungent	Pungent, which increases vata
Bitter	Pungent, which increases vata
Astringent	Pungent, which increases vata

Prabhava

Defined as 'inconceivable' effects because of the difficulty of showing a cause and effect relationship, *prabhava* describes the special quality and effect of a herb or foodstuff in your body.

Some foods have what appear to be the same energetics, but their actions are totally different. For example, lemon is sour in rasa (flavour) and thus should have a sour vipaka (post-digestive effect); however, its vipaka is for some 'unexplainable' reason sweeter than that of any other citrus fruit (hence its alkalising effect!). Honey has a sweet rasa, which would normally suggest a cooling virya (effect during digestion), but it is heating even though the vipaka is sweet again.

Certain effects seen in Ayurvedic practice can't be explained scientifically. Rather than denying the existence of certain phenomena just because the current theoretical model can't explain them (as is so often the case in modern medicine), Ayurveda offers a dedicated category to such 'inconceivable' phenomena.

Introducing Agni: The Fuel for Life

Agni, which literally means 'fire', is worshipped as a god in India. Nothing would be possible without this eternal spark that fires your being. Agni refers to the principle of transformation and how well what you take in is converted into energy to use in your daily life. The very fact that you can taste and digest your food is due to this aspect of your biology.

Your body contains more than 40 different *agnis*, or biological fires, that govern your metabolic rate. The main agni (*jathar agni*) lies in the stomach, which is filled with the enzymes and hydrochloric acid that break down your meal.

Then there are five different agnis (*bhuta agnis*) that work from your liver to separate the nutrient chyle into its five constituent elements: ether, air, fire, water and earth. Further on, *dhatu agni* works at your tissue-production level to help produce the seven *dhatus*, or life-supporting tissues, referred to in Chapter 3.

The agni inside your cells is known as *pithar agni* and operates between your cells to ensure cooperation between them. Lastly, working within your cells to maintain the production of energy and maintain your immune integrity is *pilu agni*.

The Ayurvedic qualities of agni are sharp, hot, subtle, mobile, dry and light. (See Chapter 2 for more on Ayurvedic qualities.) Thus any substance which enhances these characteristics can boost your digestion. For example, sharp, hot and light ginger aids your digestion, particularly if you add a little salt and lemon juice and chew it 15 minutes before your main meal.

According to Ayurveda, a healthy condition of your agni can confer on you the following benefits:

- ✔ A beautiful clear complexion with a lustrous glow

- ✔ Plentiful energy, body warmth and a good metabolism

- ✔ A strong immune system, great digestion and the ability to easily absorb all that you eat

- ✔ Plenty of enthusiasm, intelligence and energy are (the emotional attributes of good agni)

- ✔ A long life!

Examining Your Digestion

Your digestive system is the engine room of your body, and you need to nurture it. When things go wrong in the stomach, all systems are affected; this is why Ayurveda places so much importance on food. Keep an eye on your digestion so that you can spot when things are out of kilter. The four states of agni (fire) to be aware of are:

- ✔ **Sama agni.** This is your benchmark for a normal-functioning digestive system. You can digest anything within reason with no ill effects. Nothing perturbs you, irrespective of time of day, season or place. You're in good health; your energy is high and you wake up bright and full of enthusiasm for the day ahead. You maintain a constant weight and have a strong metabolism.

- ✔ **Tikshna agni.** This state is related to pitta dosha. You notice burning sensations, dryness in your mouth and throat and heartburn. Your appetite is voracious; you want to eat often and in large quantities. You experience swings in blood sugar and have an intense desire for sweet things for a quick fix. If left unchecked, the excess pitta creeps into your system and results in gastritis, colitis, nausea, hypoglycaemia, migraines and inflammatory conditions of your body. The accompanying emotions are irritability, lack of patience and envy.

✔ **Manda agni.** This condition is related to kapha dosha and displays all its qualities. You experience dullness and heaviness after eating that often results in indigestion. You notice an increase in salivation and mucus in your system, and a loss of appetite. Even a lettuce leaf seems to add a pound to your waistline, because nothing is effectively burned off. You feel lethargic and lack any real enthusiasm. This situation can lead to diabetes, congestion and obesity. Emotionally you have accompanying feelings of depression, greed, possessiveness and attachment.

✔ **Vishama agni.** This type of digestion is related to vata dosha and displays all its characteristics. If this is applicable to you, the most recognisable trait of your digestion is changeability – sometimes it's fine and sometimes it isn't. You experience bloating, flatulence, burping and sometimes accompanying pain, especially when you eat raw food. You may alternate between diarrhoea and constipation. You often notice a gurgling in your intestines. You may notice your skin and hair becoming drier. Your joints may feel achy and crack as you move them. After some time, your sleep may be disturbed and you may develop muscle tics as well as feeling anxious and fearful.

The following two chapters (11 and 12) can help you to choose the best foods for your personal health and keep your digestion in tip-top condition.

Chapter 11

Selecting the Right Diet for Your Type

*W*hen you're young, you have about 10,000 taste buds, but this reduces to around 2,000 by the time you reach 80 years old. Guard what you have with the best quality food.

Corruption of the sense of taste can lead people to poor food choices that not only disrupt the sense of taste but also harm the taste buds.

Taste isn't the whole picture of diet, of course, and within this chapter I tell you about the effects of food – and combinations of foods – on your body and your moods. I talk about general nutrition and about dietary aids to nutrition and for the different doshas. You don't have to know your constitution for this chapter, but you get more out of it if you do. (Read Chapter 4 to determine your constitution.)

The Effect of Flavour on Your Emotions

Ayurveda states that all foods have emotional analogues. That means if you're feeling unloved, for example, you tend to favour sweet tastes to pacify your emotion. Table 11-1 shows you how each of the flavours connects with different traits and emotions.

Table 11-1	Emotional Analogues Of The Six Flavours	
Taste	**Positive**	**Negative**
Sweet	Love, compassion, care, wholesomeness, grounding	Attachment, greed, temptation, laziness
Sour	Alertness, attentiveness, realism, focus, discrimination	Judgemental, critical, rejecting, drawing wrong conclusions
Salty	Energy, enthusiasm, stimulation, ability to digest ideas, faith	Attachment, anger, grief, temptation
Bitter	Renunciation, austerity, celibacy, happy with solitude, clarity	Isolation, loneliness, separation from others
Pungent	Increases the ability to digest ideas and makes the mind more probing, motivation	Anger, envy, hatred, jealousy
Astringent	Stability, groundedness spirituality, surety, asceticism	Fear, insecurity, anxiety, withdrawal

To strictly follow an Ayurvedic diet, you'd eat food in a prescribed order: sweet, sour, salty, pungent, bitter and then astringent. (I tell you more about flavour in Chapter 10.) So, for example, you'd start a meal with rice and move on to sour pickle, ginger with rock salt, and so on. I admit that I, and most Ayurvedic practitioners I know, don't follow this practice, but now you know the theory!

Eating organic to support taste

We violate taste more than any of the other methods of human perception, mainly because we have lost regard for the land and contaminated it with fungicides, pesticides and fertilisers, as well as subjecting it to mechanisation. This has led to monoculture on a major scale, in which farmers grow nothing but their primary crop.

Your food is also subject to freezing, irradiating, genetic modification and often long transport times. All of these factors have a negative effect on the delicate flavours and aromas of the food you consume.

If you haven't the means to grow your own food and find organic products too pricey, I suggest that you make your entire intake of dairy food and oil organic; for example, use organic milk and olive oil. This is because all the additives that are in non-organic dairy and oil are fat-soluble and stay lodged in your tissues, creating *ama* (or toxins; refer to Chapter 5 for an explanation of ama). Organic dairy and oil are more nutritious than their non-organic counterparts, with greater amounts of omega 3 fatty acids and vitamins, which promotes good health.

Food and the Three States of Energy

If you eat roast beef and Yorkshire pudding, you feel more sluggish than if you consume a fresh green salad with olive oil drizzled over it. You've probably found this to be true in your own experience (and with various different foods and combinations). The effect of combinations of food has to do with the three states of energy, known as *gunas*. (I discuss these in detail in Chapter 2.)

The three states of energy, the gunas, are:

✔ **Sattwa:** Potential energy, linked to light nourishing foods

✔ **Rajas:** Kinetic energy from energising foods

✔ **Tamas:** Inertia, caused by heavy and hard-to-digest foods

Referred to as God itself in the ancient text *Taittiriya Upanishad*, food is much more than simple nutrition. According to Ayurveda, when you eat, you assimilate the essence of creation within your body and turn it into the building blocks of bodily tissues.

Food also affects your mind and your emotional states. Ayurveda divides foods into three categories according to their effects:

✔ **Sattwic foods** are sweet and cooling by nature and have a calming effect on your mind. This group includes:

- Dairy products
- Fruits
- Honey
- Nuts
- Wheat

✔ **Rajasic foods** confer stimulation to your mind and rouse your passions. They include highly spiced and salty foods, which are hard to stop eating after you taste them.

Alcohol is included in this group, and you've probably felt the terrific lift when you drink it, but you've probably also felt the sleepiness when the kick is over.

Garlic, fried foods and caffeinated drinks also give you a buzz, but if you consume them too often, they can become quite addictive.

✔ **Tamasic foods** increase laziness, pessimism and dullness of mind. Avoid these foods at all costs when you're ill, and don't make them the mainstay of your diet when you aren't. They include:

- Canned foods

- Processed foods

- Heavy meat such as red meat and manufactured meat products

- Powdered milk

Sadly, much of the fast food available today falls into the tamasic category. This food is simply a filler, with no nutrients. When you eat food like this, you tend to eat more because your body is searching for nutrients.

Many people are surprised to learn that an Ayurvedic diet is not vegetarian. In fact, the qualities of many types of meat are spoken about in the *Charaka Samita* (an important Ayurvedic text), from quail to elephant. Traditionally, when meat was consumed it was eaten in small quantities and as a sacrament.

Table 11-2 is a list of foods and how they affect your mood by creating sattwa, rajas and tamas if you focus too much on one guna. The way to go with this list is to always include foods from the sattwic section in your meals, and include a few from the other groups in measured quantities.

Table 11-2	Food and the Gunas		
Guna	Fruit / Vegetable	Dairy / Fluids	Meat / Grain
Sattwic foods	Mango, coconut, lettuce, yams, yellow squash, kidney beans, figs, pears, pomegranates	Milk, ghee, panneer, yogurt, lassi, water	Mung beans, basmati rice, tapioca, quinoa, amaranth
Rajasic foods	Apples, oranges grapefruit, persimmon, garlic, onion, asafoetida (hing), potatoes, tomatoes, pickles	Goats cheese, Gournay cheese with pepper	Millet, rye, buckwheat, corn, red lentils, fish, chicken, rabbit, shellfish, wine
Tamasic foods	Bananas, avocado, pumpkin, mushrooms	Hard, aged cheese, tofu, soy milk, margarine	Brown rice, wheat, urad dal, pinto beans, black beans, beef, pork, lamb, spirits

Eating to Enhance Your Digestion

Naturally, what you eat has a lot to do with how well your digestive system functions. Take in a lot of heavy or processed foods and you tax your system. Or dine on fresh whole foods and feel the increased energy you get from not asking your system to work overtime.

Truly enhancing your digestion and keeping your system free from toxins depends on an array of factors, however. Within the following guidelines, you probably recognise a lot of the rules as advice your granny gave you:

- Food that's been cooked and that you eat when it's warm is much easier to digest than raw food.

- Perfectly ripe food (neither unripe or overripe) is the friendliest to your system.

- Avoid eating heavy food at night; eat at least three hours before bed.

- A short walk after a meal helps you to digest it.

- Don't drink iced water with food; it reduces your gut motility, which in turn impedes the action of your *agni* (fire) in the stomach and creates indigestion.

- The stomach needs to be a third full of food, a third with fluid, and a third empty to allow your digestion to work correctly.

- After eating, don't do heavy mental or physical work as it can impede the process of digestion.

- To help the flow of digestive juices, try chewing a slice of ginger with a squirt of lemon and a pinch of salt on it about ten minutes before you eat your main meal.

- Leftovers can have less vital force, or *virya*. Eat freshly prepared food whenever you can.

- When you're under a great deal of stress, adrenalin surges around your system and your gut pretty much shuts down. Be extra vigilant during these times.

  One-pot cooked foods like casseroles, in which all the favours blend together, are easy for you to digest at these times.

- Avoid drinking water at least 15 minutes before eating, so that you don't dilute the precious digestive juices. Sipping water with the food is fine, but keep it to a minimum.

- Eat at fixed times. Your body loves routine.

✔ Whenever possible, eat your main meal at midday. Your digestion aligns with the sun and so is strongest at this time.

✔ According to the *Ksema-kuntuhala*, a Vedic cookbook from the 2nd century AD, eating in pleasant surroundings with good company is as important as the food itself.

✔ Don't eat when you're upset or angry. Your body can't process food correctly during these times.

✔ Include a selection of all six tastes to feel most satisfied.

✔ Keep your kitchen and utensils as clean as possible, and wash your hands before and after eating your food.

✔ Consume foods that are appropriate to the season and climate. A leafy salad won't build a strong immune system in the middle of winter.

Identifying Incompatible Food Combinations

Foods don't just react with your body chemistry but with each other, along with the elements of place, time, process, and so on. Certain food combinations deposit toxins or ama in the tissues if you eat them habitually. Avoiding detrimental mixtures helps you stay in tip-top condition.

The ancient texts identify many combinations to avoid, and suggest that you consider:

✔ **Place (desam):** Avoid food that emulates the area, like rice and crackers in arid lands or wet and sweet foods in marshy spots.

✔ **Time (kalam):** Don't eat cold and dry foods in a cold season, or really hot foods in summer. So no ice cream or salad in winter!

✔ **Fire (agni):** Steer clear of heavy foods if you have low digestive capacity. Your ability to digest food and convert it into tissue is innate. Certain individuals with a very light frame don't cope well with heavy foods.

✔ **Dose (matra):** Certain doses, or quantities of mixtures, of foods should be avoided. For example don't mix honey and ghee in equal quantity. Post-digestively, honey is heating and ghee is cooling, so they work in opposition to each other.

✔ **Process (samskara):** The way food is produced affects it. For example, pressed rice is heavy and puffed rice is light. If you're on a weight-loss diet, rice crackers are far less likely to put weight on your midriff than pressed sticky rice in sushi.

✔ **Potency (virya):** Avoid the following combinations of foods, which have incompatible potencies. (You can find out about these effects in Chapter 10.)

- Milk has a cold potency and fish has a warm potency, therefore the common English dish of fish with parsley sauce isn't such a good idea because the sauce contains milk.

- Meat with honey, milk, germinated grains, radish or molasses.

- Meat of domestic animals with game.

- Milk with sour substances such as cherries or with yeast-containing products, meat, melons or bananas.

- Milk with oxalic-acid-rich vegetables like spinach, radish, melons, tomatoes or potatoes.

- Fruits with potatoes.

- Dates with yogurt or corn.

- Heated honey or cooked honey, which creates an insoluble mass that blocks the srotas. (I describe the *srotas*, or passageways, in Chapter 2.)

- Eggs with milk, lemon, fish, bananas or cheese.

- Mangoes with cucumber or cheese.

- Fruit with meals.

- Lemon with tomatoes, milk, cheese, yogurt or cucumbers.

- Corn with raisins, dates or bananas.

✔ **Alimentary canal (kostha):** Make sure you don't eat too small a quantity of food, which leads to undernourishment. By the same token, don't eat too much; it may make you overweight and subject to a myriad of complaints.

✔ **Condition (avastha):** Avoid foods that increase a dosha; for example, you don't want a vata-increasing food when you have excessive fatigue in your body and you have a vata constitution.

✔ **Order (krama):** Avoid eating when you have an urge to use the toilet.

✔ **Must (parichara):** Don't drink hot water after eating a lot of pork. Pork is very heating to your system and along with hot water can create too much heat.

✔ **Obey (upachara):** Refrain from consuming cold items after eating ghee. Ultimately, both substances are cooling and so will create ama in your system.

✔ **Cooking (paka):** Avoid eating partially cooked, overcooked or even burned food, which is more likely to form ama and can clog up your system.

✔ **Combinations (samyoga):** The previous list for potency shows you food combinations to avoid.

✔ **Heart (hrd):** Steer clear of tasteless processed food and unpleasant food.

✔ **Quality (sampat):** Don't use substances of poor quality, such as old or spoiled food.

✔ **Rules (vidhi):** These rules apply to cooking and eating:

• Eat in a quiet place, if possible. Eating mindfully, by really concentrating on your food, is important so that you chew properly and encourage proper digestion. You're also less likely to eat too much.

• Keep your kitchen fresh and clean. Traditionally in India, the kitchen was only used for cooking and was separated from the main dwelling. Outdoor clothing and shoes weren't worn in the kitchen.

• Don't eat too much dry food. Moist food is considered easier to digest.

• Use well-seasoned carbon steel, cast iron, earthenware, ceramic and glass cooking utensils. Avoid aluminium and Teflon cooking pots.

Matching Diet to Dosha

Given the intricate interplay between your mind and body and the foods you eat, it's easy to see that your basic constitution plays into which foods are most appropriate for you. What buoys a kapha constitution may be detrimental to someone who is pitta dominant. The upcoming sections show you how to match diet to constitution.

Eating for kapha

Kapha dosha is smooth like custard, soft like marshmallow, cold like ice-cream, stable like bread, moist like melon, heavy like banana and sticky like treacle.

If you have a kapha constitution:

✔ Focus on light, dry and warm food.

✔ Seek pungent, bitter and astringent tastes.

✔ Avoid cold, heavy foods and drinks.

✔ Pass on rich desserts. (Sorry.)

✔ Skip really salty foods to keep weight from piling on (although a little is okay and even encourages salivation and enjoyment).

✔ Make your food spicier to increase digestive power. Add black pepper or ginger. Wasabi paste and mustard also give pep to your diet.

✔ Leave oily fried foods out of your diet. You can't digest them easily, and they end up around your waist and not burned off with activity.

Kaphas already have strong, well-built bodies and therefore need less of the body-building foods like bread, pasta and rich desserts, which should make up a smaller proportion of their daily menu.

Stick to low-fat food choices when you have the opportunity. Oils that are appropriate for you because they are slightly heating are sunflower and corn oil. Ghee in moderate quantities is useful to you because it increases your precious digestive fire.

All foods become easier to digest if you roast or toast them, because they become lighter and drier. So if you want to eat bread, for example, toast it. Dry snacks such as popcorn, unsalted tortilla chips and dry crackers work well for kaphas.

Table 11-3 shows you the foods that are best for a kapha diet.

Table 11-3	Balancing Foods For Kapha
Vegetables	All bitter greens, cabbage, cauliflower, Brussels sprouts, sweet-corn, green beans, leeks, lettuce, peas, potatoes, mushrooms, carrots, celery, broccoli, garlic, onions, green/red peppers, beetroot, kale, watercress, turnips, swede, radish, cooked tomato, bok choy
Fruits	Apples, cherries, mango, pears, figs, pomegranate, prunes, plums, raisins, apricots, cranberries, star fruit, kiwi, persimmon, peaches, berries, dried fruit snacks
Dairy	Avoid dairy in general, but focus on ghee, goat's milk, lassi, goat's milk butter, paneer and buttermilk when you must have dairy
Legumes/seeds	Split peas, rice cakes, black-eyed beans, mung beans, red lentils, tur dal, chickpeas, soya milk (heated), tofu (hot), aduki beans, sunflower seeds, pumpkin seeds, flax (toasted)
Grains	Millet, barley, corn, oats (dry), seitan, polenta, rye, buckwheat, quinoa, small quantities of basmati rice
Meat	Chicken, turkey, rabbit, quail, pheasant, fish, shrimp, venison, eggs
Oils	Corn, canola and sunflower oil, and almond oil in small amounts
Herbs/spices	Black pepper, chilli, ginger, mustard, nutmeg, cloves, bay leaves, allspice, cardamom, cayenne, marjoram, cumin, caraway, cinnamon, basil, anise, asafoetida, turmeric, sage

Preparing foods for pitta

If you're predominantly pitta dosha, your qualities are lightness, liquidity, sharpness, heat and slight oiliness. Throughout the year, but especially in hot weather, you benefit from nourishing, cooling and sweet foods.

Pittas have voracious appetites and need to be mindful of not eating too much in one go.

To keep your constitution in balance, favour the naturally sweet, bitter and astringent foods that Table 11-4 shows, and follow these guidelines:

- You can eat raw foods and enjoy salads and refreshing cool drinks – especially in the summer. These foods tend to contain bitter and astringent flavours, which are good for you.

- Eating only light or dry foods aggravates pitta, so make sure you include a good quality protein. Beans are excellent, because they provide astringency.

- Wheat products and heavier foods help keep you in balance. Try spelt bread, which is made from an older form of wheat and is easier to digest.

- Tofu in all its various forms is a good choice for you because it's cooling in nature and made of soya beans, which have an astringent quality.

- Keep your fluids high in hot weather and take advantage of the abundance of fresh sweet fruits.

- Don't eat when you're upset or angry; you'll suffer from indigestion and headaches.

Table 11-4	Balancing Foods For Pitta
Vegetables	All bitter greens, fennel, asparagus, cucumber, artichoke, broccoli, squash, cabbage, cauliflower, celery, parsnip
Fruits	All sweet ripe fruits, pomegranate, figs, dates, melons, pears, pineapple, prunes, raisins, coconut, grapes, mango
Dairy	Ghee, unsalted butter, cottage cheese, goat's and cow's milk, mild soft cheese, sweet lassi, sorbets, buttermilk
Grains	Barley, quinoa, cooked oats, rice (brown, wild, white), amaranth, wheat, spelt

Legumes/ seeds	Mung beans, chickpeas, soya beans, tofu, soya milk, oat milk, almond milk, split peas, tempeh, green lentils, kidney beans, haricot beans, butter beans, lima beans
Meat/eggs	Brown trout, rainbow trout, rabbit, chicken, turkey, egg white
Oils	Avocado, coconut, olive, sunflower, soy, walnut, hazelnut and sesame oil (all in moderation)
Herbs/ spices	Fennel, aniseed, turmeric, cinnamon, coriander, mint, liquorice, lemon grass, rose water, saffron, peppermint, dulse

Choosing wisely if you're vata

If vata is prominent in your constitution, you are by nature delicate; your digestive capacity is erratic and prone to problems with gas. Therefore, your daily diet should be light, warmed and slightly oily, so that your digestive system has less to do.

The following guidelines help keep a vata constitution functioning optimally:

- Soak dried fruits before you eat them to avoid gassiness.

- Don't skip breakfast; your energies are too subject to fluctuations. A bowl of porridge cooked with cloves and cinnamon is great for you and will keep your blood sugar stable throughout the morning.

- Avoid products with yeast, which create gas.

- Nuts are a good snack for you and are best if you eat them little and often. They tend to be oily and heavy in large quantities, but have very high food value in small doses.

- Avoid caffeine if you can; if not, stick to black tea in moderate amounts, because it's astringent. Caffeine in large amounts taxes your already delicate nervous system.

- Warm milk is very comforting to you if taken with a little saffron, which helps to remove the mucous qualities of milk.

- Spices stimulate the flow of digestive enzymes and so are a help to the underactive vata constitution.

Overall, the message to those with a vata constitution is to consume moderate amounts and keep a regular dietary schedule to protect your precious digestion. Table 11-5 shows foods that are especially good for you.

Table 11-5	Balancing Foods For Vata
Vegetables	Asparagus, carrots, cooked onions, cucumber, leeks, olives, sweet potato, parsnip, pumpkin, watercress, courgettes, well-cooked greens, green beans, garlic, avocado, seaweed
Dairy	All dairy and ghee is acceptable in moderation
Fruit	All sweet fruits, rhubarb, peaches, papaya, mango, lemons, limes, grapes, grapefruit, figs, coconut, dates, berries
Grains	Cooked oats, all types of rice, amaranth quinoa, wheat, couscous
Legumes/seeds	Lentils, split mung beans, miso, soya milk, oat milk, flax seeds, sunflower seeds, pumpkin seeds, sesame seeds, macadamia, all nuts
Meat	Beef, chicken, duck, turkey
Oils	Most oils, such as sesame, peanut and olive oil
Herbs/spices	Saffron, black pepper, salt, , tamari, ajawan, anise, sage, turmeric, rosemary, fennel, dill, cayenne, asafoetida, cinnamon, bay leaf, cumin, basil

Chapter 12

Optimising Your Diet: A Recipe for Success

*Y*ou're nothing short of a walking miracle. Your digestion has achieved the marvel of being able to implement what alchemists through the centuries have attempted to do – to reconcile the opposites of fire and water by way of the perfect balance of acid and water in your stomach. You reap great benefits when you cooperate with your system in any way that you can. This chapter helps you do so with tips to ensure that your diet is nourishing.

There's absolutely no substitute for a decent diet. One way or another, the food you choose to power your engine ultimately affects how you feel and your ability to ward off illness.

You can get away without knowing your constitution in this chapter, but you may want to refer to Chapter 4 to help tailor the information to your profile.

Highlighting High-Energy Foods to Include in Your Day

All foods are not created equal, especially when it comes to sustaining you through whatever your day brings. In this section I describe four foods that are well-known for providing long-lasting energy, with two from those wonderful workers, the bees.

Your body engages important systems to produce energy and sustain endurance, such as your adrenal glands, thyroid and liver. Carbohydrates are the key to strength and endurance; they promote the storage of muscle fuel and are easily absorbed without excess fat. Carbohydrates are considered to be the mainstay of your diet in Ayurveda, in the form of whole grains, vegetables, fruits, rice and beans.

Basmati rice

In India, basmati rice is considered a holy grain; it's sweet and fragrant, and so it helps curb a strong appetite. It's a very nutritious grain that's low in sodium and cholesterol and is a rich source of manganese and selenium.

Basmati rice is produced by being soaked in lukewarm water and then steamed until it softens or partially cooks. The fluid is then drained off and the grains are spread out in the sun to dry. After that, the rice is hulled to reveal its unique, rich, fragrant flavour. Contrary to what you might think, this ancient practice preserves the nutrient content at the highest level at the centre of the grain.

Rice in large quantities can cause gastric distress. Any brown rice retains its outer covering (or *pericarp*), which makes it more difficult to digest, but is rich in folate and niacin. Adding some light, warming spices such as cinnamon, cardamom or cumin when you cook rice can help you avoid this problem.

If you're worried about blood sugar and insulin resistance, choose brown basmati or a product known as *converted white rice*, which comes very low on the glycaemic index (low-glycaemic-index food gives you energy for longer).

Almond milk

You can easily buy almond milk, or you can use my very simple recipe to produce this high-protein alkaline drink which is also very tasty. You can use almond milk on cereals, in soups and desserts, or drink it on its own, unless of course you have a reaction to nuts.

Almond milk builds *shukra dhatu*, which is reproductive tissue. Almonds are rich in minerals, particularly bone-building calcium and magnesium, which helps release energy from your cells. One ounce of almond contains 25 per cent of your recommended daily amount of protein. Almonds are also a very good source of the antioxidant Vitamin E.

Those of you who suffer with colitis, constipation, irritable bowel syndrome (IBS) or Crohn's disease can use almond milk therapeutically. Often these conditions are related to lactose intolerance, so almond milk is a useful substitute. Soya milk often makes sufferers with gut problems quite gassy. Peeled almonds appear to have a protective effect on the colon.

To make your own almond milk, follow these steps:

1. **Soak 100 grams of almonds in apple juice overnight.**
2. **Drain the juice from the nuts. Remove the outer skins from the almonds and discard.**
3. **Blend the nuts with 1 litre of water in a food processor.**

   If you like, flavour the almond/water mixture with honey and a teaspoon of orange blossom water.

Honey

Ayurveda mentions many types of honey, but by far the most nutritious and bioactive is simple bee's honey, which has been used for centuries by people everywhere. According to Ayurveda, raw unpasteurised organic bee's honey builds something called *ojas*, which is a store of the finest energy in your body. This produces your aura, transmits energy from your mind to your body, and maintains the integrity of your immune system.

Honey has a property known as *yogavaha*, which means that it augments the effects of any medicines given along with it – rather like a helping hand to get the medicines deeper into your tissues.

For all its benefits, honey does have a shortcoming. You don't want to cook it, because cooked honey forms an indigestible mass that blocks the channels of the body known as *srotas*.

Taking honey with warm water helps disperse mucus. Honey is rough, sharp and drying, which makes it useful for kapha disorders. Taken in the morning, it can be useful as part of a weight-loss programme, because unlike sugar, honey's effect is heating. Medicinally it can be used for sore throats, ulcers, nausea and asthma.

Bee pollen

As well as honey, bee pollen is a great addition to any diet, especially a vegetarian diet, because it not only boosts your energy levels but also contains all the essential amino acids.

You need 22 building blocks or amino acids to make up all the protein structures in your body. The vegetarian diet doesn't generally provide these unless you work to combine foods to cover the full gamut of amino acids.

You can add bee pollen to your breakfast cereal or porridge, apple juice or yogurt. Take a couple teaspoonfuls and mix them with a little cinnamon – it tastes really good. You can even add it to a smoothie or the lassi recipe later in this chapter.

Certain people may find bee pollen a bit too stimulating to take before bed, because it's such a concentrated foodstuff. Some schools of thought suggest soaking it overnight to make it more digestible, so bear this in mind if your digestion is sluggish.

Bee pollen provides you with a source of 5,000 enzymes and co-enzymes. Bee pollen is made up of 3 per cent vitamins and minerals: vitamin B complex, vitamins A, C and D, beta carotene, selenium and lecithin. In other words, bee pollen is packed with life-enhancing nutrients.

Test whether you may be allergic to bee pollen by placing one granule on your tongue. If you experience no reaction, add a couple more. If you experience itching, swelling in the throat, and watering of the eyes and nose, stop there and avoid bee pollen in future.

Improving Your Digestion with Lassi

A common drink in India, *lassi* is made primarily of water and yogurt. It's very refreshing by itself and after a meal.

An Ayurvedic favourite for helping you to digest your food, lassi also prevents bloating and kindles *agni* (the essential digestive fire). This is possibly because it supplies your gut with probiotics that keep your digestive tract healthy. Lassi also provides a valuable source of calcium and vitamin B12.

Choose the lassi that's right for your constitution from the choices in this section. If all's well with your digestion, you can try all of them with impunity.

Lassi tends to create mucus, so may not be helpful during cold, cool or damp weather. Some Ayurvedic practitioners don't recommend it for people living in countries with a cool climate.

Vata lassi

If your digestion is erratic, the following lassi recipe is best for you. This recipe is designed for those with a vata constitution:

2 cups of water

½ cup of organic yogurt

Pinch of rock salt

One teaspoon of roasted cumin seeds

Mix the ingredients with a hand whisk or blender and serve at room temperature.

Pitta lassi

If you tend to get gastritis and burning, make your lassi as follows:

2 cups of water

½ cup of organic yogurt (use goat's milk yogurt if you can)

2 teaspoons of jaggery or another sweetener

1 teaspoon of organic rosewater

Mix ingredients with a hand whisk or blender and serve at room temperature. For a change, you can add ½ teaspoon of coriander powder and finely chopped green coriander leaves.

Kapha lassi

If your digestion is sluggish and you put weight on easily, choose this recipe for you kapha types:

2 cups of water

½ cup of organic yogurt

½ teaspoon of ginger powder or 1 teaspoon of grated fresh ginger

Pinch of salt

Mix the ingredients with a hand whisk or blender and serve at room temperature.

Fasting for General Health

Fasting – reducing your food intake – is an age-old practice that many cultures include in their rituals. According to Ayurveda, *langhana*, or lightening of the dietary intake, is the first line of treatment against most diseases, especially in the case of fever. Known as *ksut nigraha* in Sanskrit, which means 'to control hunger', fasting involves abstaining from all food or certain foods, or eating a 'mono diet' of just one food.

Don't undertake fasting of any kind without first consulting your doctor, especially if you have a health condition.

Understanding the benefits of fasting

For a sense of how fasting can help, you need to know about something called *ama*, the Ayurvedic equivalent to toxins in your body. Ama is generated by such things as:

- Poor diet
- Environmental pollution
- Ingesting heavy metals
- Chronic stress
- Electromagnetic contamination
- Undetected dental disease

Chapter 5 can help you determine whether ama is affecting you.

These factors – on their own or in combination – upset your intestinal flora (the good bacteria that help you assimilate your food) and thicken the blood and lymph circulating in your body. These changes shift the alkalinity of your internal landscape and allow pathogens to invade and create disease.

Most – in fact, about 80 per cent – of the body's defences reside in the small intestine. Poor dietary habits eventually prevent it from effectively performing its task.

A fast activates T-lymphocytes – white blood cells that are the vanguard of your immune system. These cells help to clear your body of unwanted elements.

Ayurveda frowns on long-term fasting. Pulling the pendulum too far to one side with an extended fast generally means your diet is going to swing back just as far in the other direction. It's an effect that yo-yo dieters are well aware of. Even in fasting, moderation is a good call.

Knowing which fast is right for you

Follow these few simple guidelines before thinking about fasting:

- ✔ Don't fast in very cold weather. You need calories to keep you warm.

- ✔ If you're ill, you may be put on a fast as part of an Ayurvedic treatment known as *panchakarma*. This is a strong treatment for your body and needs to be supervised by an expert.

- ✔ Don't fast if you're pregnant or suffering from any physical or mental illness. Checking with your doctor before fasting is always best.

- ✔ Don't fast if you're weak, fatigued, a child or aged.

- ✔ Don't fast if you're under a lot of personal or professional stress; you need to feel in a good place emotionally.

How you fast can depend upon your constitution. The following guidelines give you some ideas for maximising your own fast according to your profile:

- ✔ **Vata:** Try a day's fruit fast during which you eat only papaya, mangoes and other sweet fruits – the naturally sweet taste pacifies vata dosha. Sip warm water or vegetable broth throughout the day.

  The main seat of vata dosha in your body is the colon, so you may be subject to constipation. Therefore you might also want to take a half teaspoon of triphala at night to keep you regular (available at any health-food shop).

  Because your system is so delicate, avoid fasting for more than two days. Doing so can knock your system off balance for an extended period.

- ✔ **Pitta:** Your very strong digestion enables you to fast for three to four days. You can eat sweet fruits such as pomegranates, grapes and cooked apples as often as you like, because they pacify pitta dosha. Avoid sour fruits. Try vegetable juices like celery and parsley, and salads.

  Drink mineral water at room temperature throughout the day. Hot water's good, too.

✔ **Kapha:** Your constitution actually enables you to fast longest – for up to a week – but your comfort-seeking personality means you're unlikely to want to do so! Quite a catch-22. Bitter vegetable juices and cranberry juice are the best choices for you, because they're a tonic and cleansing to your system.

Drink cooled ginger tea with a little honey added to help dislodge ama from your system. Avoid sweet and sour juices, because they increase kapha dosha.

Your system will appreciate the well-earned rest of a once-a-week fast or even a day of drinking just juice or ginger tea. An even more accessible form of fasting is to give up desserts or fried food for a while; doing so helps an over-taxed system.

If, during your fast, you can abstain from talking, too, you'll find much more energy available to you and gain greater mental clarity.

Fasting isn't necessarily a good choice for everyone, or at any time. Think carefully before fasting, and listen to what your body is telling you.

Lightening your diet with kicheree

By far the easiest way to lighten your diet is to eat a mono diet of *kicheree* three times a day. This is a fundamental dish in Ayurveda that is very cheap, quick and easy to produce. Kicheree includes split mung beans, which are very light and easy to digest and which, with rice, form a complete protein.

The dish helps eliminate toxins from your system and can form the base for any chopped vegetables you may want to add.

Ingredients:

½ cup of yellow split mung beans

1 tablespoon of ghee

1 teaspoon of black mustard seeds

2 inches of cinnamon bark

2 cardamom pods, bruised

¼ teaspoon of turmeric

1 inch of finely chopped ginger

½ teaspoon of cumin seeds

¼ teaspoon of coriander seeds

Pinch of rock salt

Pinch of asafoetida

1 cup of basmati rice

6 cups of water

Method:

1. **Wash the mung beans and allow them to soak for about 30 minutes.**

2. **Put the ghee into a frying pan and melt.**

3. **Add the black mustard seeds and cook until they pop.**

4. **Add the rest of the spices and sauté for a few minutes to release their fragrance.**

5. **Add the rice and beans and mix well with the ghee and spices.**

6. **Add the water and bring to a boil.**

7. **Cover with a lid and simmer until all the juices have been absorbed (in 15 to 20 minutes). Stir occasionally and add more water if necessary.**

You can easily customise this meal to your constitution. Add coconut and more ghee if you're a pitta; more ginger and spices if you have a tendency towards kapha; and more fluid with a bay leaf or garlic if you're vata.

Eat the kicheree three times a day for one or two days to cleanse your system.

Introducing Ghee, the Cream of the Milk

Ghee – clarified butter – and its advantages to health are legendary in Ayurveda. Cows process the essence of plants and produce milk, which in turn is churned to form butter. Then the essence of the butter is modified and refined by heating and removing the fat solids to form ghee.

Discovering ghee's benefits

Ghee is said to nourish all the different tissue elements in the body, and maintain the agni and all the subtle fires at tissue level. Ghee also:

✔ Strengthens the immune system by increasing *ojas*, a superior form of subtle energy in the body

✔ Enhances the intellect and improves memory

✔ Boosts your digestive capacity without aggravating pitta dosha – the fire principle in your body

✔ Dissolves wastes and toxins known as ama in your tissues, and carries them to your digestive tract to be expelled

✔ Helps in the healing of peptic ulcers and gastritis

✔ Relieves wounds, skin rashes and burns

You can also use ghee with herbal decoctions because it has the capacity to deliver the medicine directly to the tissues.

The qualities of ghee are heavy, unctuous and oily, so those of you who are kapha dosha should use it in moderation. Ghee pacifies both pitta and vata.

Whenever possible, make your own ghee (use the recipe in the next section) or at least buy an organic version. The versions of ghee commonly available in the supermarket are either of vegetable origin or they contain preservatives. In my experience, their taste is a far cry from the sweetness and fragrance of your own blend.

Making delicious ghee

Creating your own ghee is a very simple process. Just buy the best unsalted organic butter you can find and then follow these steps:

1. **Melt two packets (about 500 grams) of butter in a saucepan at medium heat for about 20 minutes.**

   As the butter dissolves, froth will rise to the surface.

2. **Reduce the heat.**

   The butter will turn golden brown.

3. **Test the ghee by putting a drop of water in the pan.**

   If you hear a cracking sound, the ghee is ready. At this point, you'll see that the solids have sunk to the bottom.

4. **Gently pour the liquid through a strainer, decanting the clear golden fluid into a sterile container.**

Always use a clean utensil when you want to scoop out some ghee. Doing so prevents contamination.

You don't need to put the ghee in the fridge, because it keeps well at room temperature. In fact, like wine, the older it gets more it is prized. Some ghees in India called *mahaghrita* are over 100 years old!

Making special ghees

Medicated ghees are an important part of Ayurveda's extensive toolbox. They can be time-consuming to make, but are hard to come by and so worth the effort. Ghee is what's known as an *anupana* in Ayurveda, which means that it effectively delivers herbs deep into the system. Common examples are Brahmi ghee, which is used as a brain tonic and applied daily to the nose on the tip of the little finger, and triphala ghee, which you can use in cooking to cleanse the channels, improve your skin and enhance digestion.

As a rough guideline, you need a ½ ounce of herb per 2 ounces of ghee. Fresh herbs are ideal, but sometimes powdered ones – which also work just fine – are all you can get.

To make medicated ghees, follow these steps:

1. **Calculate the amount of water you need.** Use four times the amount of water as the amount of ghee you want to produce. So if you're aiming for 8 ounces of ghee, use 32 ounces of water.

2. **Simmer the herbs** (use ½ ounce for every 2 ounces of ghee you hope to produce – so if you're making 8 ounces of ghee, use 2 ounces of herbs) in the water until the liquid is reduced by 75 per cent.

   Simmering concentrates the active ingredients of the herbs.

3. **Gently mix in the ghee and heat to a slow simmer.** Be careful not to burn the mixture. Regulate the temperature.

4. **Once all the water is removed by gentle heating, the herbal ghee is ready.**

5. **Strain the mixture into a screw-top jar through five or six layers of cheesecloth placed in a strainer.**

If your mixture doesn't solidify after a time it has too much water in it, so reheat it to get rid of all the water. The whole process takes practice, so be patient.

Bread of Heaven: Wheat-free Recipes for an Excellent Loaf

According to Ayurveda, wheat is sweet and heavy in nature, so overuse of it can put on the pounds if you're a kapha dosha or indeed if you already have excess weight. Modern wheat has been tinkered with a lot to increase the yield, so many people find that they have an adverse reaction to it. As an alternative to regular flour in recipes, try spelt flour, poetically known as *dinkel* in Germany, where it's used a lot. Spelt is an old, traditional form of wheat, so your system has more chance of recognising it so that it can be digested properly.

Here I offer you two tasty wheat-free bread alternatives, which are easy to make.

Serbian cornmeal bread

This recipe makes a delicious loaf.

Ingredients:

> 1 tablespoon of dried yeast
>
> 100 millilitres of lukewarm milk
>
> 25 grams of potato flour
>
> 1 tablespoon of molasses or agave syrup
>
> 50 grams of fine cornmeal
>
> 2 tablespoons of soya flour
>
> Pinch of salt
>
> 1 egg, beaten
>
> 1 tablespoon of corn oil or sunflower oil

Method:

1. Put the yeast, milk and molasses or agave syrup in a bowl and allow to stand for 10 to 20 minutes somewhere warm.

2. Now put the dry ingredients into a bowl. Then add to the bowl the beaten egg, oil, and the yeast and milk combination, and mix together.

3. Spoon the mixture into an oiled, lined loaf tin. Leave it in a warm place for half an hour.

4. Bake in a pre-warmed oven at 180°C/350°F for 40 to 45 minutes.

5. Let the loaf cool thoroughly on a wire rack before you eat it.

African millet bread

This recipe makes tasty individual bread patties.

Ingredients:

4 tablespoons of lukewarm milk

Pinch of sugar

1 teaspoon of dried yeast

100 grams of flaked millet

½ teaspoon of salt

225 millilitres of lukewarm water

Method:

1. Mix together the milk, sugar and yeast and leave in a warm environment for about 15 minutes.

2. Grind the millet flakes in a grinder until fine then put them in a bowl with the salt.

3. Make a well in the centre of the ground millet and pour in the water and the yeast mixture, stirring all the time using a wooden spoon to form a smooth batter.

4. Beat for one minute and then cover the bowl with a cloth and leave for about an hour until the mixture becomes frothy.

5. Now cook the batter on a lightly greased and heated griddle or in a heavy-based frying pan. Drop the batter into the pan in spoonfuls and cook for about six minutes on both sides until the patty is crisp and honey-coloured.

Crafting Super Spice Mixes for Everyday Use

Spices are highly prized in Ayurveda for their health-giving benefits and for their excellent flavour. You can make your own blends that correspond to your doshic balance.

For all the mixes, get non-irradiated varieties if you can. In Europe and the United States, spices are irradiated to prevent fungal growth, so when I travel outside these areas I bring the fresh spices back with me. I once went to the Yemen, and the flavour of non-irradiated pepper is fragrant and more pungent than that of the pepper we get here.

Use 25 grams of each individual spice, as follows, to make your concoctions:

- **Cooling pitta spice mixture:** Turmeric, coriander, fennel, aniseeds
- **Warming vata spice mixture:** Ginger, clove, cardamom, cumin, asafoetida, ajwan
- **Heating kapha spice mixture:** Ginger, black pepper, mustard seeds, kalonji, cumin

Now put your spices in a coffee grinder, but don't make them too fine; leave them quite granular because they keep their flavour longer that way. Then place the mixtures in separate labelled screw-top jars so that they're ready when you need to cook with them. Use the spice mixes in seasonal cooking, assuming you're balanced and well.

Chapter 18 gives you information on ten super spices for your kitchen.

Adding Herbs to Your Diet

A very simple way of adding to the much-needed spectrum of tastes in your daily diet is by adding herbs. The more variety of the six tastes mentioned in Chapter 11 you can ingest, the more likely you are to feel satisfied with less food. You eat more if your body is crying out for nutritious food. So often, the modern fast food diet is devoid of minerals and vitamins, which are essential for health. Get into the habit of adding fresh herbs to your shopping list.

Listed in Table 12-1 are short lists of herbs for each dosha.

Table 12-1	Choosing Herbs for Your Dosha	
Vata	Pitta	Kapha
Basil	Green coriander	Horseradish
Parsley	Mint (in moderation)	Rocket
Chervil	Chicory	Parsley

Head to Chapter 17 for ten wonderful herbs to use liberally.

Quenching Thirst with Pure Water

There is much to say about the life-giving substance of water, and I can only marvel at the minds that revealed this knowledge to us in the Vedas.

Every cell in your body is dependent on water. Water serves as a heart tonic and a pacifier of pitta dosha due to its cool potency.

The amount of water you need depends largely on your exercise levels, on air-conditioning, heating and the seasons, and on your constitution. I so often see large ladies forcing big bottles of water down themselves and thinking it will flush the kidneys, but in many cases they're doing more harm than good because they're diluting their precious *agni* or digestive fire.

Nature gave you such a concentrated environment in your stomach so that you digest everything that you put in! So as a general rule, drink:

- ✔ Five to six cups of water daily if you have a pitta constitution
- ✔ Seven to eight cups of water per day if you have a vata constitution
- ✔ Roughly four cups of water per day if you're kapha

Drink water at room temperature without ice, to aid your digestion. If you serve water in a copper vessel for optimum agni, this has the added bonus that it helps to neutralise chlorine. Drinking from a clay pot is said to be good for all doshas.

Bottled water is readily available but varies greatly in its content:

- ✔ Bottled waters with a low mineral content, such as Evian or Volvic, are good for babies and general use.
- ✔ Mineral waters like San Pellegrino and Contrex are rich in calcium, and so are advised to promote healthy kidneys and healthy bone tissue.
- ✔ Those waters with a high mineral content, such as Vichy, are good for short-term use for the bones and kidneys, and are also useful as part of a fast. They're also believed to be helpful if you have hypertension, arthritis, low immunity and digestive problems. Badoit, which is high in magnesium, is a personal favourite and is excellent for sufferers of cystitis and anyone with liver problems.

Avoid plastic bottles, because the chemicals used in the plastic can enter the water; glass is much better.

Part IV
Fitting Ways to Enhance Healing

Go to www.dummies.com/extras/ayurvedauk for free online bonus content.

In this part . . .

- ✔ Boost your digestive fire with herbs, oils and friendly bacteria.

- ✔ Fight the flab the Ayurvedic way.

- ✔ Discover simple yet incredibly effective and soothing breathing exercises.

- ✔ Get rid of congestion and clear your head.

- ✔ Improve mobility and stability.

- ✔ Find Ayurvedic treats for your skin and hair, including a special Ayurvedic massage with a myriad of benefits.

Chapter 13

Stoking the Fire: Caring for Your Digestive System

In This Chapter

▷ Looking at ways to manage indigestion

▷ Relieving gas

▷ Improving bowel function

▷ Coping with weight gain

▷ Dealing with irritated bowels

*W*hen things go wrong within your digestive system, nothing in your body feels right. In fact, most diseases begin in the *alimentary tract* (basically, the tube that runs from your mouth to your other end, and which is where your digestive processes take place).

Through the process of digestion, the food you eat enters your bloodstream and eventually gives rise to all the tissue elements in your body. If the right components of a healthy diet aren't in place, you experience problems farther down the line. Trouble may not happen immediately, but a poor diet eventually leaves its mark. A patient once came to me with osteoporosis aged 45 – quite an early age for it. I found out that in her late teens and early 20s she'd been anorexic, and even her current diet was low in calcium.

What you put into your body and how you stress or nurture your digestive system shows up in your health. This chapter shows you some of the ways your digestive system calls attention to issues, and how to help them.

How you eat, as much as what you eat, can affect your digestion. Your best bet is to eat slowly, chew your food well, and avoid worry and tension at mealtimes. While you eat, salivary enzymes mix with food and start to turn sugars into starches at the beginning of their journey down the alimentary canal. Giving this process a thorough start helps smooth the rest of digestion.

Cool Approaches to Hyperacidity

The more I acquaint myself with the human body, the more I realise that it's a work of genius. Take for example the stomach: it has the capacity to digest a steak without eating itself. Your stomach achieves this miracle by having tiny little cells that produce hydrochloric acid (known as *packak pitta*) alongside a thick lining of mucous membrane (known as *kledak kapha*).

This amazing system works perfectly – until stress and poor eating habits breach the barrier, causing what's known in Ayurveda as *amala pitta* (literally, sour bile), and in the West as *gastritis*.

The upcoming sections show you how to combat amala pitta.

Eating to reduce acidity

Amala pitta, which is inflammation of the stomach lining, is the result of what's known as *tikshna agni*, when too much fire causes burning and pain in your stomach. This condition has different presentations according to your constitution, but in general you experience burning, burping of sour or bitter fluids, nausea, pain and indigestion, leading to loss of appetite.

If you find yourself dealing with amala pitta, cut down on all foods that stimulate acid production. That includes tea, coffee and fizzy drinks. (Most popular colas are a weak solution of phosphoric acid – a substance that you can clean the loo with, and which disrupts the production of healthy bone tissue.) You also need to reduce the amount of pungent, sour and salty foods. (Chapter 10 tells you more about the various flavours of foods and their effects on your body.)

Also avoid alcohol with its attendant sharpness, because this quality is also one of the attributes of pitta, which you're trying to pacify. Avoid fried foods as well as anything oily or pickled. These foods are difficult to digest and create more acidity and, in the long-term, form *ama* (toxins, explained in Chapter 5).

You may also need to eradicate certain food combinations that leave toxic residues in your body. An observable example of this is mixing sour fruits with cream or milk; you can see for yourself that the milk curdles. These toxins build up over time and make hyperacidity symptoms worse. Check out the rules for eating that are outlined in Chapter 11, and take note of unsuitable food combinations and the pitta-reducing diet, both of which will aid you greatly.

Sugary foods promote a greater flow of acid into the stomach. Even though your body probably craves sweets because it's 'running hot', you're better off eating naturally sweet foods like ripe peaches, figs, courgettes and ripe pomegranates. Sweet tastes pacify pungency in your body. Figs are particularly good, because they're very alkaline and this works to neutralise acidity.

Try adding roasted coriander seeds to your food; they're not only tasty but also help with dyspepsia.

Applying cooling herbs

When your body is running hot, as it is when gastritis is an issue, a wealth of herbs are available to help cool things down.

Perhaps the easiest one to find is amalaki. Taking two teaspoons in warm water three times a day helps to effectively calm any inflammation in the lining of your stomach. A form of Indian gooseberry, amalaki is regarded in Ayurveda as a major rejuvenator and tonic.

Fresh coconut water provides plenty of minerals and works as an antacid. You can take fresh coconut water as you need it.

Avipattikar churna is a super mixture of balancing spices that gently removes any symptoms of acidity without causing you harm. Take a half teaspoonful in a little water three times a day after eating. Avipattikar churna is widely available from well-stocked Indian grocery stores, but make sure it contains trivrut, which is a vital cooling ingredient of the mixture.

Looking at hot emotions

Inappropriately expressed fear and anger are said to have a lot of bearing on digestive health. The stomach is where people 'digest' feelings – an idea that shows up in our language in terms like 'gut feelings' and something 'eating away' at you.

If you fail to appropriately deal with hot emotions such as anger and aggression, your stomach undergoes an increased acid reaction in an effort to cope. That strategy leads to caustic fluid being pushed upwards, resulting in heartburn and gastric ulcers.

If you think that your emotions may be contributing to your gastritis, sit quietly and answer the following questions. What is it that I can't swallow? Why am I deliberately avoiding conflict? How can I express my feelings in a non-destructive way? If you can identify what's bothering you, you can begin to work through the issue. In cases where you have a hard time working through your emotions, you may need help in the form of counselling or psychotherapy.

Fit to Burst: Relief from Flatulence and Bloating

I am old enough to remember a health-food restaurant in central London that become very popular in the 1970s – it served great food, but the food was very heavy and raw. I often came out of there bloated and with enough wind to play a trumpet voluntary!

I'd bet you've found yourself in a similar situation. It happens a lot if you eat too much raw food. One of my teachers has always said that raw food has more *prana* (energy) in it, but if you can't digest it properly, eating raw food is worse than not eating at all.

A yoga posture that offers great benefit when you find yourself fighting flatulence is the wind-relieving posture, which I show you in Chapter 7. Read on to find more solutions.

Preventing gas

Gas is essentially a problem of vata, which is a combination of air and ether elements. Vata is light and expansive, therefore foods that have the opposing properties need to be the focus of your diet. Increase your intake of naturally sweet, sour and salty foods. Foods that cause many people a problem are pulses, potatoes and fatty fried food.

For more details about foods that balance vata, check out Chapter 11.

Relieving wind with herbs

Hinguvastak churna is a good gas-reliever, and you can make it yourself if you're unable to get hold of any ready-made. Blend equal parts of ginger powder, long pepper powder, asafoetida powder (available in Indian grocery shops, and sometimes called hing), black pepper powder, cumin seed powder, caraway seeds, ajwan (celery seed, available widely in Indian shops) and ground rock salt. Take two teaspoons in warm water each day on an empty stomach.

A decoction of ginger with a teaspoon of castor oil can effectively manage the pain from trapped wind in the stomach and lower back. Kumariasava, a herbal preparation of one ounce of aloe taken with one ounce of water twice daily after meals is very helpful.

Moving Things Along: Coping with Constipation

Constipation is so common these days that many people consider it normal. Hours spent inactive at the computer and poor eating habits are generally the root of this distressing situation.

The colon is the main seat of vata in the body, so a good bowel habit is essential for preventing the toxicity that occurs when waste sits too long in your colon. This situation leads to a fuzzy head, loss of appetite, inability to digest food, skin complaints and lethargy.

To check your 'transit time', eat some beetroot and see how long it takes to pass through your system. It should take between 16 and 20 hours, on average. If it stays in there for longer, you're in danger of generating toxins called *ama* in Ayurveda. (Chapter 5 tells you more about ama.)

Strategies for lightening the load

Your first step for alleviating constipation is to implement the vata-pacifying diet in Chapter 11. An important element of that diet is eating foods that are cooked and warm. Avoid raw foods, because they tend to be rough and hard to digest. Start using light, warming spices in your diet, such as ginger, clove and cinnamon. You'll see the results from this strategy within a week.

Your bowel is made up of a band of circular muscle, which needs something to grasp as it pushes the contents along. You can increase the bulk of the stool by taking isabgol, also known as fleaseed or psyllium husk; take two teaspoonfuls in warm water before bed.

Make sure that you avoid refined foods, which contain very little insoluble fibre, and increase the transit time of wastes from your body.

Other important steps to relieve constipation include:

- ✔ Regularise your schedule so that you take meals at fixed intervals.
- ✔ Give yourself plenty of time to open the bowels in the morning.

✔ Train yourself to go at the same time every day; even if very little happens at first, the colon eventually regularises itself.

✔ Include some good-quality oils in your diet to lubricate your colon.

✔ Drink warm milk with ghee in it before retiring; this can be a good way to lubricate the colon while ensuring a good sleep.

✔ Walk for, at the very least, 30 minutes each day. Your bowels will never work properly if you don't do a certain amount of exercise. Squatting postures are also really helpful.

Introducing triphala

Triphala is a blend of botanicals that you drink like tea or take in capsule form for its therapeutic effects. In a nutshell, triphala cleanses and tones your colon. Its mild scraping action cleans the little pockets in your colon (known as *rugae*), where crud lodges over time. Triphala is very gentle in its action. I've never known anybody react badly to it.

At night, take two tablets, or one teaspoon of powder with warm water. Some people find it easier to take triphala first thing in the morning, because it can have a mild diuretic effect. If you have a particularly sensitive colon, put one teaspoon of triphala powder in water at night, let the sediment fall to the bottom of the cup overnight, and drink the water in the morning.

Taking the Weight off Your Feet: Digestive Tips to Fight the Flab

Being overweight and suffering from its attendant diseases – diabetes, osteoarthritis, hypertension and hypercholesterolaemia, to mention only a few – is now at epidemic proportions throughout the world. This sad fact is ironic, given that other people starve to death from lack of food.

In the Ayurvedic view, people may become overweight in these characteristic ways, according to their constitution (refer to Chapter 4 to determine your constitution):

✔ **Vata:** An essentially slim individual begins to eat too much in order to calm fear and anxiety in the body. Sweet, sour and salty tastes are very attractive to these individuals. Vata individuals often eat to calm their sensitive nervous systems in an effort to ground themselves.

- **Pitta:** People of pitta constitution are usually of average build, and can put weight on but also lose it fairly easily. Pitta individuals hate it if life feels out of control, and in those situations develop a pattern of poor eating habits and use alcohol, because fire attracts fire. A craving for the sweet taste also arises in an effort to put out that emotional fire.

- **Kapha:** These individuals include those of us who are naturally rounded and curvaceous – more Kate Winslet than Kate Moss. You just have to sniff a lettuce leaf and a pound goes on. Kaphas are naturally very loving. When no solace exists, they find it in food – especially sweet, sour and salty tastes, which have an anabolic effect and so build tissue.

Understanding the set point

Western medicine talks about a *set point*, a certain weight that the body maintains to protect the optimum amount of fat tissue – *meda dhatu* in Sanskrit – within it. That's why it isn't necessarily your fault if you can't lose those extra pounds.

Part of the chemistry behind the set point is the hormone leptin, which is secreted by fatty tissue (meda dhatu). This in turn stimulates the hypothalamus – the brain's centre of appetite and metabolic rate. As you increase in weight, leptin responds to curb it. This process goes wrong when leptin resistance steps in. The body loses its natural cellular intelligence (known as *tejas*), and you pile on the pounds.

You can put a stop to leptin resistance by avoiding certain foods. An inflamed hypothalamus may be the reason why those of you with the resistant state have dramatic swings in blood sugar which can lead you to feel the need to eat all the time because you feel so drained. The main culprits appear to be starchy carbohydrates such as those found in pasta, bread and some breakfast cereals, and some omega-6 fatty acids that you find in some margarines and vegetable oils.

Lightening your diet

If you're working to lose weight, simple aids to your digestion can help support your efforts. Try considering the following tips in your diet plan:

- **Avoid cold drinks and iced food.** Cold food and drinks slow the process of digestion and reduce *gut motility* – that's a technical way of saying food passes slowly through your system, giving it a greater chance to create toxins. Contrary to current beliefs, drinking a lot of water isn't a positive thing according to Ayurveda, because it tends to reduce the stomach fire (*jathar agni*). Drinking four to six glasses of fluid per day is sufficient.

✔ **Drink honey water first thing in the morning.** In Ayurveda, honey increases the *agni* (digestive fire) and satisfies the craving for a sweet taste. Mix one teaspoon of organic honey in a glass of warm water.

✔ **Match input to output.** You can't lose weight without including some type of exercise. Exercise increases your basal metabolic rate. (Your muscle tissue burns calories even when you aren't exercising.) A half hour of brisk walking, for example, will really make you feel good and build your stores of biologically active tissue. The more exercise you do, the more insulin-sensitive your tissues become (the insulin receptors on cell membranes work better, and as a result glucose can enter cells rather than accumulate in the blood); thus your body's ability to handle sugars improves, and you're less likely to develop diabetes.

✔ **Try going without breakfast.** Instead, wait for the agni in your stomach to give you real hunger. Doing so is especially helpful if you're a kapha individual.

✔ **Focus on proteins at breakfast.** Doing so helps prevent surges in your blood sugar and staves off hunger. Have a boiled egg and some smoked salmon if you eat fish. Vegetarians may like to add quinoa flakes to their porridge or spelt porridge.

✔ **Avoid margarine.** Margarine is a highly manufactured product that has undergone heating to convert fatty acids to trans fatty acids, which aren't recognised by your system and form ama in your body. Using organic butter in small quantities is far better, and using ghee is even better. Ghee has a rather paradoxical action in that it increases tejas while reducing pitta, to improve digestion. See Chapter 12 for more about ghee, including how to make it.

✔ **Stimulate your thyroid (if you need to).** Your thyroid gland helps to control energy, so an underactive thyroid can contribute to weight gain. Bee breathing (see the nearby sidebar 'Humming like a bee to stimulate the thyroid') stimulates the thyroid gland and improves circulation in the throat region. This exercise is also said to improve your intuition, relieve anxiety and help insomnia.

Include seaweed such as dulse, arami, wakame or nori in your diet to keep up supplies of iodine, which is essential for a healthy thyroid gland and something that most people in the West are severely short of.

✔ **Try a fast.** A light fast (see Chapter 12) can wake up the system, but don't attempt it in the winter, when you need heavier food – the body will do everything it can to hold on to the fat for insulation against cold weather. One day a week, eat just a small portion of rice and vegetables twice during the day, and drink plenty of warm water or ginger tea throughout the day.

- ✔ **Kickstart digestion before a meal.** Increase enzyme-rich secretions in your stomach by eating a slice of ginger with a little lemon juice and a pinch of salt before you eat your meal.

- ✔ **Try massage.** If you have a large amount of adipose tissue, especially on the thighs, find an Ayurvedic practitioner who can administer a type of dry-powder massage called *udvartana*. This technique really helps to break down fatty tissue and improve the circulation.

- ✔ **Include more of the pungent and lightly spiced foods like black pepper, ginger, cinnamon and cardamom in your diet.** These spices are slightly warming and encourage the flow of your digestive juices. Avoid salt and salty foods; they attract water, which weighs a lot.

- ✔ **Eat cooked, warm food.** It satisfies you for longer and is easier to digest.

- ✔ **Get adequate sleep.** Studies have shown that too much (or too little) sleep is connected to weight gain.

- ✔ **Avoid or at least moderate alcohol consumption.** Alcohol is full of empty calories.

- ✔ **Avoid junk food.** It's so nutrient-poor that it leaves your body screaming for more food in order to compensate.

Humming like a bee to stimulate the thyroid

This simple exercise gets your thyroid humming along and, because this is the gland that controls how you use your energy, can help you feel more energetic:

1. Sit in a cross-legged or comfortable position with an erect spine.

2. Close your eyes and mouth and let your chin drop to your chest.

3. Place your hands with your arms bent at the elbows horizontally on either side of your nostrils. Block your ears with your thumbs so you can't hear external sounds.

4. Now place your index fingers either side of the root of your nose between your brows, and the middle fingers either side of the flare of your nostrils.

5. Allow your fourth and fifth fingers to rest lightly on your upper lip just below your nose.

6. Next make a low humming sound in your throat as you exhale. You'll feel your throat vibrating as you focus on the sound. Repeat up to ten times.

7. Exhale and bring your hands to rest on your knees, and observe the calming effect.

Herbal help to encourage weight loss

Certain herbs can help spur your digestion, which in turn helps your weight-loss efforts pay off.

Here are a few herbal remedies that are particularly helpful:

- A herbal combination called Trikatu contains long pepper, black pepper and ginger. Take two tablets (or 300 milligrams of the powder form) twice daily after food to get the digestive fires burning bright.

- Triphala Guggulu removes ama from your system and increases the fire at tissue level. Guggulu also has an anti-inflammatory action, which can help the hypothalamus. Take two tablets twice daily after food.

- Shilajit, which is a mineral tar that exudes from rocks in the Himalayas, is an invaluable medicine in terms of weight loss. It strengthens kidney energy and helps to break down fat. Take two tablets twice daily after food.

- Guduchi, which is referred to as *amrita* (immortality) in Ayurveda because of its ability to preserve youthfulness and vigour of the user, offers fat-decreasing effects. Take two tablets twice daily with meals for at least six weeks.

Make sure you obtain advice from a qualified Ayurvedic practitioner before taking any herbal remedies.

Gut Reaction: Taking Care of Your Bowels

In this section, I talk about two conditions that can affect the gut: irritable bowel syndrome and inflammatory bowel disease.

Irritable bowel syndrome (IBS) brings the discomfort of abdominal pain, bloating, diarrhoea and constipation. IBS can be a very disabling disease, because it really affects what you can do from day to day.

IBS is known as *grahani roga* in Ayurveda. *Graha* means 'to grasp', which refers to the fact that the small intestine grasps and digests input. IBS, as often related to stress. Some authorities note that individuals with this illness are inclined towards criticism and excessive analysis of a situation. This isn't always the case, but is worth bearing in mind. The body is always trying to speak to us, and we need to listen to it and interpret its message.

Inflammatory bowel disease (IBD), which presents as either ulcerative colitis or Crohn's disease, can cause diarrhoea, cramping, fatigue and weight loss. The symptoms of ulcerative colitis are similar to those of Crohn's disease but include bloody diarrhoea.

Always see a doctor if you're suffering from symptoms like these.

Caring for the colon and alimentary canal

Try the following tips for boosting the action of your digestive system:

- ✔ If the stomach and the intestines are inflamed, as with IBD, try an ounce of fenugreek seeds in a pint of warm water to get relief.

- ✔ Drink buttermilk with a little ginger powder and powdered dry fig leaves if you can get them. This concoction helps soothe your gut.

- ✔ Eat small portions of cooked, warm food. Make sure that you allow plenty of time to digest your food and eat in a stress-free environment.

- ✔ Avoid refined sugar, green lentils and all products made with white flour.

- ✔ Remove most spices from your diet. They can cause more inflammation to your gut lining.

- ✔ If you do eat fish, meat and eggs, do so in small quantities. These foods can build up acidity in the body and create more inflammation in the lining of the intestine.

- ✔ Try taking lassi after food (see the recipe in Chapter 12). Doing so can really help to improve digestion.

- ✔ The Ayurvedic herb *Boswellia serrate*, or Indian frankincense, which in Sanskrit is called kundara, has been found to be efficacious for IBD because it's an anti-inflammatory.

In very acute cases that don't respond to the tips above, seek a registered practitioner for a procedure known as *anuvasti*, which is an oil enema, to really soothe your irritated colon.

Improving intestinal health with friendly bacteria

Introducing friendly bacteria into the gut is a strategy that seems to be gaining ground. Increasing evidence shows that supplementing with large numbers of beneficial bacteria to crowd out the bad ones helps not only allay gas production but prevents inflammation. I've found a supplement probiotic called ProVen very useful.

Chapter 14

The Respiratory System: Breathing Life into Your Body

In This Chapter

▷ Breathing exercises for your lungs

▷ Clearing nasal blockages with a neti pot

▷ Using herbs for respiratory care

*H*ow your lungs function is paramount to your overall health. The way you feel about your life manifests in the way you breathe: your breathing is shallow and rapid when you're agitated, and is slow and deep when you're feeling relaxed and serene.

In this chapter, I explain practices that increase your *vital capacity*, which means that your breath reaches more of your lungs, infusing them with vital *prana* (energy). I also include information on using herbs and spices for improved lung capacity, and the practice of cleansing the nostrils using a neti pot.

If you have any form of lung disease and practise the exercises in this chapter, you can help to improve your condition. I know many asthmatics who no longer use their inhalers after learning pranayama breathing techniques. If you have a form of lung disease, I recommend that you enlist the help of a qualified Ayurvedic practitioner to reap the maximum benefit from the breathing exercises.

To get the most out of this chapter, it's helpful but not essential to know your Ayurvedic constitution type. Go to Chapter 4 to determine which constitutional type you are.

Introducing Pranayama and the Benefits of Breathing

Pranayama are controlled breathing techniques that help to alleviate stress, refresh the body and improve concentration. *Prana* is the subtle life force which invigorates the mind and all organs of the body; *ayama* connotes the control and direction of these subtle energies. The mind and the breath are intimately connected to the word *spirit*, which literally means 'breath'. The rishis, the great teachers of the Vedas, say that if you control the breath, you control life.

Your breathing is controlled by sensory and motor functions of the brain. So when you're stressed or upset, your breathing reflects this and becomes shallow. In some cases, the chest becomes sunken and you can feel down. By the same token, great fear can cause you to hyperventilate, and airborne pollutants can make you wheeze.

Your lungs are a perfect reflection of nature if you look at them as inverted trees – with your *bronchi*, or major channels, as the trunk, and the *bronchioles*, or minor channels, as the branches. The tiny balloon-like pockets at the end known as the *alveoli* are akin to the leaves, where oxygen is absorbed and carbon dioxide is returned to the atmosphere in exchange.

When you are 'inspired' during the inhalation of your respiration, your whole being is filled with life-giving *prana*, or energy, and by the same token when you exhale, your energy is lost or depleted. The ultimate exhalation is expiration.

Energising your digestion with agni sara breathing

Digestion is at the heart of Ayurveda. The stomach is seen as the powerhouse, where *jathar*, the most important fire in the body, resides. If the systems connected to your stomach aren't working properly, nothing else does either.

Poor posture, bad eating habits and stress disrupt your digestive system. To combat the effects of modern life and keep your digestive system operating smoothly, practise agni sara.

Agni means 'fire', of which your body has many sources – although the agni sara exercise focuses on the one contained in the stomach. *Sara* has several meanings, but in this case it means 'essence'.

The benefits of doing the agni sara exercise include:

✔ Easing digestive disorders such as gastritis and indigestion

✔ Assisting sluggish bowels, which cause constipation

✔ Massaging the internal organs and bringing life-enhancing prana to the thorax and abdomen

✔ Maintaining fitness if you're in good shape, and preventing abdominal problems

✔ Helping get rid of belly fat

Don't attempt the agni sara exercise if you've had recent abdominal surgery, heart problems, a hernia, stomach ulcers or you have moderate to high blood pressure.

The best time to do the agni sara exercise is early in the morning, on an empty stomach. Follow these steps and see Figure 14-1:

1. **Stand in a wide stance with your knees bent and your hands pressing on top of your knees.**

2. **Look down at your stomach as you pull it in, drawing it upwards.** Breathe out and hold your stomach in until you need to breathe in.

3. **Pump your abdomen in and out in a rhythmic way 5 to 15 times.** Don't strain in any way, and breathe when you need to.

4. **Take a breath, then exhale and do between 5 to 15 more pumpings.**

The whole process should take just two to five minutes, so it's well worth the effort for so little time.

Breathing through alternate nostrils

Known as *anuloma viloma* and *nadi shodhana*, this breathing exercise is beneficial for those with a vata constitution and anyone who wants to feel more relaxed. Practising this pranayama can help your digestion, promote sleep and calm your mind. During this exercise, your neural activities are harmonised by balancing both hemispheres of your brain.

Alternate-nostril breathing also purifies the *nadis* – conduits for the nervous system – easing the flow of energy through them. The stream of power through your nadis can be impeded due to pollution, stress and an irregular schedule. Blockage in the nadis creates what Ayurveda calls *negative space* where disease can begin to manifest. (For more information on the nadis, see Chapter 3.)

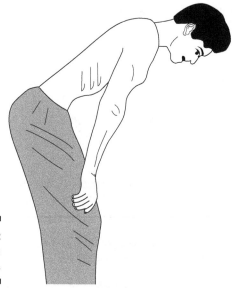

Figure 14-1:
Agni sara
breathing.

Follow these steps for alternate-nostril breathing:

1. **Sit comfortably with your back straight.**

   If you can sit cross-legged that's great, but don't let it stop you if you can't.

2. **Place one hand in your lap and form a *mudra* with your other hand, folding your first and second fingers into the palm of your hand.**

3. **Raise your mudra hand to your face and use your ring finger and little finger to lightly close your left nostril.** This gesture is known as *pranav mudra*. See Figure 14-2.

4. **Inhale deeply and slowly through your right nostril.** *Jalandrabhandha* should also be engaged, which means bringing your chin down to your neck.

   Don't force an inhalation; just breathe comfortably.

5. **Hold your breath.** Without strain, when it feels comfortable to breathe out, remove your fingers from the left nostril and use them to close the right nostril. Release the breath through your left nostril, while slowly and smoothly exhaling.

6. **Inhale again through your left nostril, keeping the right one closed.**

7. **Closing the left nostril, exhale through the right.** Continue this alternation.

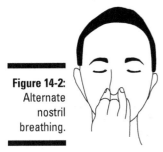

Figure 14-2:
Alternate
nostril
breathing.

Start by performing three rounds a day and gradually increase the number to ten. Your breath should be silent, with no strain.

The inhalation is the shortest phase, and the holding and exhalation should be longer, in a ratio of 1:2:2 – inhale for one count, hold your breath for two counts and exhale for two counts. You can do a 1:4:2 ratio if that's easier for you.

Whenever you do a task that requires your complete concentration, such as when you thread a needle, you often hold your breath. By the same token, when you're emotionally upset or angry, your breath changes markedly. Breathing exercises can help you calm your mind sufficiently to still the body and give you some control over your emotions.

Creating cool sounds with sitkari

Sitkari is most beneficial for those with a pitta dosha. *Sitkari* involves pronouncing 'sit' as you breathe in (a sort of reverse hissing) and exhaling through your nose, as follows:

1. **Sit comfortably with your spine straight but your chin down on your neck and your eyes closed.**

2. **Clench your teeth together, stretch your lips as if in a smile, put your tongue where your teeth meet and draw in air to the sound of 'si'.**

3. **Push your tongue farther against the back of your teeth and say 'ta' (known as a dental sound) on the exhalation.**

   Keep a ratio of 1:2:2 (inhale for one count, hold for a count of two and then exhale for a count of two). Don't strain.

4. **Repeat the exercise five or six times.**

The nose has it

If you pay attention to your breathing through-out the day, you notice that the dominant nostril changes in 60- to 90-minute intervals. Certain activities are more conducive to one phase than the other. The left nostril dissipates heat from your body, causing you to be more relaxed, while the right nostril creates warmth and energises you for action.

If you want to open the right nostril because you want to be alert and active, or the left nostril to be more chilled and relaxed, lie on the 'opposite' side to the nostril you want to be dominant (so your right side if you want to open your left nostril), place a cushion under the armpit of your arm on the bed, and stay there for 15 minutes.

This breathing exercise is particularly helpful for those of you with hypertension, stomach acidity or burning sensations in the body. It can also increase your lung capacity and improve your concentration, because it removes lethargy. Ayurveda also says that if you practise this technique you'll become a *kamadeva* or god of sex!

The sitkari is a great exercise to practise in the open air when the weather is warm, but don't do it in a cold place, because you may predispose yourself to a cold.

Shining your skull with kapilabharti breath

Translated, *kapilabharti* means 'shining skull'. I don't know about the outside of your head, but this exercise helps expel mucus, so it cleans out your sinuses anyway. It's also a purification practice that rids the lungs of stale air. It invigorates your mind after only a few breaths.

If your blood pressure is very high, don't do kapilabharti. Also, if you suffer from insomnia, don't practise this breathing exercise before bedtime, because it may be too stimulating.

This breathing practice is balancing for all three doshas, but it's particularly good for those with a kapha constitution.

Follow these steps:

1. **Sit comfortably with your back not resting against anything, and exhale quite sharply by contracting your belly muscles, raising your diaphragm and pushing air out of your lungs.**

Breathe fairly quickly to set up a pumping action, forcing a column of air out of your lungs.

2. **Inhale passively by allowing your belly to relax. You will naturally breathe in.**

   Make sure your breathing is regular and rhythmic.

3. **Practise ten exhalations, holding each exhalation for a count of two.**

4. **Repeat for three to four rounds.**

The benefits are immediate: you feel cleansed, and a joyous, peaceful feeling radiates through your body. You can only know this feeling if you try the exercise, so give it a go.

Cleansing Your Nose with a Neti Pot

With the ever-increasing exposure to airborne pollutants, respiratory infections are on the rise. To rid yourself of some pollutants and decrease your risk of respiratory and sinus infections, use a neti pot to clean your nostrils.

You can buy the pot itself – Figure 14-3 shows a sample – from a health-food shop or from the suppliers listed in Appendix C.

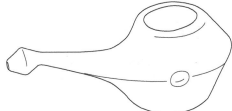

Figure 14-3:
A neti pot.

Getting rid of gunk in your nose and sinuses takes about five minutes and offers many benefits:

✔ Improves your breathing

✔ Makes your sense of smell more acute

✔ Cleans out not only your nose and sinuses, but also your eyes, ears, throat and lungs

Here's the method:

1. **Add one teaspoon or less of fine sea salt to about a one pint of body-temperature water.** The amount of the mixture that you use depends on whether you have a cold, lots of mucus or clean nasal passages. The more mucus you have, the more mixture you'll need. Adjust to your needs. This ratio creates an isotonic solution that has the same ratio of salt to liquid as human blood does.

2. **Standing over a sink, open your mouth to allow a free flow of breath and put the nose cone of the pot into your right nostril, tilting your head back to make sure the cone is securely in your nostril.**

3. **Tilt your head to the left so that the salt water in the neti pot flows gently into your nose.**

   Your left nostril should be the lowest point of your face. After a few seconds, the water starts running out of this nostril. Keep the flow going into your right nostril in a continuous stream.

4. **After using half the solution, remove the neti pot from your nostril, bring your head up and gently expel any remaining mucus.**

5. **Repeat Steps 2 to 4 with your left nostril.**

You can perform this exercise daily. If your nostrils feel dried out afterwards, use your little finger to apply a smear of sesame oil to them.

Caring for Your Lungs

This section outlines some herbal medicines commonly used in Ayurveda to promote lung health, and is of help for those of you who are subject to seasonal colds.

Defending yourself with chyavanprash

Prevention is always better than cure, and the best way to ensure that your lungs stay healthy throughout the year is to build up your immune system. Allow me to introduce you to a very special substance known as chyavanprash, which is probably the most famous of the innumerable herbal formulations used in Ayurveda (for suppliers, flick to Appendix C). Chyavanprash nourishes all your body tissues (and also tastes great!).

The recipes vary; chyavanprash can contain 70 to 80 ingredients. Its principle constituent is amalaki, a type of gooseberry that contains more vitamin C by weight than any other food substance. This makes chyavanprash a significant antioxidant for you, and it also protects your liver. It's particularly good in the treatment of asthma and coughs.

The Vedic sage Charaka said that chyavanprash bestows 'intelligence, memory, comeliness of body, freedom from disease, longevity, strength of the senses, great pleasure in the companionship of women, great increase in strength of digestive fire, and improvement of the complexion'. You can't get better than that!

Take 10 grams a day – 5 grams after breakfast and 5 grams after dinner. Increase the amount to 30 grams if you have a cold or an immune system imbalance – but use no more than this, otherwise you get a laxative effect. Chyavanprash comes as a type of jam, and you can eat it straight off the spoon or add it to warm milk (unless you have a cold; milk can aggravate congestion).

Taking tulsi

The tulsi plant, also known as holy basil, is perhaps the most sacred of herbs. It's prized in Indian kitchens as a household protector because the plant purifies the air around it. Scientific studies show that tulsi liberates ozone and energises the atmosphere with negative ions.

Tulsi has a wide variety of uses, and it's a very effective remedy for coughs, colds, bronchitis and asthma. Those with respiratory disorders find it especially beneficial because of its warming properties.

Make a tea by steeping a few tulsi leaves in hot water and adding half a teaspoon of ginger. You can add a little sugar if you like. Drink the tea three times a day if you have a cold or flu, or enjoy as a daily tonic if you want a boost.

Snuffing out a cold with spices

If all your airways are blocked and you're having trouble breathing at all, you might like to try your own blend of snuff to release the blockage. Simply blend together an equal quantity of ground black pepper, ground cinnamon, powdered cardamom and powdered seeds of *Nigella sativa*. Then place a pinch of the mix on what's known as the *anatomical snuffbox* – the groove on the upper side of your hand, at the base of your thumb by the junction with your wrist – and inhale it through one nostril at a time, blocking the opposite nostril. Have a handkerchief ready, because you'll let out a much-needed sneeze and clear away the blockage.

Strengthening with pippali milk

Pippali is closely related to black pepper but has a sweet post-digestive effect as opposed to black pepper's pungent one. (Chapter 10 explains tastes and their effects.) Whole, it comes in long corns, but you can also get pippali in powder form. Take half a teaspoon of powder with honey to aid your lungs.

You can use pippali to strengthen the lungs for winter by using it as a *rasayana*, or rejuvenative.

To prepare pippali, boil peppercorns in a cup of milk and then drink the milk. Start with one peppercorn the first day and add one peppercorn each day until you reach 20 peppercorns. Over the next 20 days, reduce the number of peppercorns by one each day until you're down to just one peppercorn, and then stop the treatment. Complete this process before the onset of winter. The whole procedure takes 40 days in all, but it really improves your lung energy.

Chapter 15

Flexible Approaches for Your Musculoskeletal System

*N*o one passes through life without physical pain or strain of some kind, at some point. The lucky among us get only minor issues of the muscles and skeleton, such as simple stiffness in the morning. Others deal with more serious and even debilitating issues like arthritis.

Exercise and stability strategies can help address some of the issues of your musculoskeletal system, and I give you suggestions for these approaches within this chapter. I also suggest aids for arthritis, particularly the types I see most in my practice – osteoarthritis and rheumatoid arthritis.

To get the most out of this chapter, refer to Chapter 4 to ascertain your constitution.

Maintaining Mobility with Simple Stretches

Over time, the human skeleton loses mobility. You probably know this if you've tried to get down on the floor to play with a child (who can plop right down, pretzeling his or her legs with no trouble at all), or if you've felt challenged by bending over to grab something from the floor.

As you age, your joints tighten up from wear and tear and because the inherent juice in the joint capsules and surrounding tissues dries up. But you can definitely help your joints by adjusting your diet and doing regular gentle stretching.

I suggest a careful approach to stretching. Yoga is the discipline par excellence for managing flexibility, in part because any movement you make is made up of many accessory movements. For example, an outward stretch of the arm is accompanied by an outer rotation. Combining the movements means you get more out of the practice. Head to Chapter 7 for a whole chapter about yoga.

You can easily overdo it, even with a generally soothing practice like stretching. Make sure that you never stretch to the point where you feel pain.

Frequency outdoes intensity with stretching. You get the most out of flexibility training when you do it faithfully, not when you do it in short, hard bursts of activity.

The following flexibility training should take no longer than ten minutes per day. It's designed to lengthen the muscle groups, which in turn increases agility and the range of motion in your joints.

A note here for those of you with inflammatory arthritis of any kind: joint dysfunction from poor habitual use makes the pain much worse. So implement these stretches only during pain-free phases.

If all is going well for you, do this programme of stretches on a daily basis, but be gentle with yourself. Don't delay with this strategy for health, because it will provide you with invaluable protection against musculoskeletal problems associated with ageing.

The stretches are:

- ✔ **Hip mobility:** Sit on the floor with your knees bent out to the sides and the soles of your feet together as close as possible to your body. Bend forward slightly and grasp your feet, allowing your knees to drop towards the floor. Move your knees up and down like a butterfly's wings. Repeat slowly ten times.

- ✔ **Achilles stretch:** Stand at the bottom of stairs, facing up, with a hand on the wall for support. Balance your forefoot on the edge of a step, allowing your heels to drop and stretching the Achilles tendon.

- ✔ **Quadriceps (front of the thigh) stretch:** Standing upright, with your right hand on a wall for balance, bend your left knee and grasp the top of your foot behind you with your left hand so that your heel touches your buttock. Release, turn and repeat on the other side.

✔ **Opening the chest:** Stand facing the corner of a room with your arms raised at shoulder height and push out with equal pressure on both walls. This can open your chest after stooping over a computer for hours.

✔ **Neck stretch:** Interlink your hands behind your head. Bend your neck and chin towards your chest as far as is comfortable. This stretches the muscles at the back of your neck. Bring your head back to level, release your hands and turn your head gently from side to side.

✔ **Leg and back stretch:** Lie on the floor, legs straight, and fold one knee, leaving the other leg outstretched. Now, grasping the front of your knee with both hands interlinked, bring it towards your raised head and hold for about 90 seconds. Repeat with the other leg.

✔ **Supine rotation:** Lying on the floor with your arms outstretched to either side for stability, bring your knees to your chest, keeping your arms on the floor, and allow your knees to drop to the left without your back leaving the floor. Turn your head to the right to really rotate your spine and give flexibility to your lower back. Repeat on the other side.

✔ **Lower back strengthening:** Lie face-down on the floor, breathe in, and squeeze your buttocks. Raise your hands, arms straight out in front like Superman, and lift your upper body as high off the floor as you can without strain. You probably won't be able to hold this position for more than a few seconds. Be very careful; this can be quite a difficult back bend. Work up to raising your legs as well if you want to go a little bit further.

Every time you go through a door, stretch up to the lintel with both hands. You give your back and shoulders a quick stretch several times throughout the day.

Coping with Cramp

Called *khalli vata* in Ayurveda, cramp is an uncontrolled spasm in the muscles and can be the bane of your life if you suffer with it. Cramp can occur after many repetitions of the same movement, wearing high heels when the body is trying to tell you to stop or, very irritatingly, when you're in bed and just about to nod off.

Vyana vayu, which is the force that regulates *prana* (energy) to the legs, gets aggravated by the accumulation of *ama* (toxins; in this case lactic acid) and deposits itself at the nerve endings to cause cramping.

Here are some easy steps to help eliminate cramps:

- ✔ **Stay hydrated.** In general, Ayurveda discourages drinking a lot of water, because it reduces the delicate digestive fire; however, exceptions include before exercise to prevent cramping in hot weather.

- ✔ **Add a pinch of salt and lemon or lime juice to your water.** If you cramp during exercise, drink the solution when the attack occurs.

- ✔ **Keep warm.** Cold keeps your body contracted.

- ✔ **Massage your legs daily with warmed mustard oil or mahanarayan oil.** This encourages circulation.

- ✔ **Consider taking a multi-mineral supplement.** Calcium and magnesium are important for fighting cramps, because they encourage muscle relaxation. The modern diet tends to be low in both minerals.

- ✔ **Take half a teaspoon of triphala at night before bed, if you're constipated.** This should do the trick by helping to purify your system and facilitating the removal of excess lactic acid.

- ✔ **Always do warm-ups before exercise.** The receptors in your muscles then tell the brain that they're ready for use.

- ✔ **Eat potassium-rich foods.** Pineapple, bananas, parsley, almonds, buckwheat, kelp and sunflower seeds are all good sources.

- ✔ **Try taking Vitamin E.** A dose of 400 IUs/day can improve the circulation.

Addressing Osteoarthritis and Rheumatoid Arthritis

Osteoarthritis is known as *sandhi gata vata* in Ayurveda, and occurs when the cartilage of your joints wears away. The bones begin rubbing against each other, causing pain and restricting motion. This process usually happens in one or two joints of the body, like the hip or knee, and is usually due to wear and tear.

Rheumatoid arthritis, or *ama vata*, is a systemic disease, which means that the whole body is involved. It's an autoimmune disease in which the immune system attacks the membranes that line the joints, causing fluid to build up. The joints in turn become inflamed and painful.

According to Ayurveda, both of the types of arthritis described here have a common origin; you can see that in the name, because they both contain the word *vata*. The vata dosha is very subtle and easily disturbed in your body. (Chapter 2 explains the doshas in detail.)

If you're struggling with arthritis, your first step is to avoid the common factors that aggravate arthritis:

- Exercising beyond your capacity
- Suppressing natural urges (refer to Chapter 5 for more on this)
- Staying awake at night or sleeping excessively
- Exposing your body to excessive wind and cold
- Eating incompatible food combinations such as milk together with fish (Chapter 12 explores food combinations)

Looking at dietary principles and arthritis

One way to reduce stiffness and heaviness in the body is to improve the *agni*, or stomach fire. You can do this by:

- **Langhana,** or lightening the diet by restricting the intake of food. One effective way to practise this technique is to eat well-cooked rice broth with cumin, ginger, clove and mustard seed three times a day over a couple of days until your tongue is clear (looks pink and healthy) and you feel a sense of lightness in your body. (Head to Chapter 12 for more about fasting.)

- **Trut nigraha,** or restricting your intake of liquid and sipping hot water only. If you like, add some herbs such as ginger, nutgrass and cloves. Add 10 grams of these herbs to a litre of water and simmer until half the amount remains. Keep it in a flask and sip it throughout the day. Doing so helps to remove any residue of ama residing in your joint spaces and your muscles.

Other dietary practices help arthritis sufferers reduce symptoms. Try the following:

- **Include herbs like guduchi and ginger:** These keep the digestion ticking along nicely and prevent build-up of ama. These herbs increase your digestive fire and promote enzyme production, so you're less likely to form toxic residues which eventually find their way into your joint spaces and cause inflammation.

- **Emphasise naturally sweet foods and a moderate amount of sour and salty tastes in your diet:** These tastes pacify vata dosha, the humour which in general is the initiator of the problem. Eating these foods is useful for osteo-arthritis in particular.

✔ **Eat mung beans:** You can eat mung beans, a source of high-quality protein, in moderate quantities, because they are very easy for your body to process.

✔ **Choose food that's fresh, cooked and warm:** Such food is far easier for you to digest, and therefore less likely to form toxins. Eating this way is also one of the first-line treatments for soothing vata dosha in your body.

Certain foods only encourage your symptoms. If you suffer from arthritis, you're better off steering clear of the following:

✔ **Fried foods:** These are heavy to digest.

✔ **Stale food and leftovers:** These don't contain the same vital forces as freshly cooked meals and can also leave a residue (ama), which eventually lodges in the joint spaces.

✔ **Refined white sugar:** This acts like poison in the body. Processed sugar has no food value and increases ama. Over the long term, you may put on weight, which puts more pressure on your joints. Sugar also increases the inflammatory response, which causes you more pain.

✔ **All members of the nightshade family:** Avoid aubergines, tomatoes, tobacco, chillis, peppers and potatoes for at least a month, to see whether you regain some joint mobility. These foods affect some people, but not everyone.

✔ **Dairy:** Such foods can be hard to digest and can douse the biological fires known as *agnis*. Dairy has kapha qualities, which are heavy, cloudy, dense and cold.

In addition, avoid eating fish with milk or dairy of any kind. Fish is heating and dairy is cooling in quality; post-digestively, together they form ama, which can lodge in your joints creating pain and inflammation.

✔ **Red meat:** It increases arachidonic acid in your body; this in turn causes your body to produce more inflammatory substances.

Happening upon the effects of nightshade

Dr Norman Childers, Professor of Horticulture at Rutgers University, observed that when cattle were unable to find their usual feed and wandered into a field of potato plants, they became very stiff in the joints in the following days, and the severe pain caused them to feed on their knees until they had metabolised the toxins from the plants. Having osteoarthritis himself, he removed all members of the nightshade family from his diet and regained full joint mobility (and, incidentally, lived to be 100!).

Healing herbs

A number of herbs have proven helpful to arthritis sufferers. I recommend that you start with garlic and then move through other herbs to determine what works best for you. To use garlic, add two or three crushed cloves to a cup of milk and heat gently until the mixture reduces by a quarter. (Dairy isn't recommended for arthritis, but consuming it this way acts as a vehicle to deliver the medicine to the tissues and removes the irritating pungent qualities of the garlic.) Drink this combination at bedtime, but warn your partner first!

Guggulu helps rid the joints and tissues of old, deep-seated ama or toxins. When mixed with other herbs, it really cleanses the body and gets rid of the sludge that creates inflammation in the tissues.

Take guggulu as follows, according to your constitution (explained in Chapter 4):

- ✔ **Vata types:** To benefit, take half a teaspoon of triphala guggulu two or three times a day.
- ✔ **Pitta types:** Take 20 milligrams of kaishora guggulu twice daily with water.
- ✔ **Kapha types:** Try 100 milligrams punarnava guggulu twice daily.

For pitta and kapha arthritis sufferers, half a teaspoon of triphala with warm water at bedtime can keep your bowels clean, which is very important in these conditions, and improves the surfaces of your alimentary canal for absorption of nutrients.

Consult an Ayurvedic practitioner for help and advice, and see the list of suppliers in Appendix C.

Using oils, inside and out

Oiling is useful for joint health, both inside as well as out! If you eat fish, you may find a daily 1,000 milligram capsule of krill oil some benefit; if you're vegetarian, try 1,000 milligrams of flaxseed oil for at least a month to see whether it helps you. Oils have a very effective anti-inflammatory activity in your body.

Many medicinal oils are available in the practice of Ayurveda, but a few are easily available and particularly good to use in arthritis (but *not* rheumatoid conditions).

Here's a list for you to try:

- **Mahanarayana Tailam:** The main ingredient in this widely used oil is shatavari, which is known for its vata-pacifying qualities when applied externally to your body. Warm it slightly and massage it onto your body to relieve joint pain and sciatica.

- **Dhanvantari Taila:** Dhanvantari is the god of Ayurveda, and this healing oil reflects that fact. It contains 17 herbs, which work in synergy to balance the doshas and to reduce the effects of arthritis and the associated inflammation and swelling.

- **Ksheerabala Tailam:** The primary ingredients of this oil are bala and sesame. Lightly applied to the affected part of the body, it's anti-rheumatic, analgesic and anti-inflammatory. It tends to be more cooling than Mahanarayan oil, so it's useful if you have burning sensations and in fibromyalgia. Ksheerabala Tailam soothes and strengthens the muscles, and relieves stiffness and vata in the joints.

Introducing castor oil

Castor oil is an invaluable treatment for inflammatory arthritis. Derived from the evergreen *Ricinus communis*, it acts as a pain reliever and a bowel cleanser. It's pungent in quality but can be used by all constitutions, including pitta individuals, during a flare-up.

You can apply warmed castor oil externally twice a day to benefit aching joints and burning pain in your body. Take it internally by drinking one tablespoon with half a teaspoon of ginger powder in a cup of hot water once a day. This procedure is best undertaken with a practitioner who will know how to guide you through it. It may make you very loose or even cause diarrhoea if you use bigger doses.

Castor oil also has steroid-like properties and can be used on a daily basis to remove inflammation from the system, by taking it in doses of one to two teaspoons per day in hot ginger tea at bedtime. You may want to adjust the dose according to your needs, but take no more than four teaspoons a day.

You can also use castor oil to effectively sweat ama from a joint, when you use it as a poultice. Place a thick pad soaked in castor oil on the affected joint. I find that a cut-up baby's nappy is best. Place a hot-water bottle or a heat pad over it and keep it in place for as long as you can.

Regaining Stability: Strategies for Chronic Fatigue Syndrome

Chronic fatigue syndrome (CFS) and its closely linked cousin chronic fatigue and immune dysfunction syndrome (CFIDS) are becoming more common. Both refer to a kind of tiredness that lasts more than six months, disrupts your daily activities and obstructs the proper functioning of your senses. I've included it here because some of the main symptoms affect the musculoskeletal system.

Diagnosing CFS

Common features of CFS include the following:

- Muscular pain and weakness
- Recurrent headaches
- Flitting joint pain
- Sleep disturbance – either excessive or less sleep than is normal for you
- Recurrent sore throat
- Mild fever
- Enlarged or tender lymph nodes
- Impaired memory
- Prolonged fatigue after little or no exercise

Causes of CFS include the following:

- Stress
- Depression
- Epstein–Barr virus
- Low adrenal function
- Hypoglycaemia
- Food intolerances
- Anaemia
- Hypothyroidism
- Impaired liver function

From an Ayurvedic point of view, CFS is a reaction to a build-up of toxins in the body due to diet, lifestyle and stress. Ultimately these factors lead to what's known as *oja kshaya*, or loss of energy.

The great Ayurvedic physician Sushruta said that you should manage a disease according to its symptoms. Because CFS involves many factors, the protocol should be tailored to your individual presentation, with a spectrum of interventions.

If you suspect that you have CFS, don't try to treat it on your own. Involve your doctor and get a full set of blood tests to establish whether you have an infection, liver malfunction, thyroid malfunction, or urea or electrolyte problems. Also, a urine analysis to find protein or sugar is helpful for ruling out common causes of fatigue.

Coping with CFS: Herbal remedies

You can supplement your CFS treatment with herbal remedies, as follows:

- **Ashwaghandha powder:** Take 5 grams in a small glass of milk twice a day to help relieve muscle pain, lymph-node enlargement, joint pain and a sore throat. It also helps you sleep.

- **Trikatu:** Two tablets twice daily before food works to improve the digestion and helps reduce inflammation or allergy. It also protects the liver.

- **Guduchi:** Two caplets twice daily is helpful if you have a fever, headache or lymph node enlargement.

- **Mandukaparni:** Two caplets twice daily can help if you have mental fatigue, decreased memory and mental stress as part of your symptoms.

- **Amalaki.** This is known as a *rasayana*, which means it's a rejuvenator – which is very useful if you have CFS. Amalaki can help if you have a fever. Try two capsules twice daily.

- **Shatavari.** Also a rasayana. Take two capsules twice daily.

Consult a qualified Ayurvedic practitioner to guide you, and always keep your GP informed of your treatment.

Chapter 16

The Secrets of Healthy Skin and Hair

*Y*our skin is a reflection of who you are and how you're doing; it's your outermost boundary. A brief look at someone's skin can even tell you a lot about that person's personality. For example, very sensitive skin indicates a highly sensitive soul, while excessively sweaty flesh suggests someone with a nervous disposition. A tough, resilient skin usually belongs to someone you'd call thick-skinned.

Your skin reflects every disturbance of your inner organs. Its close connection to your feelings is suggested in language when you exclaim how 'touched' you are by something beautiful or when someone offers you a kindness. Ayurveda addresses the care of your skin and scalp (which affects your hair's health), including the treatment of common skin problems.

Read on to find practices that keep your skin and hair at its best.

Skin deep

According to Ayurveda, skin has a total of seven layers. The skin is one of the most remarkable organs in the body; it protects you from the outside elements, extremes of temperature, dangerous chemicals and the sun's rays. Your skin produces essential vitamins and proteins, and retains moisture; it's the largest organ in the body, measuring 2 square metres (22 feet) – that's the size of the average doorway. The average adult's skin weighs about 3.6 kilograms (8 pounds). It is constantly changing and you shed about 40,000 skin cells per hour; that's why there's so much dust around! Your skin regenerates itself every 35 days, so you have to be patient when looking for change.

Your skin has certain characteristics, according to your predominant dosha:

Vata-predominant Skin	Pitta-predominant Skin	Kapha-predominant Skin
Dry, fragile	Fair, easily burns	Thick, pale, cool
Dark patches	Freckles, wrinkles	Oily, smooth
Cold	Warm	Pale

Saving Your Skin with a Simple Massage Routine

According to Ayurveda, one of the most important things you can do for yourself is to regularly oil your skin. Your skin is a true mirror of your internal status, whether it be your emotions or the condition of your organs such your spleen, liver, heart, spleen and stomach. Oil massage alleviates vata dosha by pacifying it with warming and lubricating properties. (Chapter 2 explains the doshas.) Not only does it soothe your endocrine and nervous systems, oil massage can increase your resistance to bacteria and improve your muscle tone. Massage is said to strengthen your skin while facilitating the removal of impurities. Finally, massage is said to remove fatigue, improve sleep and keep the ravages of age at bay.

You can use raw organic sesame oil for your massage, or you can choose an oil that's appropriate for your constitution by flipping back to Chapter 8. This simple form of massage is called *abhyanga* in Ayurveda, and is a general technique which you can use at any time.

If you've never used sesame oil, apply a little on the inside of your forearm overnight. If there's any sign of redness, itching or a rash, choose another oil that doesn't irritate you.

Follow these steps for a wonderful self-massage:

1. **Apply a small amount of warmed oil to the scalp on the crown of your head.**

   This spot is the *adipati marma* (the father of all points), which is often slightly tender, and so needs a little more attention.

2. **Release tension in the scalp by massaging with both hands using the fingertips.**

3. **Focus pressure on your temples.**

4. **Move to your ear lobes and stretch them gently with your thumb and index finger.**

   The ears often hold a lot of tension.

5. **Use the tip of your first finger to gently massage the inner part of your ear.**

6. **Finish massaging your ears by rubbing the bony prominence that sticks out behind the ear.**

7. **Beginning at the top of the shoulders, with a little oil in your hand, draw it down your arm, stopping at the elbow and wrist joints to massage in a circular motion.**

   Repeat the action with your other arm.

8. **Apply oil to your torso. Begin with your chest from your sternum or breastbone at the centre of your torso and work to the outer edges, circling the breasts and then pressing lightly between the ribs.**

9. **Massage your stomach by rubbing in a circular clockwise motion from your navel outwards.**

10. **Draw your oiled palm from the top of your thigh down to your foot with firm pressure.**

11. **Apply oil to the back of your thighs and calves in a downward direction.**

12. **Rub each buttock in a circular motion with your palms open, continuing around the waist.**

13. **Reach each hand over its opposite shoulder, stretching as far as you can to apply oil to your upper back and shoulders.**

14. **Bathe or shower to allow your pores to open and the oil to penetrate.**

General tips for skin maintenance

Sleep is very important to the lustre of your skin. Insomnia and general lack of sleep increases vata dosha with its attendant qualities of dryness, which causes dark circles around the eyes. Excessive sleep is also not advised because it increases the production of fat, which ultimately causes looseness of the skin with associated pimples and rashes.

Avoid consuming food after 7 p.m. in the evening to allow plenty of time for digestion. Sip hot water with a small piece of ginger root throughout the day to cleanse the system.

Make sure that you have a walk for at least 20 minutes a day to keep your circulation in good order. Allied to this, don't spend long hours doing repetitive things to the point of exhaustion.

Try to avoid suppressing anger; express it constructively if you can. Anger is not only bad for your digestion, but is related to the presence of rashes and itching – things 'getting under your skin'.

Identifying Foods Your Skin Will Love

What you eat and drink is recorded on your skin's surface. Too much alcohol manifests as broken, spider-like red veins. Tobacco and too many caffeinated drinks increase dryness and lead to wrinkles.

So in general eat a balanced diet of fresh fruits and vegetables, and eat organic when possible. Avoid excessively salty and spicy foods.

The following list contains foods that are particularly good for your skin (this list assumes that you're in good health and that your digestion is working effectively):

- Barley
- Butter
- Castor oil
- Chana dal (split yellow gram)
- Cow's milk
- Garlic
- Ghee
- Honey
- Linseed oil

✔ Mango

✔ Mung beans

✔ Saffron

✔ Sesame oil and seeds

When you're plagued with acne, the excruciating scaliness and itching of psoriasis (see the next section) or the presence of unsightly warts on your feet and hands, you can greatly help reduce these conditions either by taking a supplement of zinc or increasing the number of zinc-rich foods in your diet. See Table 16-1 for some good sources of zinc.

Due to modern farming techniques and the use of fertilisers, which bind the precious mineral, much of our food is zinc deficient. This fact, along with low-calorie diets and food processing, leads to a widespread decrease of zinc in your diet.

Warts are caused by a virus that invades the skin and begins to produce painful growths, especially under the feet, where they are known as verrucae. This virus occurs because your immune system is challenged, and all my years of practice have shown that zinc is part of the key to recovery.

So why is this mineral so important to you? Zinc is implicated in many functions of the body, the most important of which are protein synthesis, enzyme function and carbohydrate metabolism.

Table 16-1	Zinc-rich Foods to Include in Your Diet
Food	*Zinc Content (mg) per 100 grams*
Oysters	148.7
Ginger root	6.8
Pecans	4.5
Split peas	4.2
Oats	3.2
Brazil nuts	4.2
Egg yolk	3.5
Peanuts	3.2

Attacking acne

I remember when I had a pimple on my face when I was young, it always felt like Mount Vesuvius. I thought that everyone else was only looking at it.

In Ayurveda, acne is known as *mukhadooshika* (pustules) and *yauvanpidaka* (puberty). The *dhatu*, or tissues, mainly affected by acne are *rasa* (lymph), *rakta* (blood) and *meda* (fat).

Treatment for acne needs to address both vata and kapha doshas, and dietary intervention is of major importance in managing this very distressing condition.

Balancing the Scales: Helpful Ways to Settle Psoriasis and Eczema

Psoriasis is a very debilitating disease in which the skin produces silvery scales called plaques, which become red and then itch and burn. In more advanced cases, joint stiffness and pain results.

Eczema, a common condition when the skin becomes rough, itchy and blistered, is no less distressing than psoriasis but is easier to manage. In Ayurveda, it's known as *vicharchari*.

Eczema is commonly caused by allergic reactions to both metals and foods, and is often related to asthma.

Skin symptoms vary according to your doshic manifestation (Chapter 4 can help to determine your constitution):

✔ **Pitta:** If your skin condition is pitta in nature it will be hot, red, make you irritable and become worse with heat. It's definitely worth your while trying an antiallergenic diet, removing pungent and sour foods listed in Chapter 11, and trying bitter herbs such as sariva and manjishta to purify your blood.

Apply oils such as Brahmi and bringaraj to your hair and face, while organic coconut oil and aloe gel can work well on your body. Turmeric cream and Psorolin Ointment may help if you have psoriasis.

✔ **Kapha:** Your condition will be oozing with swelling and itching involved. Dampness and exposure to cold air will make it worse. An anti-ama diet is important for you, which means no dairy, yogurt or oily, heavy or sweet foods. Triphala guggulu, gokshura guggul and neem are helpful to take. Apply Lippu Ointment for eczema.

✓ **Vata:** When this dosha is out of balance, the good news is it's the easiest to cure. It will appear as dry, scaly and fissured skin made worse by wind and cold. Adopt a diet of cooked warm food and follow the vata-pacifying diet in Chapter 11. Taking triphala guggulu and rasna is helpful in this case, as is applying Dhanvantari oil, sesame oil or ghee to your skin.

Consult an Ayurvedic practitioner to help in determining the best treatment for you.

For all cases of psoriasis and eczema, the following tips are useful:

✓ Use a non-pore-blocking soap to cleanse your skin, like Biotique Bio-Neem body cleanser or Psorolin soap.

✓ Don't use soap powders with enzymes to wash your clothes; they can cause dermatitis and itching.

✓ Make sure you properly dry your skin after washing.

✓ Try not to do anything that makes you sweat.

✓ Cut down on alcohol and all processed foods.

✓ Visit spas with sulphur-rich waters.

✓ Eat more sulphur-rich foods, including:

• Eggs

• Brussels sprouts

• Beans

• Garlic

• Cabbage

✓ Up your intake of zinc-rich foods or take a zinc supplement (see the previous section). Psoriasis causes a very rapid turnover of skin cells, and so increases your requirement for zinc.

✓ Expose your skin carefully to sunlight to enhance the production of vitamin D in the body.

✓ Take one teaspoon of mahatikta ghrita, morning and evening, for six weeks.

✓ Avoid using very hot water when you shower, and don't languish too long in the bath; it can aggravate the skin and cause folliculitis.

✓ Avoid coming into contact with rubber or nickel, and don't wear synthetic fabrics, because they are occlusive and prevent the skin from breathing.

Stepping Out with Chicken Soup for the Soles

The skin of your feet faces quite a lot of challenges every day. It's the part of you that meets the floor and bears your weight over and over, all day long. Nowhere else does your skin take as much consistent and heavy contact – usually while cooped up in socks and shoes (some of which may not be exactly right for your feet or what you ask of them). Naturally, the skin on your feet may encounter some problems.

The upcoming sections give you suggestions for addressing common foot complaints. If none of these strategies is effective after three weeks, visit your local podiatrist for further help.

Simple solutions for corns

Corns are small, painful areas of thickened skin. They result from pressure on bony areas, usually around the fourth and fifth toes.

To help prevent corns, make sure that your shoes fit properly. You can also keep your toes separate with a piece of chiropody felt or lambswool.

If it's too late for prevention, apply a paste made from one teaspoon of aloe vera gel with a quarter of a teaspoon of turmeric. Strap the paste to the offending toe with a plaster, and leave overnight. Follow this procedure for a week, and then lift out the corn.

For soft corns, apply a drop of castor oil.

Coping with a callus

A *callus* is a thickened area of skin that arises from pressure or friction. It can be caused by shoes that are too high, too tight or even too big, which causes your foot to jam into the front of the shoe as you slide forwards with each step.

For immediate relief, soak your feet in an Epsom salt bath and then use a pumice stone to smooth the surface of the skin. Follow with an emollient cream such as zinc and castor oil or calendula.

At night, rub a little castor oil into your feet and wear socks in bed to help it soak in. Not so good for your sex life, but your feet will soften!

Fixtures for fissures

A *fissure* is a crack in the skin, usually found on the heel. A fissure can be very painful, especially when you walk or stand for long periods, and because the cracks can go deep, they leave you open to problematic infections.

Prevent fissures from occurring by oiling your feet, especially in autumn, so that your feet are ready for dry winter.

You can treat a fissure with a paste of ground nutmeg and a little water. Apply the mixture into the cracks and cover it with a dry dressing.

Check that your diet provides you with plenty of essential fatty acids, which keep the skin moisturised. Udo's Choice Ultimate Oil Blend is a good start to mix into food and drink, and for vegetarians, use cold-pressed flaxseed oil. For really bad cases, I've had great success with Petroleum 6X, a homeopathic remedy, taking one tablet a day for two weeks. Also Haelan Tape, available from your chiropodist.

Managing ingrown toenails

An *ingrown toenail* – one in which the tip of the nail becomes embedded in the skin – is a very common problem that many people experience at one time or another. You're less likely to run into this problem if the toe box of your shoes is big enough. You should be able to raise your big toe without feeling undue pressure from the top of your shoe.

Always trim your toenails in line with the top edge of the toe, resisting the temptation to go down the sides, because this is when problems start.

If the nail is infected, apply neem oil or cream to it and apply a dry dressing.

Reducing the pain of heel spurs

A *heel spur* is a calcium deposit that grows out of the heel, usually in a formation that looks like a hook. It's a fairly common condition that used to be known as policeman's heel, because it usually occurs as a response to too much walking on unrelenting surfaces.

To relieve the pain of a heel spur, use a heel cup – available at most pharmacies – to raise your heel slightly. Or cut a felt pad the size of the underside of your heel and remove a small circular section of felt in the spot where you feel the pain, and affix it with flexible strapping. This isn't a particularly Ayurvedic solution but it works! Heel spurs sometimes go away on their own.

Heading in the Right Direction with Scalp Massage

Hair care has been part of Ayurveda for a very long time, and indeed the word *shampoo* came into our language in the 17th century from trade with India. Asian women have always been admired for their beautiful hair, and one of their secrets is oil application.

Scalp massage not only ensures that your hair is strong and lustrous but also improves your ability to handle stress. The skull is the headquarters (so to speak) of the nervous system. All the senses are located in the head region, and massage helps promote their normal functioning.

Head massage also:

- Helps to prevent greying
- Aids sound sleep
- Helps to prevent refraction errors of the eyes
- Treats tension headaches
- Nourishes the roots of your hair, which can help alleviate hair loss

Some of the major *marma points* (focal points of energy) are located on the head. Three important ones are adipati marma, which is where the fontanel is located (the soft spot that slowly knits together after you're born). The other marma points are the brahma randra, two finger-widths in front of the adipati marma, and the sivarandha, which is the point two finger-widths behind.

Choose an oil that matches your constitution:

- **Vata:** Himsagara or almond oil
- **Pitta:** Brahmi or amala
- **Kapha:** Neem or triphaladi

If you want to address premature greying, choose bringaraj oil, which is known as *keshraja*, the king of hair. It promotes dark colour and lustrous locks. You can take bringaraj powder internally, as well. It's an excellent rejuvenator.

Using lukewarm oil, follow these steps to massage your scalp:

1. **Locate the adipati marma.**

   Place your hand on your forehead, with the base of your wrist on the ridge of the brow bone. Where the middle finger falls on the midpoint of your skull is the adipati marma.

2. **Rub the oil into the adipati marma with the tips of your fingers.**

3. **Move two finger-widths up on the same line to the *shika*, and give it a gentle clockwise tug.**

   The *shika* is the little tassel of hair you see on Hindu monks, who leave it long when they shave their heads. They maintain this growth so as not to disrupt the energies, because this is the site of the crown chakra, an energy centre located on a subtle energy pathway which begins in the base of the spine.

4. **Spread the oil over the whole of your scalp using both hands.**

5. **Let your head drop forwards and part the hair at the back of the head to apply oil to the hollow at the base of the skull.**

   Massage the area with your thumb.

6. **Release tension in your cranium by gripping your head with both hands, interlocking the fingers from either side, just above your ears.**

   Apply firm pressure.

7. **Use picking strokes as if lifting a tuft of hair with the tips of your fingers, to stimulate circulation to your hair roots.**

   This motion is a great stress reliever.

8. **Grasp the hair in little clumps and twist in a clockwise direction.**

   Each hair has a tiny muscle attached to it, and these muscles tighten when you get stressed. The grasping manoeuvre rids you of tension in the scalp and improves blood flow.

9. **If you can, leave the oil to soak in for a bit, and shampoo it out when you bathe.**

   Use a mild, preferably pH-balanced shampoo. Many Ayurvedic shampoos are available. Maharishi Ayurveda Healthy Scalp is very good and a personal favourite. See Appendix C for suppliers.

Part V

the part of tens

Go to www.dummies.com/extras/ayurvedauk for super online bonus content, including an extra Part of Tens chapter: 'Ten Wonderful Ways to Enhance Your Health with Ayurveda'.

In this part . . .

- ✔ Find herbs to boost your immune system, aid digestion and clear up colds.

- ✔ Use spices to improve circulation, soothe toothache and relieve headaches.

- ✔ Discover how best to cook with herbs and spices, and also how to use them in poultices and pastes on your skin.

Chapter 17

Ten Herbs for Maintaining Health

In This Chapter

▷ Identifying ten commonly used herbs in Ayurveda

▷ Using herbs to support good health

*A*yurveda has a wonderful medicine chest available that covers every possible need. This chapter lists some easily available herbs which are safe for you to use on your own. However, for full benefits, consult a registered Ayurveda practitioner.

The way that Ayurveda perceives the action of herbs is through the six flavours. These individual flavours have an effect on you as they pass through your body, starting with the taste in your mouth, which is a short-term effect, followed by the longer-term influence known as the potency, or *virya*, whether heating or cooling to your system. Finally comes the result of the essence of the substance at tissue level, which is more long term; this is referred to as *vipaka*, or the post-digestive effect. To learn more about this fascinating subject, which is unique to Ayurveda, see Chapter 10.

You can use herbs externally by applying a paste to your skin, or internally as a decoction:

- ✔ To make a herbal paste (known as *kalka*), simply crush a fresh plant until a paste forms, and apply externally. If fresh material is unavailable, use the powdered version of the herb with a small amount of water.

- ✔ A hot infusion or decoction is known as *phanta*. To make one, use one part plant to eight parts cold water and leave to infuse overnight. Alternatively, simply place a half to one teaspoonful of dried herb in one cup of warm water and drink.

Ashwaghanda (Withania somnifera) Winter Cherry

Ashwaghanda, or winter cherry as it's commonly called, is the big herb in Ayurveda healing. Its power comes primarily from the fact that it helps to produce *ojas*, the fine energy guarding your immune system. Ashwaghanda's specific action is to rejuvenate and promote strength, including boosting sperm production (the name means 'vitality of a horse'), which makes it a popular addition to many aphrodisiac formulas. Ashwaghanda is related to ginseng, which is widely used in Chinese medicine (thankfully, ashwaghanda is much cheaper to buy).

Ashwaghanda works to pacify vata, which connects to the wind element in the body, and kapha, which is the heavier moist quality in your system. It has a calming effect on your body and mind. This herb contains somniferin, a bitter alkaloid with a hypnotic action that makes it helpful in promoting sleep.

Ashwaghanda benefits bone, muscle, fat, the nervous system and the reproductive system. It's said to inhibit ageing by preventing tissue degeneration, and is a great tonic herb when you're feeling overworked and exhausted. It also has expectorant qualities, which are helpful if you have respiratory conditions like coughs and asthma. However, if you think you have a lot of toxins in your body or have severe congestion, using ashwaghanda is not advisable.

You can massage ashwaghanda as an oil (which you can purchase from the suppliers listed in Appendix C) into your body to give strength and warmth to your muscles.

Ashwaghanda's primary tastes are bitter and astringent, and its potency is hot. (This means that it produces warmth in the body when you first take it.) Its post-digestive effect is pungent, meaning that after it's been digested, heat is still produced. Those of you with high pitta or with heat in the body should use it with caution. To gain more of an insight into this aspect of tastes, see Chapter 13.

Put between 250 milligrams to 1 gram of ashwaghanda in some cold or warm milk with either ghee or honey. The powder can also be added to basmati rice cooked in milk. Start with a low dose first and increase it gradually over a week.

Ashwaghanda has been shown to help stabilise pregnancy, especially if the mother is weak or fatigued. Combine 5 grams of the powered herb along with 10 grams of ghee and 250 milligrams of milk and a little natural sugar for a good tonic, which also helps ease pre- and post-delivery backaches.

Ashwaghanda is a member of the nightshade family, so if you're unable to digest tomatoes, potatoes and peppers, you'll probably want to avoid it.

Bala (Sida cordifolia) Country Mallow

In Sanskrit, *bala* means 'providing strength', which is what this herb does to your body. Its major component, which is found in the seeds, is an alkaloid containing ephedrine, which is a central nervous system stimulant similar to amphetamine without the side effects. So its specific action is to promote vigour, enhance the complexion and alleviate vata dosha, which has the attributes of dryness, lightness, mobility and coldness. Bala promotes healing of wounds, is anti-inflammatory and encourages cell growth. It's a stimulant, soothes and promotes the action of your nervous system, and functions as an aphrodisiac. Bala is what's known as a *rasayana*, which means that it's a rejuvenating tonic, especially if you have general debility.

Besides working on all the tissue elements in your body, bala rejuvenates and maintains nerve tissue and bone marrow, keeping them in a healthy state. This makes it particularly useful for the common nervous impairments such as sciatica (radiating pain from the low back to the leg) and neuralgia (nerve pain).

Bala is helpful as a heart tonic and aids lung function in cases of bronchiectasis (an obstructive lung disease) or impaired breathing. It acts as a diuretic and can be useful in alleviating painful urination.

Bala's potency is cooling to the system, and both its taste in your mouth and its post-digestive effects are sweet, which means that it can be used to soothe both vata and pitta conditions of your body.

To take bala internally, add from 250 milligrams up to 1 gram to a glass of milk.

Externally, you can use bala as a paste to alleviate swelling, numbness and pain. Bala oil is available for the same purpose.

Vacha (Calamus) Sweet Flag

The word *vacha* comes from the Latin root *vox* and means 'speaking'. It's appropriate then that this herb is said to help with talking, because it stimulates and nourishes the speech centres of your brain. It has an affinity to all of the seven tissues in the body except blood.

Vacha was held in high esteem by the Vedic seers because of its ability to revitalise the nervous system and stimulate brain function. Put a half teaspoon of vacha in one teaspoon of honey and give it to your children every day to give them a brain boost.

Vacha is used in the treatment of anaemia and blood disorders. It can also be used to improve the digestion by alleviating flatulence and indigestion, as well as for clearing your mouth of any coatings on the teeth and tongue.

This herb is pungent, bitter and astringent to the taste, with a heating potency. Because of its pungent effect, it can help alleviate problems related to vata and kapha doshas and clear your channels of subtly occurring blockages. (Chapter 2 tells you about the subtle pathways of your body, which are subject to obstruction by toxins.)

Vacha promotes lactation, so breastfeeding mothers can mix a half teaspoon with one strand of saffron and a quarter teaspoon of long pepper in a glass of milk.

When in need of its benefits, take 250 milligrams of the powder in warm milk twice a day. You can also use it as a paste by adding a little water or oil to ease the pain of an arthritic joint.

Don't take more than the recommended dose, because it can cause vomiting. And don't use vacha if you're prone to bleeding disorders such as piles or nosebleeds.

Pippali (Piper longum) Long Pepper

This herb is an excellent delivery vehicle, moving whatever it's taken with to the tissues of your reproductive, muscular, nervous and circulatory systems, as well as to your fat stores.

Pippali contains a volatile oil and resin called *piperine*, which is pungent to the taste, and this makes it invaluable against kapha and vata situations.

Pippali acts as a decongestant, expectorant, carminative (meaning it relieves gas and distension) and analgesic. It's strongly heating, which makes it very useful for promoting good digestion and getting rid of toxic build-up in your body, and is useful if you have constipation.

Pippali can be used to treat anaemia and blood disorders and helps regulate spleen and liver function. Commonly used to treat coughs, pippali can also be used to strengthen your lungs.

To prepare pippali, boil the peppercorns in a cup of milk then drink the milk. Start with one peppercorn the first day and add one peppercorn each day until you reach 20 peppercorns. Over the next 20 days, reduce the number of peppercorns by one each day until you're down to just one peppercorn, and then stop the treatment. Complete this process at least 40 days before the onset of winter.

You can also apply the medicated oil externally when your circulation is sluggish. Boil 250 to 500 milligrams of powdered pippali in half a pint of water, or take up to three peppercorns with a little honey in the morning to remove excess mucus in your system – a great treatment for winter chills.

Don't use pippali when your tissues are inflamed or when your pitta is high. High pitta translates to the qualities of heat, oiliness and sharpness in your constitution. (See Chapter 4 to determine your constitution.) Don't take more than the recommended dose, because it can aggravate all the doshas.

Haritaki (Chebulic myrobalan) Indian Gall Nut

Haritaki is a special medicine connected to the god Shiva. Its name means 'that which carries all disease away'. It contains five of the six tastes – all but salty – and pacifies all three doshas, which makes it a very powerful and useful force in Ayurveda. Its potency in your body is heating and it has a sweet post-digestive effect.

Haritaki can serve as a laxative, aphrodisiac and general rejuvenating tonic. It stimulates digestion and has the special property of being able to work on all tissue elements in your body. Therapeutically it can be used to relieve coughs, piles, skin disorders, vomiting, colic and spleen disorders. In its capacity as a rejuvenator, it works by clearing various waste products from your system.

If you take it after eating, it can help alleviate all doshas aggravated as a result of unwholesome food and drink.

Externally, you can use it as an anti-inflammatory. As a decoction to cleanse wounds, mix one teaspoon of ground haritaki with one cup of cooled boiled water before applying it to the affected area. Take 3 to 5 grams once a day as a gargle for problems in the throat and mouth. Take a 1-gram dose when you want to use it as a rasayana, or tonic.

Because of its rough qualities, don't use haritaki if you're pregnant, debilitated or malnourished in any way. If your pitta is increased, use haritaki with caution.

Amalaki (Emblic myrobalan) Indian Gooseberry

Amalaki is like a nurse when it comes to its healing capacity. The Indian gooseberry is said to have been the first tree in the universe, and so is found on the top of towers in north Indian temples. Amalaki is said to produce *sattwa*, or calmness of mind.

Amalaki is an excellent source of vitamin C, carotene, nicotinic acid (a form of vitamin B3) and riboflavin, in combination with many other compounds.

Amalaki serves as a diuretic and laxative. It's cooling, calming and is good for your stomach. It works on all your tissues. It's said to stop hair from greying as well as prevent hair loss (hot heads usually lose their hair very early!). It can be very useful in the case of anaemia, because it helps in the absorption of iron. Amalaki's predominant tastes are astringent, sour and sweet. Its potency is cooling and its post-digestive effect is sweet.

Therapeutically, it's very close to haritaki in its uses (see the preceding section), but amalaki is especially helpful for pitta situations.

Take one teaspoon or 1 gram per day in the form of herbal jelly known as chyavanprash as a tonic in the winter to ward off colds. A general dose for daily use to ward off illness is 250 milligrams to 1 gram per day.

Guduchi (Tinospora cordifolia) Moonseed

Another very special plant with a multiplicity of uses, this climbing shrub, widely available in India, has an Ayurvedic name that reflects its therapeutic properties: 'one who protects the body'. Guduchi contains, among many things, tinosporin and berberine, which are terrific tonics for the body and your liver in particular.

Guduchi's tastes are predominantly bitter and astringent, its potency is hot and its digestive effect is sweet to the tissues.

Guduchi acts as a digestive stimulant and nourishes and rejuvenates your body. It helps with blood circulatory problems and improves reproductive tissue; specifically it alleviates pitta dosha but soothes all your doshas. Guduchi is also an aphrodisiac, which seems like a great side benefit to me.

Externally, you can use guduchi oil for dermatological conditions, rheumatoid arthritis and gout. Internally, you can use it as antacid, to relieve abdominal pain, to stop vomiting and to improve your appetite.

The dosage as a decoction is 60 to 100 millilitres a day in a cup of water, or 1 to 3 grams of the powder in a cup of water.

Shatavari (Asparagus racemosus) Wild Asparagus

Meaning 'one who possesses a hundred husbands', the translation of this plant's name refers to the fact that shatavari has very many rootlets. Its taste is sweet and bitter in the mouth, and post-digestively it's sweet. It acts to cool things down. Shatavari is a wonderful tonic for pitta, the blood and the female reproductive system. Shatavari pacifies both vata and pitta doshas and works on all seven tissues in the body.

Shatavari is absolutely invaluable if you're a woman having issues with your reproductive system, because it acts as a foetal tonic, milk producer and aphrodisiac. It can aid in the treatment of painful periods and is useful to men who suffer from a low sperm count.

Be aware that if your system is toxic (you feel heavy and unable to digest your food) and has a lot of mucus, shatavari may produce even more.

Add a quarter of a teaspoon of powder to a cup of warm milk with one teaspoon of ghee and a little honey. Taken as a powder, it's safe to use three to six grams a day. If you have pippali available (mentioned earlier in this chapter), add a pinch of that as well and drink this tonic once a day. Externally, you can use shatavari as a cream, massaging it in to stiff and painful muscles.

Brahmi (Hydrocotyl asiatica/Bacopa monnieri) Indian Pennywort

This attractive creeper is commonly found tracing its way across the ground in India. One of its names in Sanskrit is Saraswati, who is the goddess of knowledge. Brahmi is said to give you knowledge of Brahman, or the supreme. Yogis use brahmi as a brain tonic to enhance meditation practice, because it's said to balance both hemispheres of the brain and opens the crown chakra.

Brahmi balances all three doshas by virtue of its bitter and astringent taste in the mouth, sweet digestive effect and a cooling potency.

Brahmi operates mainly on your blood and the tissues of your nervous system. It's very useful for dealing with mental upheavals.

Take half a teaspoon of powder in a cup of water and drink as a tea with honey. Use it with milk as a nerve tonic or prepare it with ghee (clarified butter) to use as a rejuvenative. Make a paste with a little water to apply to skin conditions, or you can buy it as oil and use it for anxious tension in the body.

Kumari (Aloe vera indica) Indian Aloe

Kumari means . . . wait for it . . . 'to impart youthful vitality on you and bring forth the expression of the feminine nature'. This name is borne out, because kumari is a great tonic for your liver, blood, spleen and for the female reproductive system. It calms all the doshas of your body when used in its liquid form. Be careful with the powder form, because it can aggravate vata dosha. Kumari is both bitter and sweet to the taste with a pungent post-digestive effect, while its action is cooling to your body, which makes it great for burns.

Because kumari works on all of the tissues of your body, you can use it widely for many conditions. It can even act as an antidote to poison, although I hope you'll never need to use it for this purpose!

To mention a few external uses: kumari treats inflammatory skin conditions; applied as a poultice to your forehead, it eases headaches; the juice soothes red eyes. In your digestive system, kumari is invaluable, because it promotes good bowel health and bowel movements and increases secretions in the small intestine. You can use kumari juice as a general tonic, because it helps ignite all the fires of your body at tissue level.

Externally, use the fresh plant by stripping the outer skin off and applying the sticky contents to the skin. Internally, use in doses of 500 milligrams to 1 gram of powder as a decoction in half a cup of water. If you purchase it freshly prepared as juice, follow the manufacturer's directions.

Chapter 18

Ten Super Spices for Your Kitchen

In This Chapter
▶ Learning about spices and their culinary uses
▶ Implementing spices for healing

*Y*ou may not realise it, but you have a pharmacy in your kitchen. Food is your best defence against ill health, and you can boost its effectiveness by using the spices in your kitchen cabinet. This chapter runs through ten spices worth keeping and using to enhance flavour and health.

Turmeric

Turmeric is a little tuber that packs quite a force and has been used as a spice, medicine and colouring agent since time began! It really became prominent when modern science discovered that it's a powerful antioxidant with anti-tumour properties.

You can use turmeric in myriad ways. It's an anti-inflammatory, a digestive and a cholesterol-lowering agent. It makes a very good antibiotic, because it purifies the blood and improves intestinal flora. Also, it's been proven to help balance blood sugar.

If you have a family history of cancer, have been exposed to smoke or inhaled chemicals, you may like to take half a teaspoon of turmeric twice daily on food. An easier option is to take two capsules twice daily; they're available from your local health-food shop.

For respiratory allergies and asthma, mix honey with turmeric.

Cinnamon

You can use cinnamon, one of my personal favourites, in almost anything. Highly prized as an antioxidant, cinnamon appears for sale as oil, powder or sticks of bark excised from the tree. Its benefits include:

✔ Improving heart health, because it helps thin the blood and strengthen the heart muscle

✔ Promoting the flow of the energy known as *vyana vayu*, which promotes circulation in your body

✔ Improving the digestive fire known as *agni* and therefore helping the digestive tract expel toxins

For those of you suffering with colds and sinus infections, try a teaspoon of manuka honey with half a teaspoon of cinnamon powder in warm water, two or three times per day.

A great treat on winter days is Langdale's Essence of Cinnamon. Add a teaspoon to a cup of warm milk or water. If you have a cold, you can have this three times a day (unless you're a man hoping to soon become a father, because cinnamon affects sperm production).

Black Pepper

Ubiquitous black pepper is a household remedy with a wide reach, including:

✔ Encouraging your stomach to secrete saliva and gastric enzymes

✔ Increasing the motility of your gut

✔ Helping you release trapped wind

✔ Burning toxins in the digestive system by stimulating your digestive fire

✔ Comforting coughs and colds by helping your body sweat them out

If you have a cold, you can use a pinch of freshly ground pepper with two cloves of garlic in a glass of warm water three times a day, or try a pinch of turmeric powder and a quarter of a teaspoon of black pepper in boiled, cooled milk.

One of pepper's best applications is to counter the effects of cold raw food; a crack of pepper improves digestibility.

Pepper is not advisable if you have any gastric irritation or high pitta conditions where there's a lot of heat in your body. For those of you in serious meditative practices, remember that it can cause excitement of the mind because of its pungency.

Mustard Seed

Mustard seeds are an important part of the Ayurvedic kitchen because of their pungency – they enhance the flavour of any savoury dish you put them in. Yellow mustard seeds are milder in action and taste.

The seeds help to relieve both vata and kapha doshas in your body, because they work in opposition to their cold properties.

You can find mustard seed oil in Indian grocery shops. It's great for cooking, of course, but you can also use it for body massage if you want to stimulate the circulation. I find it very effective when rubbed into my cold feet in the winter, and it aids any sign of arthritis in a joint.

For poor circulation, tie two teaspoons of mustard seeds in a cheesecloth and immerse in hot water, and then soak your feet in the water.

Don't take mustard seed if your stomach is acidic or you have an aggravated pitta condition.

Ginger

Ginger is practically a pharmacy within itself and has earned the name *vishwabhesaj*, or 'universal medicine'. It's very calming to the mind and a tonic to the heart. It earns considerable interest in the scientific community because of its antiplatelet activity in the blood (which improves circulation), its anti-inflammatory properties and its ability to treat nausea.

You can chew a piece of ginger before meals with a little salt on it to stimulate the digestion. Add ginger to food to make it easier to digest and help control any flatulence.

For painful menstruation, take a little chopped fresh ginger and boil it in a cup of water for a few minutes, add a sprinkling of cane sugar and take three times a day after food.

Dry ginger, or *sunthi*, has a hotter potency and as such is more effective than the root for relieving mucousy coughs and colds; take a quarter of a teaspoon twice daily in warm water.

Cumin

Cumin is essential in Indian cuisine. Its distinctive flavour arises from a volatile oil known as thymene. Cumin is unsurpassed as a herb for digestive and gas problems, because its mild pungency helps build the digestive fire and get the juices flowing.

If you have painful swellings you can use cumin externally, made into a paste, because it has analgesic and anti-inflammatory properties. (Remove the paste after an hour.)

You can use cumin as a diuretic by taking a glass of warm water with half a teaspoon of cumin powder and one teaspoon of raw cane sugar.

If you suffer from menstrual pain, you can get relief by roasting some seeds until the aromatic oils are released and then chewing a teaspoonful. Chase them down with one teaspoon of aloe vera juice.

In India, hiccups are relieved by smoking a cigarette made of ghee with cumin seeds. Imagine how that would smell!

Coriander

You can very successfully grow coriander in your garden, producing better-tasting seeds and leaves than you can buy. And what a good thing, because this is another essential spice for the Ayurvedic kitchen.

Coriander seeds help to soothe an excess of kapha dosha or mucus in your body, while green coriander relieves pitta dosha or heat in your system. You can steep green coriander seeds in a little water and apply the paste to your skin to relieve rashes and urticaria.

If you experience pitta problems such as rashes, nausea and irritability, you can make a decoction of half a teaspoon of cumin, one teaspoon of coriander and a little raw cane sugar to taste. Boil in a little water for 15 minutes and then add to a cup of hot milk. Take up to twice daily to soothe symptoms.

When I was in India, I got 'Delhi belly'. One teaspoon of coriander seeds steeped in hot water for 15 minutes drunk throughout the day soon got me back on track.

Coriander seeds can also act as a tonic for the nervous system. One teaspoon of seeds with a cup of boiled milk can help you in cases of memory loss, vertigo and fainting.

I should also mention that coriander's a very good diuretic and is very helpful if you get water retention, especially in the summer months, and will help to protect the kidneys, especially in cases of pitta-type diabetes. Just sprinkle the chopped leaves on your food.

Cardamom

You find two types of cardamom in common use, but I refer to the small green variety.

Cardamom is a very mild digestive stimulant and regulates the peristaltic movements in the intestines and colon.

If you have toothache, you can relieve it with cardamom oil. Simply put a drop on a small piece of cotton wool against your tooth before going to the dentist.

Eating cardamom can be very useful if you have a persistent cough, because it's an expectorant and can shift mucus sitting in your lungs.

Cardamom's also a source of manganese, which helps to metabolise cholesterol and fats in the body and gives you energy. So include cardamom regularly in your cooking.

Clove

Clove is a friend in the kitchen because it keeps well and has many uses.

Chewing on a clove not only refreshes the breath, it also cures hoarseness and helps relieve stomatitis (inflammation of the lining of the mouth, the gums and tongue) and skin disorders.

Like cardamom, clove has analgesic properties and is very effective at numbing the pain of toothache. Clove is also mildly aphrodisiac, so if you're celibate you may want to avoid it!

If you have morning sickness you can take it with a spoonful of honey; clove also helps with milk production and has the added bonus of purifying it.

Clove is a liver stimulant and is useful if you experience hyperacidity, flatulence or abdominal colic.

Nutmeg

One of the most fragrant of spices, nutmeg is best kept whole in the kitchen and freshly grated to release its sweet overtones. You can use the smallest amount to flavour milk products. I add it to mashed potatoes for a delicious flavour.

For your digestion, nutmeg removes bad tastes from your mouth, stimulates your liver and enhances your appetite, while improving absorption of chyle, especially from your small intestine.

You can use a little nutmeg powder with ginger to help alleviate a headache brought on by a cold.

Nutmeg's quality of being rather heavy and dulling to your system makes it ideal if you have a problem sleeping; try a quarter of a teaspoon in a cup of warm milk.

A word of caution here: nutmeg oil is potent stuff, so don't use more than the stated dose, and don't use it if you have an aggravated pitta condition. Anything that pungent in taste increases symptoms of heat in the body.

In India, nutmeg's used for impotency and premature ejaculation; it's applied to the penis as an oil, and then betel leaves are tied around the penis. What a cure!

Part VI

Appendices

Go to www.dummies.com/extras/ayurvedauk for super online bonus content.

In this part . . .

- ✔ A useful at-a-glance glossary of Ayurvedic terms.

- ✔ A handy reference of botanical names in English, Hindi, Sanskrit and Latin so you can always find what you're looking for.

- ✔ A comprehensive list of suppliers of herbs, spices, Ayurvedic education and yoga and meditation centres.

Appendix A

Sanskrit Glossary

Agni. Fire.

Ahamkara. Self-will, the ego, mask. The principle in man which makes himself feel separate from others.

Ajna chakra. Command centre; the centre of consciousness between the eyebrows, also known as the third eye.

Akasha. One of the finest of the elemental particles, a substratum of the property of sound.

Alochaka. One of the five types of pitta, which resides in the eyes. Its main task is to capture images of objects external to the body.

Ama. Improperly digested food which, when it becomes fetid, produces toxins that lodge in the body.

Annamaya kosha. The sheath around the body, nourished by food and aligned to the physical self.

Anandamaya kosha. The sheath of bliss which surrounds the body.

Asana. A particular posture for the practice of meditation or certain exercises to promote health.

Artha. An 'object of pursuit', referring to abundance or money.

Asthi. Bone tissue; one of the seven dhatus which supports the body, giving it shape and protection.

Ayurveda. The science of life. *Ayur* means 'life' and *veda* means 'knowledge'.

Bodhaka. One of the five types of kapha, which is located at the root of the tongue and the pharynx and enables the sense of taste.

Brahma. The creator, taking the universe as his body, manifesting the energy of creation.

Buddhi. The faculty of the mind, from *budh*, 'to awake, to understand'. The discriminative faculty.

Chakra. 'Wheel'; name of centres of consciousness which are described as being strung along the spine and related to nerve centres which govern the bodily functions.

Dhanvantari. The physician to the gods and incarnation of Vishnu, who represents the true healer in all beings.

Dharma. From *dhri*, 'to support': that which is established; law; justice; duty; the prescribed course of conduct; that which supports.

Dhatu. The basic structural tissues (there are seven) of the body, which support and nourish the body.

Dosha. Literally a fault, defect or blemish. Three humours are principally responsible for maintaining the integrity of the human body, governing all biological and psychological functions.

Ghee. Clarified butter.

Guna. Quality; three attributes which are in balance before the evolution of creation takes place.

Kama. Desire; one of the three pursuits of life, commonly ascribed to all humans.

Kapha. One of the three doshas associated with the body; the bodily fluids.

Kicharee. Dish made up of mung beans and rice, which is very easy to digest.

Kledaka. One of the sub-types of kapha which moistens the food in the stomach.

Kosha. One of five sheaths which compose the subtle body.

Mahabuhta. The five elements which make everything in the universe.

Majja. One of the seven dhatus, or bodily tissues, whose function is to nourish reproductive tissue and fill up the bones.

Mamsa. One of the seven dhatus, or bodily tissues, whose main function is to provide physical strength.

Manas. The mind.

Mano-maya kosha. The mental sheath which surrounds the body.

Meda. One of the seven dhatus, or bodily tissues, whose function is to lubricate the body.

Moksha. Liberation, freedom and release from the limitations of the ego.

Ojas. Refined essence of kapha dosha, which gives lustre, strength and a strong immune system.

Pachaka. One of the five sub-types of pitta dosha, which resides in the area between the stomach and the duodenum. Its action is comparable to that of bile and pancreatic enzymes.

Panchakarma. A system involving five different types of deep cleansing of the body.

Pitta. One of the three doshas, or bodily humours, which is responsible for all the physio-chemical reactions in the body.

Prakriti. Primal nature or matter. Also a person's constitution, which is determined at birth.

Prana. Breath or life force. One of the five vital winds governing the body, mainly responsible for respiratory and mental functions.

Pranamaya kosha. The sheath of the vital breath which surrounds the body.

Pranayama. Yogic control of the breath.

Rajas. One of the three gunas or forces governing the creation. Rajas is responsible for action.

Rakta. One of the seven dhatus responsible for the circulation of prana in the body via the blood.

Ranjaka. One of the five pitta sub-types, located in the liver and spleen, and mainly responsible for the formation of blood.

Rasa. The first of seven dhatus, closely related to lymph, which circulates nutrients to every cell in the body.

Sadhaka. One of the pitta sub-types, it is responsible for enthusiasm, intelligence and memory.

Samana. One of the vata sub-types located in the stomach and duodenal area. The most important function is the separation of food materials and wastes in the body.

Samkhya. The main philosophy which underlies Ayurveda, meaning 'to enumerate'.

Sattwa. The purest aspect of the three gunas; the sentient principle which gives harmony, purity and light.

Shleshaka. One of the five sub-types of kapha, it protects the joints by keeping them lubricated.

Shukra. One of the essential seven dhatus, shukra is concerned with reproduction.

Sphota. Sound, vibration from which the universe emanated.

Srotas. The minute channels of the body responsible for the transport of prana and nutrients throughout the body.

Tamas. One of the three gunas or states of energy related to inertia and groundedness.

Tarpaka. One of the five sub-types of kapha, which is found in the head and functions to protect the brain and sensory organs.

Tejas. The superfine essence of pitta, which among other things governs metabolism and gives radiance.

Udana. One of the five sub-types of vata dosha. Its seat is in the area of the navel, and it regulates the upward movement of prana.

Vata. One of the three doshas, or humours, governing the body. It is related to air and space, and responsible for the circulation of everything in the body.

Vedas. Important scriptures of ancient India.

Vedanta. Known as the 'end of the Vedas'. One of the six philosophical systems which underpins Ayurveda. It teaches the essence of the Vedas and was founded in the Upanishads.

Vyana. One of the sub-types of vata dosha; the 'vital air' which circulates blood in the body.

Vyanamaya kosha. The subtle intellectual sheath which surrounds the body.

Appendix B

Botanical Index

Sanskrit	Latin	Hindi	English
Amalaki	*Emblica officinalis*	Amla	Indian gooseberry
Ashwagandha	*Withania somnifera*	Asagandh	Winter cherry
Bala	*Sida cordifolia*	Bariyar, khareti	Indian country mallow
Brahmi	*Bacopa monnieri*	Jalabrahmi	Indian pennywort
Dhanyaka	*Coriandrum sativum*	Dhaniya	Coriander
Ela	*Elettaria cardamomum*	Elaichi	Cardamom
Eranda	*Ricinus communis*	Andi, rendi	Castor oil plant
Guduchi, amrita	*Tinospora cordifolia*	Giloy, gurach	Heartleaf moonseed
Guggulu	*Commiphora mukul*	Guggul	Indian myrrh, bedellium
Haridra	*Curcuma longa*	Haldi	Turmeric
Haritaki	*Terminalia chebula*	Harade, harra	Chebulic myrobalan, ink-nut
Jatiphala	*Myristica fragrans*	Jaiphal	Nutmeg
Jeeraka	*Cuminum cyminum*	Jeera	Cumin
Karpoora	*Cinnamomum camphora*	Karpoora	Camphor
Kumari	*Aloe vera*	Elua, mussabar	Aloe vera
Lavanga	*Syzygium aromaticum*	Lavang	Clove
Maricha	*Piper nigrum*	Kalimircha	Black pepper
Pippali	*Piper longum*	Pipal	Indian long pepper
Sarshapa	*Brassica juncea*	Sarson	Brown mustard seed
Shatavari	*Asparagus racemosus*	Shatavar	Wild asparagus
Sunthi (dry), ardraka (fresh)	*Zingiber officinale*	Sonth (dry), adrak (fresh)	Ginger
Twak	*Cinnamomum zeylanicum*	Dalchini	Cinnamon
Vacha	Acorus calamus	Vach	Sweet flag, calamus root

Appendix C

Suppliers

Use these helpful lists to locate herbs, spices, oils, colleges and journals, wherever you are in the world.

Suppliers of Herbs

- Banyan herbs: www.banyanbotanicals.com
- Vadic Herbs: www.bazaarofindia.com
- Indigo Herbs: www.indigo-herbs.co.uk
- Maharishi Ayurveda: www.maharishiayurveda.co.uk
- Pukka: www.pukkaherbs.com
- Setramed London Ltd (herbs, oils and education): www.setramedayurveda.com
- The Nutri Centre: www.nutricentre.com

Suppliers of Spices

- Fudco: www.fudco.net
- Indian Spice Shop: www.indianspiceshop.co.uk

Ayurvedic Education

- California College of Ayurveda: www.ayurvedacollege.com
- Department of Ayurveda, Yoga and Naturopathy, Unani, Siddha and Homoeopathy (India): www.indianmedicine.nic.in

- International Academy of Ayurveda: www.ayurved-int.com.
- The Institute of Ayurved (New Mexico): www.ayurveda.com.
- Middlesex University, School of Health and Social Science: www.mdx.ac.uk

Journals

- *Ayurveda Today*: www.ayurvedatodaymagazine.com
- Indian journals of Ayurveda: www.systematicreviewinayurveda.org
- *Journal of Ayurveda and Integrative Medicine*: www.jaim.in
- *Light on Ayurveda*: www.loaj.com

Yoga and Meditation

- The British Wheel of Yoga: www.bwy.org.uk.
- Transcendental Meditation: www.t-m.org.uk
- International Sivananda Yoga Vedanta Centres: www.sivananda.org
- The School of Meditation (London): www.schoolofmeditation.org
- The School of Economic Science (London): www.schooleconomicscience.org
- The Study Society (London): www.studysociety.org

Organisations

- Ayurvedic Practitioners Association: www.apa.uk.com
- Ayurvedic Medical Association (US): http://ayurvedanama.org
- British Association of Accredited Ayurvedic Practitioners: www.britayurpractitioners.com
- European Ayurvedic Medical Association: www.ayurveda-association.eu

About the Author

Angela Hope-Murray has dedicated her life to the practice and study of all aspects of healthcare, both complementary and orthodox. Spanning nearly 40 years, her career began as a podiatrist in the NHS. Moving to the United States in 1979, Angela gained a Master's degree in Nutrition and Health Counselling. In Boston's Lemuel Shattuck Hospital she spent five years in the ground-breaking Pain and Stress Relief Clinic both as an intern and then running the nutrition modality. This clinic, developed by Professor Ted Kaptchuk, was one of the first of its kind to treat chronic pain and stress related disorders using a multi-disciplinary approach combining complementary medicine and conventional practices.

America gave Angela the opportunity to study reflexology, Chinese diagnostics, massage and counselling. During this time she was introduced to Ayurveda by two of its foremost exponents, Dr Vasant Lad and Dr Robert Svoboda. This meeting led to training in Ayurvedic Medicine with them both over a number of years, before returning to England at the end of 1989. At the same time, she was initiated into the Advaita tradition whose perennial philosophy has guided her life like a golden thread.

In 1997 Angela gained a BSc in Osteopathy. She was the one of the first students to enroll as an Ayurvedic practitioner in the UK College of Ayurveda at Middlesex University in 2001, gaining an MSc in 2009.

Angela practises at the Hale Clinic in central London and from her home in Berkshire. As well as *Ayurveda For Dummies*, she has written another book, and many articles for journals and magazines. Outside academia she has practised yoga and meditation for 30 years. For the last 20 years she has travelled extensively around the world running retreats, lecturing at conferences and teaching students.

Angela has passed on the knowledge in this book, which she has garnered through many years, in the hope that it will find fertile ground and encourage further study.

You can contact Angela at `ahope-murray@tiscali.co.uk`.

Dedication

I would like to dedicate this book to all those individuals who have preserved the sacred knowledge of the Vedas for the peace and prosperity of humankind. May their teachings be enlivened by all of you who have come into contact with them through this book, motivating you to embrace them for the betterment of your life and that of others.

Author's Acknowledgements

Firstly, I am profoundly grateful to my dear mother Joan Cordon who has supported me through the last year with nightly encouragement on the phone. My partner, Christopher van Kampen who kept home with plenty of cups of tea and advice about computers. My yoga teacher, Jean Cosham, for freeing up the tension in my shoulders in her classes. Jo Findley, for her advice and encouragement with the book. Dr Palitha Serasinghe, Dr Joshi and Dr Mauroof Attique who have been instrumental in my education in Ayurvedic medicine.

Most importantly I am grateful to Dr Vasant Lad and Dr Robert Svoboda. They ignited in me the flame of the Vedic teachings, which have been the bedrock of my life ever since our first meeting. This book wouldn't exist without them. I also thank all those wonderful teachers to whom I am indebted, who are too numerous to mention.

Thanks to Dr Paul Lowe who has been a terrific support and provided very helpful comments in his reviews. The wise counsel and care of Swami Kailasananda and Swami Krishnadevanada at Sivanada have been invaluable to me.

The professional support from the team at Wiley has been truly exceptional, both in the domain of the mechanics of the book and on a personal level. A very big thank you to Rachael Chilvers and Kerry Laundon for all your help and advice.

OM PARAMATMAN NAMAHA

Publisher's Acknowledgments

We're proud of this book; please send us your comments at `http://dummies.custhelp.com`. For other comments, please contact our Customer Care Department within the U.S. at 877-762-2974, outside the U.S. at (001) 317-572-3993, or fax 317-572-4002.

Some of the people who helped bring this book to market include the following:

Acquisitions, Editorial, and Vertical Websites

Commissioning Editors: Kerry Laundon, Sarah Blankfield

Project Editor: Rachael Chilvers

Assistant Editor: Ben Kemble

Development Editors: Kathleen Dobie, Traci Cumbay

Technical Reviewers: Paul Lowe, Sascha Kriese

Proofreader: Mary White

Production Manager: Daniel Mersey

Publisher: Miles Kendall

Cover Photo: © Hande Guleryuz Yuce / iStock

Composition Services

Senior Project Coordinator: Kristie Rees

Layout and Graphics: Melanee Habig, Joyce Haughey

Proofreader: Lindsay Amones

Indexer: Potomac Indexing, LLC

Index

Notes

Notes

FOR DUMMIES

Making Everything Easier! ™

UK editions

BUSINESS

978-1-118-34689-1

978-1-118-44349-1

978-1-119-97527-4

MUSIC

978-1-119-94276-4

978-0-470-97799-6

978-0-470-66372-1

HOBBIES

978-1-118-41156-8

978-1-119-99417-6

978-1-119-97250-1

Asperger's Syndrome For Dummies
978-0-470-66087-4

Basic Maths For Dummies
978-1-119-97452-9

Body Language For Dummies, 2nd Edition
978-1-119-95351-7

Boosting Self-Esteem For Dummies
978-0-470-74193-1

Business Continuity For Dummies
978-1-118-32683-1

Cricket For Dummies
978-0-470-03454-5

Diabetes For Dummies, 3rd Edition
978-0-470-97711-8

eBay For Dummies, 3rd Edition
978-1-119-94122-4

English Grammar For Dummies
978-0-470-05752-0

Flirting For Dummies
978-0-470-74259-4

IBS For Dummies
978-0-470-51737-6

ITIL For Dummies
978-1-119-95013-4

Management For Dummies, 2nd Edition
978-0-470-97769-9

Managing Anxiety with CBT For Dummies
978-1-118-36606-6

Neuro-linguistic Programming For Dummies, 2nd Edition
978-0-470-66543-5

Nutrition For Dummies, 2nd Edition
978-0-470-97276-2

Organic Gardening For Dummies
978-1-119-97706-3

FOR DUMMIES®

Making Everything Easier! ™

UK editions

SELF-HELP

Cognitive Behavioural Therapy For Dummies
978-0-470-66541-1

Creative Visualization For Dummies
978-1-119-99264-6

Mindfulness For Dummies
978-0-470-66086-7

LANGUAGES

Spanish For Dummies
978-0-470-68815-1

Polish For Dummies
978-1-119-97959-3

British Sign Language For Dummies
978-0-470-69477-0

HISTORY

The Tudors For Dummies
978-0-470-68792-5

Medieval History For Dummies
978-0-470-74783-4

British History For Dummies
978-0-470-97819-1

Origami Kit For Dummies
978-0-470-75857-1

Overcoming Depression For Dummies
978-0-470-69430-5

Positive Psychology For Dummies
978-0-470-72136-0

PRINCE2 For Dummies, 2009 Edition
978-0-470-71025-8

Project Management For Dummies
978-0-470-71119-4

Psychology Statistics For Dummies
978-1-119-95287-9

Psychometric Tests For Dummies
978-0-470-75366-8

Renting Out Your Property For Dummies, 3rd Edition
978-1-119-97640-0

Rugby Union For Dummies, 3rd Edition
978-1-119-99092-5

Sage One For Dummies
978-1-119-95236-7

Self-Hypnosis For Dummies
978-0-470-66073-7

Storing and Preserving Garden Produce For Dummies
978-1-119-95156-8

Teaching English as a Foreign Language For Dummies
978-0-470-74576-2

Time Management For Dummies
978-0-470-77765-7

Training Your Brain For Dummies
978-0-470-97449-0

Voice and Speaking Skills For Dummies
978-1-119-94512-3

Work-Life Balance For Dummies
978-0-470-71380-8

12-47776–187x234mm

FOR DUMMIES®
Making Everything Easier! ™

COMPUTER BASICS

978-1-118-11533-6

978-0-470-61454-9

978-0-470-49743-2

DIGITAL PHOTOGRAPHY

978-1-118-09203-3

978-0-470-76878-5

978-1-118-00472-2

SCIENCE AND MATHS

978-0-470-92326-9

978-0-470-55964-2

978-0-470-90324-7

Art For Dummies
978-0-7645-5104-8

Computers For Seniors For Dummies, 3rd Edition
978-1-118-11553-4

Criminology For Dummies
978-0-470-39696-4

Currency Trading For Dummies, 2nd Edition
978-0-470-01851-4

Drawing For Dummies, 2nd Edition
978-0-470-61842-4

Forensics For Dummies
978-0-7645-5580-0

French For Dummies, 2nd Edition
978-1-118-00464-7

Guitar For Dummies, 2nd Edition
978-0-7645-9904-0

Hinduism For Dummies
978-0-470-87858-3

Index Investing For Dummies
978-0-470-29406-2

Islamic Finance For Dummies
978-0-470-43069-9

Knitting For Dummies, 2nd Edition
978-0-470-28747-7

Music Theory For Dummies, 2nd Edition
978-1-118-09550-8

Office 2010 For Dummies
978-0-470-48998-7

Piano For Dummies, 2nd Edition
978-0-470-49644-2

Photoshop CS6 For Dummies
978-1-118-17457-9

Schizophrenia For Dummies
978-0-470-25927-6

WordPress For Dummies, 5th Edition
978-1-118-38318-6

12-47776-187x234mm

Think you can't learn it in a day? Think again!

The In a Day e-book series from For Dummies gives you quick and easy access to learn a new skill, brush up on a hobby, or enhance your personal or professional life — all in a day. Easy!

Available as PDF, eMobi and Kindle

12-47776-187x234mm

Get More and Do More at Dummies.com®

Start with **FREE** Cheat Sheets

Cheat Sheets include
- Checklists
- Charts
- Common Instructions
- And Other Good Stuff!

To access the Cheat Sheet created specifically for this book, go to
www.dummies.com/cheatsheet/ayurvedauk

Get Smart at Dummies.com

Dummies.com makes your life easier with thousands of answers on everything from removing wallpaper to using the latest version of Windows.

Check out our
- Videos
- Illustrated Articles
- Step-by-Step Instructions

Want a weekly dose of Dummies?
Sign up for Newsletters on
- Digital Photography
- Microsoft Windows & Office
- Personal Finance & Investing
- Health & Wellness
- Computing, iPods & Mobile Phones
- eBay
- Internet
- Food, Home & Garden

Find out "HOW" at Dummies.com

CPSIA information can be obtained
at www.ICGtesting.com
Printed in the USA
BVHW08s0326070718

520825BV00011B/128/P

9 781118 306703